BEYOND THE CODE

ETHICAL DILEMMA IN THE AI ERA

BY

DR. HESHAM MOHAMED ELSHERIF

ABOUT THE AUTHOR

Dr. Hesham Mohamed Elsherif stands at the forefront of library management and research, boasting an impressive 22-year tenure in the field. Holding dual doctoral degrees, one in Management and Organizational Leadership and the other in Information Systems and Technology, Dr. Elsherif brings a unique blend of knowledge to any intellectual endeavor.

An expert in Empirical research methodology, Dr. Elsherif specializes particularly in the Qualitative approach and Action research. This specialization has not only strengthened his research endeavors but has also allowed him to contribute invaluable insights and advancements in these areas.

Over the years, Dr. Elsherif has made significant contributions to the academic world not only as a professional researcher but also as an Adjunct Professor. This multifaceted role in the educational landscape has further solidified his reputation as a thought leader and pioneer.

Furthermore, Dr. Elsherif's expertise isn't confined to one region. He has served as a consultant to numerous educational institutions on an international scale, sharing best practices, innovative strategies, and his deep insights into the ever-evolving realms of management and technology.

Combining a passion for education with an unparalleled depth of knowledge, Dr. Elsherif continues to inspire, educate, and lead in both the library and academic communities.

PREFACE

In "Beyond the Code: Ethical Dilemmas in the AI Era," we embark on a thought-provoking journey through the intricate and often controversial world of artificial intelligence (AI) and its ethical implications. This book is a timely exploration into how AI, a field that has revolutionized our world, poses complex moral and ethical questions that challenge our traditional understanding of autonomy, privacy, and fairness.

As we step into an era where AI influences almost every aspect of our lives, from healthcare decisions to social interactions, the need for a comprehensive ethical framework has never been more critical. This book delves deep into the heart of these dilemmas, examining the fine balance between technological advancement and ethical responsibility.

Chapter by chapter, we unravel the multifaceted layers of AI ethics, beginning with a historical overview of AI development and its rapid evolution. We then transition into the core ethical issues - privacy concerns, bias and discrimination in AI algorithms, the implications of autonomous systems, and the looming fear of job displacement due to AI automation. Each topic is meticulously explored, providing readers with a nuanced understanding of the ethical challenges we face.

Further, "Beyond the Code" does not shy away from the complex interplay between AI and global socioeconomic structures. It probes into how AI-driven decisions can perpetuate existing inequalities and explores the global disparity in AI development and its implications for international relations.

What sets this book apart is its multidisciplinary approach. Weaving in perspectives from leading AI researchers, ethicists, sociologists, and policymakers, the book offers a holistic view of the ethical landscape of AI. Through case studies and real-world examples, it illustrates the tangible impact of these ethical issues on individuals and societies.

As we navigate the uncharted territories of AI, "Beyond the Code" serves as both a guide and a catalyst for critical thinking. It invites readers to question and reflect upon the ethical boundaries of AI, encouraging a proactive approach to shaping a future where technology and ethics coexist harmoniously.

Happy Reading!

Dr. Hesham Mohamed Elsherif

WHO SHOULD READ THIS BOOK?

"Beyond the Code: Ethical Dilemmas in the AI Era" is essential reading for a diverse audience, reflecting the wide-reaching impact of AI on various facets of our lives. This book is meticulously designed to cater to the interests and needs of multiple groups:

1. **Technology Professionals and AI Developers**: For those at the forefront of creating AI systems, this book offers a profound insight into the ethical considerations that should be integrated into their work. It encourages developers to think beyond the technical aspects and consider the societal impact of their creations.

2. **Business Leaders and Policymakers**: Leaders and decision-makers in business and government will find this book invaluable for understanding how AI can be implemented responsibly in their organizations and societies. It offers guidance on policy formulation, regulation, and the ethical deployment of AI technologies.

3. **Academics and Students**: Scholars and students in fields like computer science, philosophy, ethics, law, and social sciences will benefit from the book's comprehensive analysis of AI ethics. It provides a rich source of information for academic study and research.

4. **Ethicists and Social Scientists**: Those who study the moral implications of technology will find in this book a detailed examination of the ethical dilemmas posed by AI, along with an exploration of potential solutions and frameworks.

5. **AI Enthusiasts and Tech-Savvy Readers**: Individuals with a keen interest in the latest technological advancements will appreciate the book's exploration of AI's ethical challenges and its implications for the future of technology.

6. **Consumers and Everyday Users of Technology**: As AI becomes increasingly embedded in everyday life, this book is a must-read for anyone interested in understanding how AI decisions are made and their implications for privacy, autonomy, and individual rights.

7. **Activists and Advocates for Social Justice**: For those who are passionate about equity and fairness, this book sheds light on how AI

can both challenge and reinforce social inequalities, offering a foundation for advocacy in the era of digital technology.

8. **Human Resources and Recruitment Professionals**: With AI increasingly being used in hiring and workplace monitoring, these professionals will gain insights into the ethical use of AI in the workplace, ensuring fairness and preventing discrimination.

9. **Legal Professionals**: Lawyers and legal scholars will find the book's exploration of the legal implications of AI, including issues of liability and rights, crucial for navigating the emerging legal landscape shaped by AI.

"Beyond the Code" is not just a book for specialists; it is a thought-provoking read for anyone interested in the future of technology and its intersection with ethical considerations. It invites readers from all walks of life to engage with the profound questions AI poses to our society and our moral frameworks.

WHY THIS BOOK IS ESSENTIAL READING?

"Beyond the Code: Ethical Dilemmas in the AI Era" is a crucial read in our rapidly evolving digital world for several compelling reasons:

1. **Timely and Relevant**: As AI technology becomes increasingly integrated into every aspect of our lives, understanding the ethical implications is not just important, it's essential. This book offers a timely exploration of these pressing issues.

2. **Comprehensive and Multidisciplinary**: The book covers a wide range of topics, from privacy and surveillance to biases in AI algorithms. Its multidisciplinary approach brings together insights from technology, ethics, sociology, and law, making it a comprehensive guide for understanding AI's impact on society.

3. **Bridges the Gap Between Theory and Practice**: "Beyond the Code" goes beyond theoretical discussions, offering real-world examples and case studies. This approach helps readers understand how AI ethics play out in practical scenarios, making it a valuable resource for applying ethical principles in real-life contexts.

4. **Accessible to a Broad Audience**: Whether you're a tech professional, a student, or just someone interested in the future of technology, this book is written in an accessible language that doesn't compromise on depth or complexity. It's designed to be approachable for readers with varying levels of expertise in AI or ethics.

5. **Encourages Critical Thinking**: The book not only presents ethical dilemmas but also encourages readers to think critically about these issues. It challenges assumptions and prompts readers to consider their stance on the ethical implications of AI.

6. **Guidance for Policymakers and Business Leaders**: In an era where ethical missteps can lead to significant public backlash, this book serves as a crucial guide for policymakers and business leaders in making informed, ethical decisions regarding the implementation and regulation of AI technologies.

7. **Focus on Future Implications**: "Beyond the Code" doesn't just look at current issues, but also explores the future implications of AI. This

forward-thinking approach is essential for preparing for the ethical challenges that lie ahead.

8. **Promotes Ethical Responsibility**: By highlighting the importance of ethical considerations in AI development and application, the book promotes a sense of responsibility among those who are shaping our digital future.

9. **A Catalyst for Change**: This book is more than just a source of information; it's a catalyst for change. It aims to spark dialogue and action among readers, encouraging them to be part of the solution in addressing the ethical challenges of AI.

10. **Global Perspective**: The book takes a global view of AI ethics, considering how these issues affect and are influenced by different cultures and societies around the world. This global perspective is crucial in a field that knows no borders.

In summary, "Beyond the Code" is an essential read for anyone looking to understand the complex ethical landscape of AI. It provides valuable insights and guidance for navigating the challenges of this transformative technology, making it a key resource for anyone interested in the future of AI and its role in society.

Table of Contents

Introduction

Welcome to "Beyond the Code: Ethical Dilemmas in the AI Era", a book that ventures into the profound and often uncharted ethical territories of artificial intelligence (AI). At a time when AI is no longer just a futuristic concept but a present reality, the ethical dimensions of this technology have emerged as a subject of critical importance.

This book is born out of a pressing need to navigate the complex moral landscape that AI presents. It is not merely about understanding AI as a technological tool, but about comprehending its role as a new actor in the tapestry of human society, with its own set of challenges and responsibilities.

The rapid advancement of AI has brought us to a pivotal moment in history. We are witnessing AI systems making decisions that were once the sole province of humans – from driving cars to diagnosing diseases, and even influencing legal verdicts. With these advancements come profound questions: What happens when an AI system makes a mistake? Who is responsible when an AI-driven decision results in harm? How do we ensure fairness, privacy, and transparency in systems that are often inherently complex and opaque?

"Beyond the Code" seeks to explore these questions and more. We delve into the ethical issues surrounding AI, such as the biases embedded in algorithms, the erosion of privacy, the impact of AI on employment, and the ethical use of AI in surveillance and security. Each of these topics is explored not just from a technological standpoint, but from a human one – considering the impacts on individuals, societies, and global relations.

However, this book is not just a catalogue of challenges. It is also a guide to potential solutions and best practices for integrating ethical considerations into AI development and deployment. We look at how ethicists, technologists, policymakers, and other stakeholders can collaborate to create a framework that ensures AI is developed and used responsibly.

Our approach is interdisciplinary, drawing on insights from computer science, philosophy, sociology, law, and more. This multifaceted perspective is crucial in understanding the many ways AI intersects with human life. We also incorporate case studies and real-world examples to illustrate how these ethical issues manifest in tangible situations.

At its core, "Beyond the Code" is a call to action. It is an invitation to technologists, policymakers, and the public at large to engage actively with the ethical dilemmas of AI. As we stand at the crossroads of a new era, it is imperative that we forge a path that recognizes the immense potential of AI, while also safeguarding our fundamental values and rights.

As you turn these pages, we hope to ignite a thoughtful and critical exploration into the ethical dimensions of AI, and to inspire a commitment to shaping a future where technology and humanity can coexist in harmony. Welcome to the journey beyond the code.

The intertwining of AI and ethics:

In "Beyond the Code: Ethical Dilemmas in the AI Era," we embark on an insightful exploration into the intricate intertwining of artificial intelligence (AI) and ethics, a convergence that is shaping the future of human society. This book is not just about the advancements of AI as a technological marvel but about understanding the profound ethical conundrums that emerge when machines start making decisions that were traditionally the realm of humans.

At the heart of this exploration is the recognition that AI is not a neutral tool. The algorithms that drive AI systems are a reflection of the values, biases, and intentions of those who create them. As these systems become more integral to our lives, influencing everything from healthcare and education to justice and employment, the ethical implications become increasingly significant and complex.

"Beyond the Code" delves into this complex relationship, examining how ethical considerations are not just add-ons but fundamental components of AI development. We explore the challenges of designing AI systems that align with human values, the ethical dilemmas posed by autonomous machines, and the societal impacts of AI-driven decisions. The book discusses key issues such as bias and fairness in AI algorithms, the erosion of privacy, the implications of AI in surveillance, and the transformative impact of AI on the workforce.

What makes the intertwining of AI and ethics particularly challenging is the unprecedented pace of technological advancement. AI is evolving rapidly, outstripping the speed at which we can typically develop ethical frameworks and regulations. This book aims to bridge that gap, offering insights into how we can thoughtfully integrate ethical considerations into the fabric of AI development and deployment.

Through a blend of theoretical discussion, case studies, and real-world examples, "Beyond the Code" invites readers from various backgrounds—technologists, ethicists, policymakers, and the general public—to engage with the ethical dimensions of AI. It challenges the reader to consider not just the technical capabilities of AI, but also the moral responsibilities that come with these powerful tools.

This book serves as a call to action for a collaborative approach towards ethical AI, encouraging a dialogue among all stakeholders involved in the AI ecosystem. As AI continues to transform our world, "Beyond the Code" is a crucial guide for navigating the moral landscape of this new era, ensuring that AI advances in a way that is beneficial, equitable, and aligned with the greater good of humanity.

"Beyond the Code: Ethical Dilemmas in the AI Era" invites readers into a profound exploration of the complex and evolving relationship between artificial intelligence (AI) and ethics. This book is not merely an examination of AI as a technological phenomenon; it is a deep dive into the moral and ethical questions that arise as AI becomes an integral part of the human experience. In this era, AI is not just a tool; it is a catalyst that is reshaping our ethical landscape.

The core of this exploration is the recognition that AI, with its vast capabilities, brings forth challenges that extend far beyond technical hurdles. These challenges are deeply entrenched in moral philosophy, social justice, and human values. As AI systems begin to make decisions in areas that affect human lives directly – from legal judgments to medical diagnoses, from financial advising to personal privacy – the ethical implications become profoundly significant.

"Beyond the Code" delves into these issues, offering a nuanced look at how AI reflects the values of its creators and the societies they belong to. We examine the ethical design of AI systems, exploring the challenges of creating algorithms that are not only effective but also fair, transparent, and respectful of privacy. The book discusses the implications of AI in decision-making processes, the balance of power between humans and machines, and the moral responsibility that comes with AI's autonomous capabilities.

A central theme of the book is the recognition of the unprecedented pace of AI development. The rapid evolution of AI technologies has outpaced our ability to develop comprehensive ethical frameworks and regulations. This gap presents unique challenges and opportunities. "Beyond the Code" aims to bridge this gap, providing insights into how we can integrate ethical considerations into AI development and usage.

We explore the multifaceted ethical issues that AI presents, including:

- **Bias and Fairness**: How do we ensure that AI systems do not perpetuate or amplify societal biases? What measures can be taken to create algorithms that are fair and equitable?

- **Privacy and Surveillance**: As AI becomes more adept at processing vast amounts of personal data, how do we protect individual privacy? What are the ethical implications of AI in surveillance and data collection?

- **Impact on Employment**: AI's role in automation raises crucial questions about the future of work. How do we address the ethical concerns of job displacement and the changing nature of work?

- **Accountability and Transparency**: Who is responsible when an AI system makes a mistake? How do we build AI systems that are transparent and accountable?

- **Global Implications**: AI ethics is not just a local issue; it has global dimensions. How do different cultures and societies approach the ethical challenges of AI? What can we learn from these diverse perspectives?

Through a blend of theoretical discussion, real-world examples, and case studies, "Beyond the Code" provides a comprehensive overview of the ethical challenges posed by AI. It is an invitation to technologists, ethicists, policymakers, and the general public to engage in a thoughtful and critical dialogue about the role of AI in our society.

This book is more than just an academic treatise; it is a call to action. It urges a collaborative approach towards ethical AI, fostering a dialogue among all stakeholders in the AI ecosystem. As AI continues to transform our world, "Beyond the Code" is an essential guide for navigating the moral and ethical complexities of this new era, ensuring that AI advances in a way that is beneficial, equitable, and aligned with the greater good of humanity.

The pressing need for a moral compass in the digital age:

In "Beyond the Code: Ethical Dilemmas in the AI Era," we confront a pivotal challenge of our times: the urgent necessity for a moral compass in the digital age. As we navigate an era where artificial intelligence (AI) and digital technologies become increasingly embedded in every facet of our lives, the lines between ethical responsibility, technological advancement, and human values become blurred. This book delves into why and how we must recalibrate our moral compass to guide us through this new and uncharted terrain.

1. Unprecedented Technological Advancement: The rapid development of AI and digital technologies has outstripped the pace at which traditional ethical guidelines and regulations evolve. This gap has created a vacuum where critical ethical considerations are often an afterthought rather than an integral part of technological development.

2. AI's Societal Impact: AI is not a standalone tool; it impacts society at multiple levels – influencing everything from individual choices to large-scale societal changes. As AI systems make decisions that were traditionally made by humans, they bring with them a host of ethical considerations relating to bias, fairness, accountability, and transparency.

3. The Complexity of AI Systems: The intricate and often opaque nature of AI algorithms makes it challenging to understand how decisions are made. This complexity raises significant ethical questions about accountability and the interpretability of AI decisions, particularly when they impact human lives.

4. The Global Reach of Digital Technologies: The digital age transcends geographical boundaries, creating a global impact that necessitates a universal ethical framework. However, the diversity in cultural, social, and legal norms across the globe complicates the establishment of such a framework.

5. Data Privacy and Security: In the digital age, data is a currency of immense value and power. The ethical handling of personal data, concerns about surveillance, and the protection of individual privacy rights are central issues that require urgent attention.

6. The Disruption of Traditional Job Markets: AI and automation present significant challenges to the traditional job market, raising ethical questions about the future of work, income inequality, and the potential for widespread economic disruption.

7. Ethical AI Design and Deployment: There is a pressing need for ethical considerations to be integrated into the design and deployment of AI systems. This involves ensuring that AI systems are not only technically proficient but also socially and ethically responsible.

8. Navigating Moral Dilemmas: As AI becomes more advanced, it will increasingly encounter situations involving complex moral dilemmas. Establishing a moral compass in such scenarios is critical to guide AI towards decisions that are aligned with human ethical standards.

9. Public Awareness and Engagement: The digital age requires an informed public that understands the ethical implications of AI and digital technologies. Public engagement and awareness are crucial for shaping policies and practices that are ethically sound and socially beneficial.

10. Collaborative Ethical Frameworks: Developing a moral compass in the digital age requires collaboration across disciplines, cultures, and borders. It calls for the collective effort of technologists, ethicists, policymakers, and the public to create frameworks that guide the ethical use of AI and digital technologies.

"Beyond the Code: Ethical Dilemmas in the AI Era" is more than just an exploration of these challenges; it is a call to action. It urges us to collectively forge a path where ethical considerations are at the forefront of technological innovation. In doing so, we can ensure that the digital age is not only marked by technological advancement but also by a deep commitment to ethical responsibility and human values.

Chapter 1: The Foundations of AI Ethics

In the opening chapter of "Beyond the Code: Ethical Dilemmas in the AI Era," we lay the groundwork for understanding the fundamental concepts of AI ethics. This chapter serves as a crucial foundation, providing readers with the necessary context to navigate the complex ethical landscape of artificial intelligence. Here, we explore the evolution of AI ethics, its key principles, and the challenges in implementing these principles in the development and application of AI technologies.

I. Historical Context:

The chapter begins by tracing the historical development of AI, highlighting how ethical considerations have evolved alongside technological advancements. We look at key milestones in AI development and how they have raised new ethical questions, from early rule-based systems to the latest advancements in machine learning and neural networks.

In the first chapter of "Beyond the Code: Ethical Dilemmas in the AI Era," we delve into the historical context of AI ethics, providing a comprehensive overview of how ethical considerations in artificial intelligence have evolved alongside technological advancements. This exploration is critical in understanding the roots and reasons behind the current ethical debates in AI.

1. Early Days of AI: The chapter begins by exploring the early days of AI in the mid-20th century, a period marked by optimistic predictions and theoretical frameworks. We discuss the initial visions of AI, focusing on how these early concepts, such as Alan Turing's work and the Dartmouth Conference, laid the groundwork for future developments but often overlooked the ethical implications.

2. The Rise of Machine Learning: As we move forward in history, we examine the shift from rule-based AI systems to machine learning and neural networks in the late 20th and early 21st centuries. This section highlights how this transition led to new ethical considerations, particularly around the opacity of decision-making processes and the autonomy of AI systems.

3. The Proliferation of Big Data: The emergence of big data is identified as a critical turning point in the ethical landscape of AI. We explore how the vast availability of data, coupled with advanced computational power, led to significant advancements in AI capabilities, raising concerns about privacy, data security, and the potential for mass surveillance.

4. High-Profile AI Failures and Milestones: Through a series of case studies, this section looks at key moments in AI development that highlighted ethical concerns, such as the Microsoft Tay incident, the Cambridge Analytica scandal, and advancements in facial recognition technology. These examples provide insight into how ethical lapses and achievements have shaped public perception and regulatory responses.

5. The Role of AI in Society: We discuss the expanding role of AI in various sectors such as healthcare, finance, criminal justice, and social media. This expansion brought AI ethics to the forefront of public discourse, emphasizing issues like algorithmic bias, fairness, and the impact of AI on employment and societal structures.

6. The Emergence of AI Ethics as a Field: The chapter examines how the growing awareness of AI's ethical implications led to the emergence of AI ethics as a distinct field of study and practice. This includes the formation of academic programs, research institutions, and the involvement of international organizations in establishing guidelines and frameworks for ethical AI.

7. Current Debates and Future Challenges: Concluding the historical overview, this section discusses the current state of AI ethics, highlighting ongoing debates and emerging challenges. It sets the stage for understanding the dynamic and evolving nature of AI ethics, preparing the reader for deeper exploration in subsequent chapters.

Overall, this chapter provides readers with a thorough understanding of the historical context of AI ethics, illustrating how past developments and challenges have shaped the current ethical landscape of AI. This background is essential for anyone looking to grasp the complexities and nuances of ethical dilemmas in the AI era.

II. Defining AI Ethics:

We delve into what AI ethics encompasses, defining it as the study of the moral implications and responsibilities involved in the design, development, deployment, and use of AI technologies. This section explains why AI ethics is critical in ensuring that AI technologies benefit society while minimizing harm.

This section of the chapter is dedicated to clarifying what AI ethics entails, its scope, and why it is a critical field of study in the era of rapid technological advancement.

1. What is AI Ethics?: We begin by establishing a clear definition of AI ethics. AI ethics is described as the branch of ethics concerned with the moral issues arising from the development, deployment, and use of artificial intelligence technologies. It encompasses a broad range of ethical questions and dilemmas, from the design and programming of AI systems to their real-world impacts on individuals and society.

2. Core Concerns of AI Ethics: This section outlines the primary concerns of AI ethics, including issues of fairness and justice, accountability and transparency, privacy, and the societal impact of AI. Each concern is elaborated upon, explaining how AI systems can affect these areas and why it is essential to address these concerns in the development and application of AI.

3. The Importance of Ethical Consideration in AI: Here, we discuss why ethics is a crucial consideration in AI development. The section underscores the potential for AI systems to perpetuate biases, infringe on privacy rights, and make life-altering decisions. It argues that ethical considerations are vital to ensure that AI technologies are developed and used in a manner that benefits society and minimizes harm.

4. The Multidisciplinary Nature of AI Ethics: AI ethics is presented as a multidisciplinary field, drawing on principles and knowledge from philosophy, law, social sciences, computer science, and more. This part of the chapter highlights how different perspectives contribute to a more comprehensive understanding of AI ethics.

5. Ethical Frameworks and Principles in AI: This section introduces various ethical frameworks and principles that guide the development and use of AI, such as utilitarianism, deontological ethics, virtue ethics, and human rights-based approaches. It discusses how these frameworks apply to AI and their role in guiding ethical decision-making.

6. The Challenge of Implementing Ethics in AI: Implementing ethical principles in the development and deployment of AI poses significant challenges. This section delves into these challenges, such as the difficulty of translating abstract ethical principles into concrete technical requirements, and the balancing act between competing ethical values.

7. The Global Context of AI Ethics: AI ethics is not just a local or national issue; it has global implications. This part of the chapter addresses the need for a global perspective on AI ethics, considering the diverse cultural, legal, and social contexts in which AI operates.

8. Future Directions in AI Ethics: The chapter concludes by looking at the evolving nature of AI ethics as the field continues to grow. It discusses emerging areas of concern and the potential for new ethical frameworks and guidelines to arise in response to ongoing technological advancements.

By providing a clear and comprehensive definition of AI ethics, this chapter sets the stage for a deeper exploration of the specific ethical dilemmas and challenges posed by AI in the following chapters. This foundational understanding is essential for anyone seeking to engage with the ethical dimensions of AI.

III. Core Ethical Principles in AI:

The chapter outlines the fundamental ethical principles that are central to AI, such as transparency, fairness, non-maleficence, responsibility, and privacy. Each principle is explained in detail, providing readers with a clear understanding of what these principles entail and why they are important.

This section is pivotal in establishing a clear understanding of the key moral values that should guide the development, deployment, and management of artificial intelligence systems. Here, we outline and examine these fundamental principles, explaining their significance in the realm of AI.

1. Transparency: The principle of transparency is central to AI ethics. It involves the clarity and openness of AI systems, particularly in how they make decisions and process data. We explore why transparency is crucial for building trust in AI systems, allowing users and affected parties to understand how AI conclusions are reached. The chapter also discusses the challenges in achieving transparency in complex AI systems.

2. Fairness and Justice: Fairness in AI is about ensuring that AI systems do not create or perpetuate bias and inequality. This principle demands that AI systems are designed and operated in a way that treats all individuals and groups equitably. We delve into the challenges of defining and measuring fairness in AI, and how biases can inadvertently be encoded into AI systems, leading to unfair outcomes.

3. Non-Maleficence: Rooted in the medical ethics principle of "do no harm," non-maleficence in AI ethics emphasizes that AI systems should not harm humans. This principle involves ensuring the safety and security of AI systems, preventing them from causing physical or psychological harm. The chapter discusses the importance of rigorous testing and monitoring to uphold this principle.

4. Responsibility and Accountability: Responsibility in AI ethics refers to the obligation of AI developers, deployers, and users to ensure that AI systems are ethical and beneficial. Accountability goes a step further, implying that these stakeholders are answerable for the outcomes of AI systems. This section explores how responsibility and accountability can be maintained, especially in complex systems where decision-making is decentralized.

5. Privacy: Privacy is a paramount concern in AI ethics, particularly as AI systems often process vast amounts of personal data. We examine the importance of safeguarding personal information, respecting user consent, and ensuring that AI systems do not infringe on individual privacy rights.

6. Beneficence: This principle involves ensuring that AI systems actively contribute to the wellbeing of individuals and society. Beneficence in AI means designing and using AI in ways that promote positive outcomes and societal benefits. The chapter highlights the potential of AI to contribute to areas like healthcare, education, and environmental protection.

7. Autonomy: Respecting human autonomy involves ensuring that AI systems support and enhance, rather than undermine, human decision-making and independence. This principle is crucial in contexts where AI is used for recommendations or guidance, ensuring that the ultimate choice remains with the human user.

8. Sustainability: Although often overlooked, sustainability is an emerging principle in AI ethics. It focuses on the long-term impacts of AI systems on the environment and society, advocating for sustainable development and deployment practices.

This section of Chapter 1 provides a comprehensive overview of the core ethical principles that should guide AI. By laying out these principles, the chapter sets a foundation for understanding the complex ethical landscape of AI and prepares the reader for deeper discussions on how these principles can be applied and balanced in real-world AI scenarios.

IV. Challenges in Implementing AI Ethics:

This section addresses the practical challenges in applying ethical principles to AI. It discusses issues like the complexity of AI algorithms, the difficulty in defining and measuring fairness, and the challenges in ensuring transparency and accountability in AI systems.

This section is essential for understanding the practical difficulties and complexities involved in embedding ethical principles into AI systems. It explores various obstacles that practitioners, policymakers, and society face in ensuring that AI operates within an ethical framework.

1. Balancing Ethical Principles with Technical Feasibility: One of the foremost challenges is aligning ethical principles with the technical realities of AI development. We discuss the difficulty in translating abstract ethical concepts into concrete technical specifications, and how this often leads to a gap between ethical ideals and practical implementation.

2. Defining and Measuring Ethical Concepts: The chapter examines the challenge of defining and quantifying ethical concepts like fairness, justice, and harm in AI systems. These concepts can be subjective and context-dependent, making it difficult to create universally accepted definitions and metrics.

3. Dealing with Inherent Biases: AI systems are only as unbiased as the data they are trained on and the designers who create them. This section delves into the challenge of identifying and mitigating inherent biases in AI algorithms and data sets, which can lead to discriminatory outcomes.

4. Ensuring Transparency in Complex Systems: As AI systems become more complex, ensuring transparency becomes increasingly challenging. The chapter discusses how the 'black box' nature of certain AI models, especially deep learning, makes it hard for users and regulators to understand how decisions are made.

5. Responsibility and Accountability in Decentralized Systems: Another significant challenge is determining responsibility and accountability in decentralized and autonomous AI systems. We explore the 'responsibility gap' that emerges in complex systems where it's difficult to pinpoint who is accountable for AI-driven decisions or mistakes.

6. Safeguarding Privacy in Data-Driven AI: The use of vast amounts of data in AI raises significant privacy concerns. This section addresses the challenge of protecting individual privacy and complying with varying data protection laws, while still leveraging data for AI innovation.

7. Ethical Considerations in Diverse Cultural Contexts: Implementing AI ethics is not just a technical challenge but also a cultural one. The chapter highlights how varying cultural and societal norms impact the perception and implementation of ethical principles in AI, making global consensus difficult.

8. Keeping Pace with Rapid Technological Advancements: The rapid evolution of AI technology poses a challenge in keeping ethical guidelines and regulations up to date. This section discusses the need for flexible and adaptive ethical frameworks that can evolve with technological advancements.

9. Public Understanding and Engagement: Educating and engaging the public on AI ethics is essential for informed discourse and policy-making. The challenge lies in raising awareness and understanding among non-experts about the ethical implications of AI.

10. Multi-Stakeholder Collaboration: Finally, the chapter discusses the challenge of coordinating among various stakeholders – including AI developers, users, ethicists, regulators, and affected communities – to collaboratively address ethical concerns in AI.

This exploration sets the stage for subsequent chapters, which delve into specific ethical dilemmas and propose strategies to navigate these challenges effectively.

V. Ethical Design and Development:

We explore the concept of ethical AI design and development, emphasizing the importance of incorporating ethical considerations from the very beginning of the AI development process. This includes discussions on interdisciplinary approaches, involving ethicists, sociologists, and other stakeholders in the AI development process.

This section is crucial for understanding how ethical considerations can be integrated from the earliest stages of AI conception and throughout its lifecycle. It addresses the strategies, practices, and challenges involved in embedding ethics into the design and development of AI systems.

1. The Concept of Ethical by Design: The chapter begins by introducing the concept of 'Ethical by Design' in AI. This approach involves incorporating ethical considerations into the AI development process from the outset. We discuss the importance of proactive ethical thinking, rather than retroactively addressing ethical issues after deployment.

2. Interdisciplinary Approach to AI Development: Ethical AI design requires collaboration across various disciplines. The section emphasizes the need for teams that include not just technologists and data scientists but also ethicists, social scientists, legal experts, and representatives from potentially impacted communities. This diversity ensures a well-rounded consideration of ethical implications.

3. Identifying and Addressing Ethical Risks: A significant part of ethical AI development involves identifying potential ethical risks and addressing them early. The chapter outlines methods for risk assessment, including stakeholder analysis, impact assessment, and scenario planning. It also discusses how these risks can be mitigated through design choices.

4. Principles-Based Frameworks for Ethical AI: This section introduces various principles-based frameworks that guide ethical AI development. These frameworks offer a set of ethical guidelines and standards that developers can adhere to, such as transparency, fairness, and accountability.

5. The Role of Regulation and Policy in Ethical AI Development: We explore the interplay between ethical AI development and regulatory compliance. The chapter discusses how laws and policies can shape ethical AI development and the importance of developers staying abreast of legal requirements in different jurisdictions.

6. Incorporating Public and Stakeholder Input: Ethical AI development is not just about technical and regulatory compliance; it also involves engaging with the public and stakeholders. This part of the chapter examines the methods and benefits of public consultation and stakeholder engagement in developing ethical AI.

7. Continuous Monitoring and Evaluation: Ethical AI development is an ongoing process. The section highlights the importance of continuous monitoring and evaluation of AI systems post-deployment to ensure they remain aligned with ethical standards over time, especially as they learn and evolve.

8. Case Studies in Ethical AI Development: Throughout this section, real-world case studies are used to illustrate how ethical design and development principles are applied in practice. These examples provide practical insights into the challenges and successes of implementing ethical AI.

9. Challenges in Ethical AI Development: The chapter also addresses the practical challenges in ethical AI development, such as resource constraints, balancing ethical considerations with commercial interests, and dealing with the uncertainty and evolving nature of AI technologies.

By detailing the principles and practices of ethical design and development in AI, this section of Chapter 1 lays a critical foundation for the rest of the book. It equips readers with an understanding of how ethical considerations can be effectively integrated into AI development, setting the stage for a deeper exploration of specific ethical dilemmas and case studies in subsequent chapters.

VI. Case Studies and Examples:

Throughout the chapter, real-world case studies and examples are presented to illustrate the ethical challenges in AI. These examples help to ground the discussion in practical terms, showing how ethical principles are applied in real-life situations.

This section is vital for illustrating the real-world implications of AI ethics, providing tangible insights into how ethical principles are applied, challenged, and sometimes overlooked in actual AI scenarios.

1. Bias in AI Algorithms: One of the key case studies discussed is the issue of bias in AI algorithms. The chapter examines well-documented instances where AI systems in recruitment, criminal justice, and loan approvals have shown biases against certain demographic groups. These examples underscore the consequences of training AI systems on biased data sets and the importance of ethical considerations in data selection and algorithm design.

2. Autonomous Vehicles and Ethical Decision-Making: The ethical dilemmas in autonomous vehicle technology provide another rich case study. The chapter explores scenarios such as the 'trolley problem' adapted for self-driving cars, discussing how these vehicles must be programmed to make decisions in life-threatening situations and the ethical implications of these programming choices.

3. AI in Healthcare: The use of AI in healthcare, particularly in diagnosis and treatment recommendations, serves as a critical case study. The chapter looks at instances where AI has significantly improved patient outcomes, but also at scenarios where it has failed or raised ethical concerns regarding privacy, consent, and the accuracy of AI-driven medical decisions.

4. AI-Driven Surveillance: This section delves into the use of AI in surveillance, including facial recognition technologies. It examines the ethical concerns raised by AI's ability to monitor, track, and identify individuals, discussing real-world cases where AI surveillance has been used in both beneficial and controversial ways.

5. Social Media Algorithms and Echo Chambers: Another example discussed is the role of AI in creating echo chambers on social media platforms. The chapter explores how algorithmic content curation can lead to the reinforcement of biases, the spread of misinformation, and the ethical implications for free speech and public discourse.

6. AI in the Workplace: The impact of AI on employment and workplace dynamics is analyzed through various case studies. This includes examples of AI being used for employee monitoring, performance evaluation, and even hiring processes, raising ethical questions about privacy, job displacement, and the changing nature of work.

7. Ethical AI in Practice: To illustrate how ethical principles can be successfully implemented in AI, the chapter also presents positive case studies. These include AI systems designed with fairness in mind, transparent AI initiatives, and examples of AI being used to address social and environmental issues.

8. Global Perspectives on AI Ethics: The chapter includes case studies from different parts of the world, highlighting how cultural and societal contexts can influence the perception and implementation of AI ethics. These examples demonstrate the global diversity in ethical approaches to AI development and deployment.

9. Lessons Learned: Each case study concludes with an analysis of the lessons learned from these real-world examples, providing valuable insights into the successes and failures in applying AI ethics.

By integrating these case studies and examples, Chapter 1 of "Beyond the Code" effectively demonstrates the practical application of AI ethics, its challenges, and its profound impact on society. These real-world instances not only enrich the reader's understanding of theoretical concepts but also highlight the urgent need for ethical considerations in the rapidly evolving field of AI.

VII. The Role of Regulation and Policy:

The chapter also discusses the role of regulation and policy in shaping the ethical use of AI. It examines different regulatory approaches taken by governments and international bodies and how these policies impact the development and use of AI technologies.

This section is essential for understanding how legal frameworks and policies can guide and enforce ethical standards in AI development and use. It explores the complexities of regulating AI, the current state of AI regulation, and the interplay between policy and ethical AI practices.

1. The Need for Regulation in AI: The chapter begins by establishing why regulation is necessary in AI. It discusses the potential risks and harms that unregulated AI poses, such as privacy violations, discrimination, and lack of accountability. The section argues that while ethical guidelines are important, enforceable regulations are essential to ensure compliance and protect public interests.

2. Challenges in Regulating AI: This part of the chapter delves into the challenges in regulating AI, highlighting the dynamic and evolving nature of AI technologies, the difficulty in defining and measuring ethical standards, and the need for regulations that do not stifle innovation. It also touches on the global nature of AI, which complicates the enforcement of local or national regulations.

3. Current Regulatory Landscape: Here, we present an overview of the current state of AI regulation around the world. The chapter examines existing laws and policies that impact AI, such as data protection laws (like the EU's GDPR), as well as more specific AI regulations and guidelines proposed or enacted in various countries and by international bodies.

4. The Role of International and National Bodies: The chapter explores the role of international organizations (such as the OECD, EU, and UNESCO) and national governments in shaping AI policy. It discusses how these bodies are working to develop frameworks and guidelines that address ethical concerns in AI, and the impact of these efforts on global AI practices.

5. Industry Self-Regulation and Standards: In addition to government regulation, the chapter looks at the role of industry self-regulation. It discusses how tech companies and industry groups have developed their own ethical guidelines and standards for AI, and examines the effectiveness and limitations of these self-regulatory efforts.

6. Public Participation in AI Policymaking: The importance of public involvement in AI policymaking is highlighted in this section. It argues for transparent and inclusive policymaking processes that consider the perspectives of various stakeholders, including AI developers, users, ethicists, and affected communities.

7. Future Directions in AI Regulation: The chapter concludes by discussing emerging trends and future directions in AI regulation. It explores how upcoming technologies (like quantum computing and advanced neural networks) might pose new regulatory challenges and how policymakers can prepare for these future developments.

8. Case Studies in AI Regulation: Throughout this section, real-world case studies are used to illustrate how various countries and organizations are approaching AI regulation. These examples provide practical insights into the successes and challenges of implementing regulatory frameworks for AI.

Examining the role of regulation and policy in AI ethics, provides a comprehensive understanding of how legal frameworks can support and enforce ethical AI practices. This analysis sets the stage for a deeper exploration of specific regulatory approaches and policy recommendations in subsequent chapters.

Philosophy Meets Technology: A Brief History:

This section weaves a rich tapestry, tracing the evolution of artificial intelligence (AI) ethics from its philosophical roots to its current technological manifestations. It's a story that reveals how ancient philosophical inquiries have profoundly influenced modern AI development and its ethical considerations.

The Philosophical Genesis

Our journey begins in the hallowed halls of ancient philosophy. Here, the likes of Aristotle pondered the mechanics of logic and reasoning, unknowingly laying the groundwork for future computational thinking. These ancient musings on the nature of knowledge and intelligence planted the seeds for a future where machines might not only think but also make decisions.

Imagine walking through the ancient streets of Greece, where philosophers like Aristotle pondered the intricacies of logic and the essence of rational thinking. It was here, in the cradle of Western philosophy, that the foundational principles of knowledge, reasoning, and ethical consideration were first articulated. Aristotle's discourse on logic, particularly his development of syllogisms, laid the groundwork for structured thinking - a precursor to the algorithms that drive modern AI.

As our narrative winds through the corridors of history, we encounter the medieval and Renaissance philosophers who built upon these classical foundations. Their inquiries into human cognition and the nature of the mind added layers of complexity to the understanding of intelligence, both human and artificial. These were the thinkers who first dared to dream of inanimate objects imbued with intelligence - an idea that would centuries later crystallize into the concept of AI.

The story then progresses to the Enlightenment, a period brimming with ideas about human reason and scientific inquiry. Philosophers like Descartes and Leibniz contributed immensely to the discourse on human intellect and consciousness. Descartes' famous cogito ("I think, therefore I am") challenged the very notion of thought and existence, while Leibniz's work on binary systems foreshadowed the digital computations at the heart of AI.

As we transition into the modern era, the philosophical underpinnings of AI become even more pronounced. The 19th and early 20th centuries saw an explosion of scientific discovery and technological innovation. Logical positivism and other philosophical movements began to grapple with the relationship between science and philosophy, setting the stage for the eventual emergence of AI.

It was in this fertile intellectual landscape that the pioneers of computing, such as Alan Turing, emerged. Turing, often hailed as the father of modern computing, was deeply influenced by these philosophical discussions. His groundbreaking work on the Turing Machine and the conceptualization of the Turing Test were both reflections of this rich philosophical heritage. Turing's ideas blurred the lines between human cognition and mechanical computation, sparking a revolution that would lead to the development of AI.

The philosophical genesis of AI ethics is not just a historical recounting; it is a story of ideas, of dreams, and of the relentless human quest to understand and replicate intelligence. This journey through time sets the stage for the rest of the chapter, highlighting the profound impact that centuries of philosophical thought have had on the ethical considerations of AI in our modern era.

As we emerge from this historical exploration, we carry with us a deeper appreciation for the philosophical roots of AI. These roots remind us that the ethical dilemmas we grapple with today are inextricably linked to a rich tapestry of human thought, stretching back thousands of years.

The Dawn of Computational Thinking

Fast forward to the early 20th century, where figures like Alan Turing and John von Neumann emerge as the protagonists in our story. Turing, with his groundbreaking paper on computable numbers, brought forth the idea of a universal machine – an entity that could mimic human thought processes. His work blurred the lines between human cognition and mechanical computation, setting the stage for the development of AI.

As we step into this era, we encounter visionary minds like Alan Turing and John von Neumann, whose work would come to define the very essence of modern computing and, by extension, artificial intelligence. Turing, a figure often shrouded in both brilliance and tragedy, emerges as a central character in this narrative. His seminal 1936 paper, "On Computable Numbers," introduced the concept of a machine that could perform any conceivable mathematical computation – the theoretical foundation of the modern computer and a direct precursor to AI.

Turing's work was not just a technical blueprint; it was imbued with deep philosophical implications. His musings on the nature of machine intelligence, especially the famous Turing Test, proposed a future where machines could not only compute but also think – a notion that would fundamentally challenge our understanding of intelligence and consciousness.

Parallel to Turing's contributions, we meet John von Neumann, another giant in the field of computational theory. Von Neumann's architectural design for electronic computers laid the groundwork for the machines that would later run AI algorithms. His work, characterized by a blend of mathematical genius and philosophical depth, helped bridge the gap between abstract computational theory and practical machine design.

As the narrative unfolds, we witness the birth of the first computers – colossal machines of vacuum tubes and punch cards that seem archaic by today's standards but were, at the time, the cutting edge of technology. These machines were the physical manifestation of Turing and von Neumann's ideas, the realization of centuries of philosophical and mathematical thought.

But this era was about more than just hardware. It was a time of fundamental questions and bold assertions about the nature of intelligence, both human and artificial. Philosophers and scientists began to engage in earnest with the implications of computational machines. Debates sprang up around the potential and limits of these machines, foreshadowing the ethical dilemmas of AI that we grapple with today.

The dawn of computational thinking was a confluence of ideas and technology, a period where the abstract musings of philosophers merged with the concrete innovations of scientists and engineers. This fusion set the stage for the development of AI, not just as a technological endeavor but as a field deeply rooted in ethical and philosophical inquiry.

As we move forward in this narrative, the story of AI ethics begins to take shape. From the theoretical foundations laid by Turing and von Neumann, we embark on a journey towards the creation of intelligent machines, a journey that would bring with it new and unprecedented ethical challenges. The dawn of computational thinking was not just the beginning of a technological revolution; it was the opening of a new chapter in the human quest to understand and replicate our own intelligence.

AI Emerges from the Shadows

As we progress to the mid-20th century, the narrative takes us to a pivotal moment – the Dartmouth Conference of 1956, where AI was christened as a distinct field. It was a time of great optimism, where the possibilities of AI seemed boundless. However, this era was marked more by technological ambition than by ethical introspection.

In this era, the term "artificial intelligence" was coined, symbolizing a paradigm shift in the way humans viewed machines. The story takes us to the hallowed grounds of Dartmouth College in 1956, where a group of visionary scientists, including John McCarthy, Marvin Minsky, Nathaniel Rochester, and Claude Shannon, convened for the historic Dartmouth Conference. It was here that the term "artificial intelligence" was first proposed, defining a new field of research dedicated to creating machines capable of intelligent behavior.

The narrative vividly describes the atmosphere of optimism and ambition that surrounded this conference. These were the pioneering days of AI, where the possibilities seemed endless, and the horizon of machine intelligence was expanding rapidly. The discussions and ideas generated at Dartmouth laid the groundwork for decades of AI research, setting ambitious goals for the field.

As AI began to emerge from the shadows, the narrative delves into the early successes and challenges of this nascent field. We explore the development of the first AI programs, like the Logic Theorist and ELIZA, which amazed the public and academia alike. These programs, rudimentary by today's standards, were groundbreaking at the time, demonstrating that machines could not only calculate but also engage in rudimentary problem-solving and even mimic human conversation.

However, this era was not without its hurdles. The narrative addresses the early overestimations of AI's potential, where the initial burst of progress gave way to the realization that creating truly intelligent machines was a far more complex task than previously thought. This period, known as the "AI winter," saw a decline in interest and funding for AI research, as the grand promises of the Dartmouth Conference seemed increasingly unattainable.

Yet, even as AI faced these early challenges, the ethical implications of intelligent machines began to surface. The narrative highlights how, amidst the technological breakthroughs, there were voices that cautioned about the potential consequences of AI. These early ethical concerns, ranging from the impact of AI on employment to the moral status of intelligent machines, laid the foundation for the field of AI ethics that would later gain prominence.

"AI Emerges from the Shadows" is not just a story of technological advancement; it is a tale of dreams, aspirations, and the gradual realization of AI's complexity. It sets the stage for the subsequent chapters, which delve deeper into the ethical quandaries that have accompanied AI as it has grown from a fledgling field of research into a transformative force in modern society. In this narrative, the emergence of AI is portrayed not just as a scientific milestone but as a pivotal moment in the ongoing dialogue between technology and ethics.

The Awakening of Ethical Consciousness

But as AI grew in capability and complexity, so did the ethical questions surrounding it. The once-clear waters of technological advancement became muddied with concerns about autonomy, control, and morality. Thinkers and scientists began to ponder the societal impacts of AI, foreseeing issues that are at the heart of today's ethical debates in AI.

As our journey through the annals of AI progresses, we reach a period where the once-distant echoes of ethical contemplation start to resonate more loudly in the corridors of technological innovation. It's a time when the AI community, previously engrossed in the thrill of making machines mimic human thought and behavior, begins to confront the deeper questions: What does it mean for a machine to make decisions? What are the implications of delegating tasks that require moral judgment to algorithms?

The narrative brings us into the latter part of the 20th century, a time when the rapid advancements in AI technology were no longer just subjects of academic interest but were starting to have tangible impacts on society. We explore the pioneering AI systems that ventured out of research labs and into the real world, finding applications in industries, healthcare, and even the arts. With these applications came the realization that AI was not just a tool but a force capable of altering the fabric of society.

In this awakening, we encounter the early voices of caution, thinkers who foresaw the potential consequences of unchecked AI development. These were the ethicists, philosophers, and far-sighted technologists who began raising questions about privacy, autonomy, and the ethical use of AI. They warned of a future where AI systems, if not guided by ethical principles, could exacerbate societal inequalities, infringe on personal freedoms, or make biased decisions with far-reaching consequences.

The narrative captures the seminal moments of this ethical awakening: debates on the floor of conferences, landmark papers that challenged the status quo, and the formation of the first committees and organizations dedicated to the study of AI ethics. These were the initial steps in forming a dialogue between the worlds of AI and ethics, a dialogue that sought to steer the course of AI towards a more conscientious path.

One poignant story within this narrative is the transition from AI being a subject of wonderment to a subject of scrutiny. The chapter delves into the pivotal events that sparked public and academic debate, such as the deployment of AI in sensitive areas like criminal justice and healthcare, where the margin for error was thin, and the stakes were high.

"The Awakening of Ethical Consciousness" is not just a recounting of historical events; it is a tale of introspection and responsibility. It tells of how the AI community began to look inward, questioning not only the capabilities of what they could create but also the moral implications of their creations. This chapter of the story is where the ethical dimension of AI starts to gain prominence, setting the stage for the rich and complex discussions on AI ethics that form the heart of "Beyond the Code."

As this section draws to a close, it leaves the reader standing at the threshold of a new era in AI development. An era where the excitement of technological breakthroughs is tempered with a sense of ethical duty, where the question is no longer just about what AI can do, but also about what it should do. This awakening of ethical consciousness marks a pivotal moment in our narrative, where the journey of AI takes a reflective turn, intertwining the paths of technology and ethics in a way that would forever shape the future of artificial intelligence.

Philosophical Ethics Intersect with AI

The narrative then flows into the interplay between AI and ethical philosophy. It explores how AI, in its quest to emulate human intelligence, had to grapple with ethical conundrums that have been the subject of philosophical debates for centuries. Theories of utilitarianism, Kantian ethics, and virtue ethics provided lenses through which the ethical implications of AI could be examined and understood.

This pivotal moment, "Philosophical Ethics Intersect with AI," marks a profound synthesis of age-old ethical discourse with the burgeoning field of AI, setting the stage for a new era of ethical consideration.

As the 20th century waned and the new millennium dawned, the rapid advancement of AI technology began to brush against the timeless pillars of philosophical thought. In this part of the journey, we witness the awakening of AI developers and theorists to the rich landscape of ethical philosophy, a realm that had pondered the nature of intelligence, consciousness, and morality for centuries.

The story brings us into intimate contact with the way AI began to grapple with complex ethical dilemmas. For instance, utilitarianism, with its focus on the greatest good for the greatest number, became a lens through which the implications of AI's decisions could be scrutinized. The narrative explores how this and other ethical frameworks, such as Kantian deontology with its emphasis on duty and rules, and virtue ethics with its focus on moral character, started to inform the development and application of AI systems.

A vivid example of this intersection is found in the development of autonomous vehicles. Here, the age-old philosophical problem known as the 'trolley dilemma' was reborn in the context of AI, posing questions about how an AI should make decisions in life-and-death scenarios. This real-world

33

application illustrates how philosophical ethics became not just theoretical musings but practical necessities in the programming of AI.

The chapter also delves into the ethical design of AI systems, where the ideals of transparency, fairness, and justice began to take root in the digital soil. These ethical principles, drawn from centuries of philosophical thought, started to become guiding stars for AI developers, steering the course of AI applications towards more ethical horizons.

As AI applications proliferated, affecting everything from social media algorithms to judicial decision-making systems, the need for ethical guidance grew ever more pressing. The story captures the tension between the potential of AI to revolutionize society and the ethical challenges it posed, requiring a delicate balancing act between innovation and moral responsibility.

The intersection of philosophical ethics and AI also sparked new debates and collaborations. Ethicists, philosophers, technologists, and policymakers began to come together in forums and conferences, wrestling with questions about AI's impact on privacy, autonomy, and the fabric of society. These discussions laid the groundwork for the emerging field of AI ethics, a discipline that sought to bridge the gap between the theoretical world of philosophy and the practical world of technology.

"Philosophical Ethics Intersect with AI" is a chapter that encapsulates a moment of transformation - a time when the quest to create intelligent machines met the age-old quest to understand what it means to act ethically. It is a testament to the enduring relevance of philosophical thought in the modern world and a reminder that the march of technology, no matter how advanced, is forever entwined with the fundamental questions of human existence.

The Rise of AI Ethics as a Discipline

As the 20th century gave way to the 21st, AI ethics evolved into a distinct interdisciplinary field. Academic and research institutions began to focus on AI ethics, underscoring the need for guidelines and frameworks to ensure the ethical development and deployment of AI technologies.

This segment of the story marks a profound shift, where the ethical considerations surrounding artificial intelligence (AI) crystallize into a distinct field of study, intertwining the strands of moral philosophy with technological innovation.

As the 21st century unfolds, the story reveals how the ethical questions surrounding AI, once peripheral concerns, began to command center stage. With AI systems becoming more embedded in everyday life, affecting everything from healthcare decisions to social media interactions, the need for a structured approach to AI ethics became undeniable.

The tale narrates the emergence of dedicated research institutions and academic programs focused on AI ethics. Universities and tech companies alike started to recognize the importance of understanding and addressing the ethical implications of AI. Courses on AI ethics began to appear in curricula, reflecting a growing awareness of the need to equip future technologists with the tools to think critically about the ethical dimensions of their work.

In this part of the story, we witness the formation of influential committees and organizations tasked with studying and guiding the ethical development of AI. These groups brought together experts from diverse fields – including philosophers, computer scientists, legal scholars, and policymakers – to collaboratively navigate the complex ethical terrain of AI. Their work resulted in the creation of landmark guidelines and principles that sought to shape the development of AI in a manner that respected human values and rights.

Significant within this chapter is the narration of key moments and publications that served as catalysts for the field. Reports and papers that highlighted the potential risks and benefits of AI, publicized incidents where AI systems failed or caused harm, and conferences where heated debates on AI ethics took place, all contributed to the burgeoning discourse on AI ethics.

The story also touches upon the challenges that faced this emerging discipline. Debates raged over the practicality of applying abstract ethical principles to AI, the tensions between technological progress and ethical constraints, and the global implications of creating a universally accepted ethical framework in a culturally diverse world.

As AI ethics grew as a discipline, it began to influence policy and governance. The narrative highlights how governments and international bodies started to engage with AI ethics, leading to the development of policies and regulations aimed at ensuring ethical AI development and deployment. This marked a shift from theoretical discussions to actionable governance, highlighting the real-world impact of the field.

"The Rise of AI Ethics as a Discipline" is a story of convergence and maturation. It is about how the ethical questions that once simmered in the background as AI developed moved to the forefront, demanding attention and action. This chapter of the AI journey tells of the transformation of AI ethics from a niche concern to a vital component of technological progress, embedding moral considerations into the fabric of AI development and shaping the future trajectory of this transformative technology.

Contemporary Ethical Challenges

Bringing the story to the present, the chapter highlights how today's AI technologies – with their advanced machine learning capabilities and vast data processing – have reignited ethical discussions. The narrative emphasizes the importance of ongoing dialogue between philosophical ethics and technological innovation, in an era where AI is increasingly intertwined with every facet of human life.

In this era, the story unfolds to reveal a landscape where AI is no longer a distant future possibility but an integral part of daily life. AI systems are deciding who gets a loan, who sees what information online, and are even beginning to drive our cars. With these advancements come profound ethical challenges, each weaving a thread in the intricate tapestry of modern AI ethics.

One of the central themes in this chapter is the challenge of bias and fairness in AI systems. The tale recounts real-world incidents where AI has perpetuated existing social biases, making decisions that unfairly disadvantage certain groups. These stories highlight the ethical imperative to ensure AI systems are not only intelligent but also fair and just.

Privacy emerges as another pivotal theme. The narrative explores the growing concern over surveillance and data collection by AI systems, painting a picture of a world where personal information is increasingly vulnerable. This part of the story grapples with the tension between leveraging AI for societal benefits and protecting individual privacy rights.

The story then shifts to the realm of employment and the workforce, where AI's capability to automate, tasks has led to both opportunities and challenges. The narrative portrays the ethical dilemma of balancing technological progress with its impact on jobs and livelihoods, bringing to life the concerns of workers facing an uncertain future in the age of AI.

Autonomy and control form another critical thread in this tapestry. The chapter delves into the ethical implications of autonomous systems – from drones to digital assistants – and the concerns about diminishing human control in critical decision-making processes. These stories bring into question the extent to which society is willing to cede power to machines.

The chapter doesn't shy away from the global nature of these challenges. It illustrates how AI ethics is not confined by geographic boundaries, as AI technologies spread across cultures and nations, raising questions about cultural relativism in ethical standards and the need for global cooperation in addressing AI's ethical impact.

The "Contemporary Ethical Challenges," is not just a collection of problems; it is a mirror reflecting the multifaceted impact of AI on modern society. It's a part of the story that emphasizes the urgency and complexity of ethical considerations in the age of AI, calling for a concerted effort from technologists, ethicists, policymakers, and society at large to navigate these challenges. In this narrative, the ethical dilemmas of contemporary AI are not just obstacles to be overcome; they are opportunities to steer the course of technology towards a more equitable and humane future.

A Look to the Future

In concluding, the section speculates on the future ethical challenges as AI continues to evolve. It suggests a continued interplay between philosophy and technology, stressing the need for ethical guidelines that can adapt to the rapid pace of AI development.

In this forward-looking section, we find ourselves at a crossroads. The tale conjures images of a future bright with the promise of AI's potential: smart cities that adapt to our needs, healthcare systems that predict and prevent disease, and educational tools that provide personalized learning experiences. Yet, each of these prospects carries with it a spectrum of ethical considerations, painting a future that is as challenging as it is exciting.

The story then takes a turn to explore the emerging frontiers of AI ethics. It speaks of the advent of more sophisticated AI, delving into areas like artificial general intelligence (AGI) and the ethical implications of machines that could, one day, surpass human intelligence. Here, the narrative grapples with profound questions about the nature of consciousness, the rights of AI entities, and the future relationship between humans and machines.

The story anticipates advancements in ethical AI design, where cutting-edge technologies and innovative ethical approaches converge to create AI systems that are not only smart but also socially responsible. It speaks of a future where ethical considerations are embedded in the very fabric of AI development, from the drawing board to deployment.

The narrative also recognizes the global nature of AI's future. It envisions a world where international collaboration on AI ethics is not just a lofty ideal but a practical necessity. In this future scenario, global dialogues and policies on AI ethics bridge cultural and political divides, fostering a shared approach to managing the ethical challenges of AI.

"A Look to the Future" is not a set of simple predictions; it is a tableau of possibilities, a collage of potential futures shaped by the ethical decisions of today. The story acknowledges the uncertainties and complexities of forecasting AI's path but emphasizes the power of proactive ethical consideration in shaping a future where AI serves the greater good of humanity.

In this part of the story, the future of AI ethics is an open book, a narrative still being written. It invites readers to be not just spectators but active participants in crafting this future, encouraging a collective effort to ensure that as AI advances, it does so with a keen sense of ethical responsibility and a commitment to the betterment of society. As the chapter closes, it leaves us pondering our role in this ongoing story, challenging us to be architects of a future where technology and ethics harmoniously intertwine.

Through "Philosophy Meets Technology: A Brief History," Chapter 1 of "Beyond the Code" not only educates but also enthralls, providing readers with a deep understanding of the historical context of AI ethics. This narrative is a testament to how philosophical principles have shaped, and continue to influence, the ethical development of AI technologies.

Defining Ethical Parameters for Artificial Entities:

In "Beyond the Code: Ethical Dilemmas in the AI Era," the fascinating journey of AI ethics continues to delves into the complex and intriguing realm of "Defining Ethical Parameters for Artificial Entities." This segment of the story explores the profound challenge of establishing moral guidelines and ethical boundaries for entities born not of flesh and blood, but of code and algorithms.

The tale begins in the bustling laboratories and quiet studies where AI is crafted. Here, creators are faced with a daunting question: How do you instill ethical principles into a machine? The story paints a picture of developers and ethicists huddled around screens and scribbled notes, attempting to translate age-old ethical doctrines into a language that machines can understand and act upon.

As the chapter unfolds, it reveals the multifaceted nature of this task. It's not just about programming an AI to avoid causing harm; it's a deeper quest to embed a sense of fairness, justice, and respect for human values into the very core of AI systems. The narrative weaves through the challenges of defining what these values mean in a diverse and ever-changing world and how they can be universally applied to the actions of artificial entities.

An integral part of this story is the exploration of AI's decision-making processes. The chapter delves into the ethical conundrums posed by AI systems that must make choices impacting human lives. It touches on the development of autonomous vehicles, where decisions on how to avoid accidents involve complex moral calculations, and healthcare AI, where algorithms can determine diagnoses and treatments.

The narrative also grapples with the notion of accountability. It raises poignant questions: When an AI makes a decision, who is ultimately responsible – the machine, its developers, or the users? This part of the story delves into the legal and ethical frameworks being developed to address these questions, painting a picture of a society striving to keep pace with its own creations.

The tale of AI ethics moves beyond the realm of theory into the practicalities of application. It tells of the ongoing efforts to create ethical AI, from drafting guidelines and standards to implementing them in real-world scenarios. The narrative highlights both the triumphs and trials in this endeavor, showcasing examples where AI has enhanced lives while also acknowledging instances where it has fallen short of ethical expectations.

As the chapter draws to a close, it leaves readers pondering the future of AI ethics. The story suggests a continuous journey, one where the defining of ethical parameters for artificial entities is an evolving process, adapting to new advancements in AI and shifting societal values. It's a future where the relationship between humans and AI is defined not just by technological interaction but by a shared commitment to ethical coexistence.

Chapter 2: Delegating Decisions to Machines

This chapter aims to explore the implications, challenges, and potential benefits of entrusting machines with critical choices in various domains.

I. **Historical Context and Evolution**:

The chapter begins by providing a historical overview of how decision-making has evolved from human to machine-driven processes. It discusses the advent of computers and their initial roles in aiding human decisions, gradually shifting towards more autonomous decision-making capabilities with advancements in AI and machine learning.

This exploration is crucial for understanding not just how we got to where we are today, but also the implications and trajectories of this evolution.

1. **Early Computational Tools and Their Impact**: The section begins by examining the earliest forms of computational tools, such as the abacus and mechanical calculators. It highlights how these tools augmented human decision-making capabilities, setting a precedent for the reliance on technology for complex calculations and data analysis.

2. **The Dawn of Computers and Basic Decision Support Systems**: The narrative then shifts to the invention of computers and their initial applications. Early computers, though rudimentary by today's standards, were pivotal in automating basic tasks and calculations. The chapter discusses the development of the first decision support systems, which assisted professionals in fields like logistics and management with data storage and basic analysis.

3. **Artificial Intelligence: From Concept to Reality**: A significant portion of this section is devoted to the evolution of artificial intelligence. It traces the journey from theoretical concepts and early experiments in AI during the mid-20th century, through the AI winters and periods of skepticism, to the resurgence and rapid advancement in the late 20th and early 21st centuries. Key milestones, such as the development of machine learning algorithms and neural networks, are emphasized.

4. **The Internet Era and Big Data**: The narrative then examines the impact of the internet and the explosion of data it generated. This era

transformed the landscape of machine decision-making by providing unprecedented amounts of data and connectivity. The chapter discusses how this led to more sophisticated and powerful AI systems capable of making more complex decisions.

5. **Recent Advances in AI and Machine Learning**: The focus shifts to the most recent advancements in AI, particularly deep learning and reinforcement learning. The section discusses how these technologies have enabled machines to make decisions in real-time, learn from experience, and even surpass human performance in specific tasks.

6. **Societal Integration and Perception Shifts**: Finally, the section explores how societal perceptions of machine decision-making have evolved alongside technological advancements. It discusses the growing acceptance and reliance on AI in everyday life, as well as the ongoing debates and concerns about the role of AI in critical decision-making processes.

Throughout this exploration, the section provides a comprehensive historical context, allowing readers to appreciate the gradual but significant shift from human to machine-driven decision-making. This background sets the stage for understanding the current challenges, ethical considerations, and future possibilities in delegating decisions to machines.

II. **Domains of Impact**:

Various sectors where machine decision-making is prominent are explored. This includes areas like healthcare, where algorithms assist in diagnosis and treatment plans; finance, where algorithms influence trading and investment strategies; and autonomous vehicles, where decisions about navigation and safety are made in real-time by AI systems.

This section underscores the breadth and depth of the impact that automated decision-making systems have across different aspects of society and industry.

1. **Healthcare**: The chapter delves into how AI and machine learning are revolutionizing healthcare. It discusses the use of algorithms in diagnosing diseases, predicting patient outcomes, personalizing treatment plans, and even in drug discovery and development. The impact of AI on improving diagnostic accuracy, particularly in areas like radiology and pathology, is highlighted. Additionally, the section

explores the challenges, such as data privacy concerns and the need for explainability in AI-driven medical decisions.

2. **Finance and Banking**: In finance, algorithms now play a crucial role in various aspects, from personal banking to high-frequency trading. The section examines how AI is used for credit scoring, fraud detection, automated trading, portfolio management, and in robo-advisors for personal finance management. The implications of these technologies on market dynamics, regulatory challenges, and the potential risks of algorithmic trading are also discussed.

3. **Transportation and Autonomous Vehicles**: This part focuses on the transformative impact of AI in transportation, particularly through autonomous vehicles (AVs). The discussion covers how machine learning algorithms process data from sensors for navigation, obstacle avoidance, and decision-making in real-time. The section also touches on the broader implications of AVs on urban planning, traffic management, and the ethical considerations in programming decision-making algorithms in life-critical situations.

4. **Retail and E-commerce**: The chapter explores the use of AI in personalizing shopping experiences and optimizing supply chains in retail and e-commerce. It discusses how machine learning models analyze customer data to provide personalized recommendations, manage inventory, and predict trends. The impact of these technologies on consumer behavior and the changing landscape of retail is also examined.

5. **Legal and Judicial Systems**: Here, the focus is on how AI tools assist in legal research, document analysis, and even in predictive analytics for legal outcomes. The section discusses the potential for AI to increase efficiency in legal processes, but also raises concerns about bias, transparency, and the ethical implications of AI in legal decision-making.

6. **Public Policy and Governance**: The chapter also addresses the role of AI in public policy and governance, including urban planning, environmental management, and public safety. It discusses how machine learning models are being used to analyze large datasets for policy decision-making, predict social trends, and in some cases, directly influence public policy decisions.

7. **Ethical Implications and Societal Impact**: Throughout each domain, the chapter interweaves a discussion on the ethical implications and societal impact of delegating decisions to machines. This includes the risks of bias and discrimination in AI systems, the challenge of ensuring fairness and transparency, and the broader societal changes driven by these technologies.

By exploring these diverse domains, the section paints a comprehensive picture of the pervasive influence of machine decision-making in modern life. It highlights both the transformative potential of these technologies as well as the complex challenges they present, setting the stage for a deeper discussion on the balance between technological advancement and ethical responsibility.

III. **Accuracy and Efficiency**:

The chapter highlights the enhanced accuracy and efficiency that machines often bring to decision-making. It discusses how machines can process vast amounts of data more quickly and accurately than humans, leading to potentially more informed and effective decisions.

The focus is on the significant improvements in decision-making processes that machines bring, particularly in terms of accuracy and efficiency. This section thoroughly examines how and why machines often outperform humans in specific tasks, and the implications of this for various industries and societal functions.

1. **Superior Data Processing Capabilities**: The chapter begins by highlighting the fundamental advantage of machines: their ability to process and analyze vast quantities of data at speeds far beyond human capabilities. It discusses how this processing power enables more accurate predictions, assessments, and decisions, particularly in data-intensive fields such as climate modeling, financial forecasting, and market analysis.

2. **Reduction in Human Error**: An important aspect covered is the reduction in human error. Machines, unlike humans, are not prone to fatigue, emotional bias, or cognitive overload, which often affect human decision-making. The section illustrates this with examples from medical diagnostics, where AI has been shown to reduce diagnostic errors, and in manufacturing, where automated systems improve quality control.

43

3. **Consistency in Decision-Making**: Another key point is the consistency that machines bring to decision-making processes. The chapter discusses how algorithms, once trained, can apply the same criteria uniformly across numerous cases, which is particularly beneficial in areas like judicial decision-making and human resources, where consistency is paramount.

4. **Real-Time Analysis and Decision-Making**: The ability of machines to make decisions in real-time is a critical advantage in certain contexts. This is exemplified in the realm of autonomous vehicles and high-frequency trading, where decisions need to be made in milliseconds. The chapter explores how this real-time processing capability can lead to more efficient and timely responses.

5. **Enhanced Predictive Capabilities**: The section also delves into the enhanced predictive capabilities of machine learning algorithms. It discusses how predictive analytics can foresee trends, customer behavior, and potential system failures, which is invaluable for sectors like retail, maintenance, and urban planning.

6. **Scalability of Solutions**: Another point of discussion is the scalability of machine-based decision systems. Unlike human-based processes, machine learning models can easily be scaled up to handle larger datasets and more complex decision environments, such as managing large-scale logistics or global supply chains.

7. **Challenges and Limitations**: Despite these advantages, the chapter does not overlook the challenges and limitations of relying on machines for decision-making. It discusses issues like the need for high-quality data, the risks of over-reliance on algorithms, and the challenges in understanding and interpreting the decisions made by AI systems.

8. **Impact on Employment and Skills**: Finally, the section touches on the impact of increased machine decision-making on employment and skill requirements. It discusses how the demand for certain jobs may decrease while increasing the need for new skills, such as AI literacy and data analysis.

Overall, this section of the chapter provides a balanced view of the accuracy and efficiency benefits that machines offer in decision-making, while also acknowledging the complexities and challenges that come with this technological shift. It underscores the transformative potential of these technologies but also cautions against an uncritical embrace, advocating for a more nuanced and informed approach.

IV.   **Ethical Considerations**:

A significant part of the chapter is dedicated to the ethical implications of machine decision-making. This includes discussions on bias in AI, the transparency of algorithms, the accountability for decisions made by machines, and the potential for AI to perpetuate existing societal inequalities.

This section delves deeply into the moral and societal dilemmas posed by the increasing autonomy of machines, exploring various dimensions of ethics that are crucial in understanding and guiding this technological evolution.

1.   **Algorithmic Bias and Fairness**: A significant part of the section is devoted to the issue of algorithmic bias. The chapter discusses how biases in data or in the design of algorithms can lead to unfair and discriminatory outcomes. This is particularly critical in areas like criminal justice, hiring practices, and loan approvals, where biased decisions can have profound impacts on individuals' lives. The section explores the challenges in identifying, mitigating, and preventing these biases.

2.   **Transparency and Explainability**: The opacity of many machine learning algorithms poses a significant ethical challenge, often referred to as the "black box" problem. This part of the chapter addresses the importance of transparency and explainability in AI systems, especially when decisions have significant consequences. It discusses the need for algorithms to be understandable and accountable, allowing for human oversight and intervention where necessary.

3.   **Privacy Concerns**: With machines often requiring vast amounts of data to make decisions, privacy becomes a major ethical concern. The section examines the tension between leveraging data for better decision-making and safeguarding individuals' privacy. It discusses the ethical implications of data collection, storage, and usage, along with the legal frameworks and regulations like GDPR that are in place to protect privacy.

4.   **Autonomy and Human Agency**: This part of the chapter explores the impact of machine decision-making on human autonomy and agency. It

45

debates the ethical implications of delegating significant decisions to machines, potentially reducing human involvement and oversight. The concern is that over-reliance on machines might erode human decision-making skills and agency.

5. **Responsibility and Accountability**: A key ethical question discussed is who is responsible for the decisions made by machines. The section delves into the challenges of attributing accountability, especially in scenarios where autonomous systems make decisions without direct human input. It explores the legal and moral aspects of responsibility in cases of errors or harm caused by machine decisions.

6. **Societal Impact and Inequality**: The chapter also considers the broader societal implications of delegating decisions to machines. It discusses how the widespread use of AI in decision-making could exacerbate existing societal inequalities, especially if access to and control of these technologies is unevenly distributed. The potential for AI to both mitigate and exacerbate social issues is explored.

7. **Future Ethical Challenges**: Finally, the section looks forward to potential future ethical challenges as AI technology continues to advance. It speculates on issues such as the increasing autonomy of AI systems, the potential for manipulation or misuse of AI, and the ethical considerations in emerging fields like AI in warfare and advanced biotechnology.

Overall, this section of the chapter provides a thorough examination of the ethical considerations surrounding the delegation of decisions to machines. It emphasizes the importance of a proactive and thoughtful approach to these issues, advocating for the development of ethical frameworks and guidelines to ensure that the integration of AI into decision-making processes is responsible and beneficial for society as a whole.

V. **Human-Machine Collaboration:**

The chapter also explores the concept of collaborative decision-making, where humans and machines work together. It discusses how this approach can leverage the strengths of both — the emotional intelligence and ethical reasoning of humans, combined with the analytical power of machines.

This section highlights how the integration of human intuition and ethical reasoning with the analytical prowess of machines can lead to more effective and responsible decision-making.

1. **Complementing Strengths**: The chapter begins by emphasizing the complementary nature of human and machine capabilities. While machines excel in processing vast amounts of data and identifying patterns, humans bring critical thinking, emotional intelligence, and moral judgment to the table. The section provides examples from healthcare, where doctors' expertise combined with AI diagnostics lead to better patient outcomes, and in business, where strategic decisions benefit from both AI-driven insights and human experience.

2. **Augmented Decision-Making**: A key theme in this section is the concept of augmented decision-making. The chapter discusses how machines can enhance human decision-making by providing comprehensive data analysis, predictive insights, and decision support tools. This is particularly evident in fields like finance, where AI can analyze market trends but human judgment is crucial for strategic investment decisions.

3. **Interactive Learning Systems**: The narrative explores the idea of interactive learning, where humans and machines learn from each other. It discusses systems where human feedback is used to improve machine learning algorithms, and conversely, where insights from machines help humans understand complex patterns and refine their strategies. Examples from fields like urban planning and environmental management are highlighted.

4. **Ethical Oversight and Judgment**: This part focuses on the critical role of human ethical oversight in machine decision-making. The section argues that while machines can provide recommendations based on data, humans must be the final arbiters in decisions with ethical implications. This is particularly relevant in law enforcement and judicial systems, where decisions can have profound impacts on human lives.

5. **Collaborative Interfaces and Tools**: The chapter discusses the development of interfaces and tools that facilitate effective human-machine collaboration. This includes user-friendly dashboards, visualization tools, and systems that allow for easy input and interpretation of machine-generated data and recommendations. The

importance of designing these tools to be accessible and intuitive for various users is emphasized.

6. **Challenges in Collaboration**: The section also addresses the challenges in human-machine collaboration. These include ensuring effective communication between humans and machines, overcoming human biases that might affect the interpretation of machine-generated data, and managing the trust and reliance on machine decision-making.

7. **Future Prospects of Collaboration**: Finally, the chapter speculates on the future of human-machine collaboration. It discusses emerging technologies like brain-computer interfaces and advanced collaborative robots (cobots), envisioning a future where the integration of human and machine decision-making becomes even more seamless and impactful.

Overall, this section advocates for a balanced approach, leveraging the best of both worlds to achieve decisions that are not only effective and efficient but also responsible and ethically sound.

VI. **Future Prospects and Challenges**:

The chapter concludes with a forward-looking perspective, discussing future developments in AI decision-making. It speculates on the potential advancements and challenges, including the need for robust regulatory frameworks and the evolving role of human oversight in machine-driven decisions.

This section aims to provide insights into what the future might hold in this rapidly evolving field and the critical considerations that must be taken into account.

1. **Advancements in AI and Machine Learning**: The chapter starts by outlining the expected technological advancements in AI. This includes more sophisticated machine learning models capable of processing even larger datasets, improvements in natural language processing for better understanding and generating human-like language, and advances in neural networks that mimic human brain functioning. The potential impact of these advancements on various sectors, such as healthcare, finance, and transportation, is discussed.

2. **Integration in Everyday Life**: A significant focus is placed on the increasing integration of AI in everyday decision-making, both at the

individual and organizational levels. The chapter explores how this could manifest in personalized AI assistants for individuals, more intelligent and autonomous business processes, and smarter city infrastructure management systems.

3. **Regulatory and Ethical Frameworks**: The section emphasizes the growing need for robust regulatory and ethical frameworks to manage the deployment of AI in decision-making. It discusses the challenges in creating regulations that keep pace with technological advancements, ensuring fair and unbiased AI systems, and protecting individual privacy and rights.

4. **Human Oversight and Control**: The importance of maintaining human oversight and control in AI decision-making is a key theme. The chapter argues for the development of systems where human judgment is not entirely replaced but is enhanced by AI, ensuring that ethical and moral considerations are not overlooked.

5. **Challenges in Data Quality and Accessibility**: The narrative also addresses the challenges related to data quality and accessibility. The dependence of AI on large datasets raises concerns about the accuracy, privacy, and security of the data used, as well as the potential for creating digital divides where some entities have more access to high-quality data than others.

6. **AI in Global Context**: The chapter explores the implications of AI decision-making in a global context, including its impact on international relations, global markets, and cross-cultural ethical standards. It discusses how AI can both bridge and exacerbate global inequalities, and the need for international cooperation in developing AI technologies.

7. **Public Perception and Trust**: Understanding and influencing public perception and trust in AI systems is another critical aspect. The section discusses strategies to build public trust in AI through transparency, education, and demonstrating the value and safety of AI in decision-making.

8. **Emerging Ethical Dilemmas**: Finally, the chapter delves into emerging ethical dilemmas, such as the potential for AI to be used in manipulative ways in areas like marketing and politics, and the moral implications of AI decisions in life-critical situations.

Overall, this section provides a comprehensive overview of the anticipated future developments in delegating decisions to machines, balanced with a discussion of the challenges and ethical considerations that accompany these advancements. It emphasizes the need for a proactive approach in addressing these challenges to harness the full potential of AI in decision-making while safeguarding societal values and individual rights.

The Allure of Automation: Benefits and Pitfalls:

In the section, the narrative delves into the dual nature of automation in decision-making. This part of the chapter critically examines both the enticing advantages and the potential drawbacks of relying heavily on automated systems. It aims to present a balanced view, helping readers to appreciate the complexities and nuances of this technological shift.

1. **Benefits of Automation**:

   - **Increased Efficiency and Productivity**: The chapter begins by highlighting the most evident benefit of automation: its ability to significantly increase efficiency and productivity. Automated systems can process and analyze data at a pace no human team can match, leading to faster decision-making and operational speeds.

   - **Cost Reduction**: Automation is also associated with cost savings. By streamlining processes and reducing the need for manual labor, especially in repetitive tasks, organizations can lower operational costs.

   - **Improved Accuracy and Consistency**: Automated systems are less prone to the errors and inconsistencies that can arise from human fatigue or subjectivity. This is particularly beneficial in fields requiring high precision, such as manufacturing and data analysis.

   - **Enhanced Data Handling and Analysis**: Automation excels in handling vast quantities of data, extracting insights and patterns that might be impossible for humans to discern, thereby facilitating more informed decision-making.

2. **Pitfalls of Automation**:

   - **Over-Reliance and Skill Degradation**: One major concern is the over-reliance on automated systems, potentially leading to skill degradation in humans. As machines take over more tasks, there's a risk that human workers may lose critical skills or fail to develop them in the first place.

- **Job Displacement**: Automation can lead to job displacement, with machines replacing human roles, particularly in sectors like manufacturing and customer service. This raises concerns about economic and social impacts, such as unemployment and job market shifts.

- **Security and Privacy Risks**: The chapter discusses how increased automation can lead to heightened security and privacy risks. Automated systems often rely on large datasets, including personal information, which can be vulnerable to breaches or misuse.

- **Lack of Flexibility and Creativity**: Automated systems, while efficient, often lack the flexibility and creativity inherent in human decision-making. This can be a drawback in situations that require out-of-the-box thinking or a nuanced understanding of human emotions and social contexts.

- **Bias and Ethical Concerns**: There's an inherent risk of bias in automated systems, particularly if the data they are trained on is biased. The chapter also touches on the ethical concerns of removing human judgment from critical decision-making processes.

3. **Navigating the Balance**:

   - **Integration Rather Than Replacement**: The chapter advocates for a balanced approach, suggesting that the goal should be to integrate automation into human workflows rather than replacing humans entirely. This approach leverages the strengths of both humans and machines.

   - **Continuous Monitoring and Evaluation**: It emphasizes the importance of continuously monitoring and evaluating automated systems to ensure they are functioning as intended and to mitigate any negative impacts.

   - **Education and Training**: To address the challenges of skill degradation and job displacement, the chapter suggests investing in education and training programs that can prepare the workforce for a more automated future.

   - **Ethical and Regulatory Frameworks**: Finally, the chapter calls for the development of strong ethical and regulatory frameworks to govern the use of automation, ensuring that it is used responsibly and for the benefit of society as a whole.

Overall, this section provides a comprehensive overview of the enticements and challenges of automation in decision-making. It encourages a thoughtful and measured approach to the adoption of automated systems, one that recognizes their potential benefits while being mindful of their limitations and potential adverse impacts.

Can A Machine Truly "Decide"?

In the section, the narrative delves into the philosophical and practical aspects of what it means for a machine to make a decision. This contemplative section probes the nature of decision-making, contrasting human and machine processes, and questioning the extent to which what machines do can be equated with the human concept of decision-making.

1. **Defining Decision-Making**:

   - **Human Decision-Making**: The chapter begins by exploring the complexity of human decision-making, which involves not just logical analysis, but also emotional, ethical, and intuitive factors. It discusses how humans make decisions based on a blend of conscious reasoning, subconscious influences, and past experiences.

   - **Machine Decision-Making**: In contrast, machine decision-making is presented as primarily data-driven and algorithm-based. Machines follow programmed instructions to process information and produce outputs based on predefined criteria and statistical models.

2. **Limits of Machine Decisions**:

   - **Lack of Consciousness and Intuition**: One of the core arguments is that machines, as they currently exist, lack consciousness and the ability to intuit, which are fundamental aspects of human decision-making. The chapter debates whether machine outputs based on data processing can be equated with the human cognitive process of making a decision.

   - **Dependence on Human-Defined Parameters**: The section highlights that machines operate within the parameters set by humans, including the selection of data and the determination of what constitutes a 'correct' decision. This raises the question of whether machines truly 'decide' or merely execute sophisticated calculations and pattern recognitions.

3. **The Illusion of Autonomy**:

   - **Perceived Versus Actual Autonomy**: The chapter discusses how the increasing complexity of algorithms can create the illusion of autonomy in machines. However, it emphasizes that this autonomy is limited to the scope defined by human programmers, and machines do not possess self-awareness or independent goals.

4. **Ethical and Philosophical Implications**:

   - **Responsibility and Accountability**: A significant focus is on the ethical implications of attributing decision-making to machines. The section questions who holds responsibility for a machine's decisions, especially when those decisions have moral or legal consequences.

   - **Redefining Decision-Making**: The chapter also philosophically examines the need to potentially redefine what is meant by 'decision-making' in the context of advanced AI and machine learning technologies.

5. **Future Prospects**:

   - **Evolving Capabilities of AI**: Looking to the future, the chapter speculates on how advancements in AI might blur the lines between human and machine decision-making. It discusses the potential for machines to simulate aspects of human thought processes, such as learning from experience or adapting to new information.

   - **The Possibility of Artificial Consciousness**: The section concludes by exploring the theoretical possibility of artificial consciousness and its implications for decision-making. It discusses ongoing research in this area and the profound philosophical questions it raises about the nature of intelligence and decision-making.

Overall, this section of the chapter provides a deep and nuanced exploration of the concept of decision-making in the context of machine intelligence. It challenges readers to consider the fundamental differences between human and machine processes and to critically assess the implications of these differences in the evolving landscape of AI and automation.

Case Studies: Autonomous Vehicles and The Trolley Problem:

In the section, the discussion centers around a critical examination of how autonomous vehicles (AVs) handle complex ethical decisions, particularly in scenarios akin to the classic trolley problem. This section uses case studies to explore the challenges of programming ethics into machines and the implications of these choices.

1. **The Trolley Problem Explained**:

   - **Background**: The chapter introduces the trolley problem, a famous ethical dilemma used in philosophy. The basic premise involves a runaway trolley headed towards a group of people. One can choose to pull a lever to switch the trolley to a different track, where it will kill fewer people, but taking action will directly cause these deaths.

   - **Relevance to AVs**: This thought experiment is adapted to the context of autonomous vehicles. The chapter discusses how AVs might be programmed to react in situations where a collision is unavoidable, and the vehicle must 'decide' between two harmful outcomes.

2. **Programming Ethics into Machines**:

   - **Algorithmic Decision-Making**: The section delves into the complexities of programming ethical decision-making into AVs. It discusses the challenges in translating human ethical principles into algorithms and the variability in ethical standards across cultures.

   - **Responsibility and Liability**: There is a focus on the implications of these programmed decisions in terms of responsibility and liability. The chapter raises questions about who is accountable for a machine's decision in a critical situation - the manufacturer, the programmer, or the vehicle itself.

3. **Case Studies of Autonomous Vehicles**:

   - **Real-World Scenarios**: The chapter presents various case studies where AVs have faced complex decision-making scenarios. These include instances of unavoidable accidents and how the vehicle's programming dictated its response.

   - **Analysis of Outcomes**: Each case study is analyzed to understand the implications of the AV's decision, questioning whether the outcomes align with societal ethical standards and exploring public reaction to these incidents.

4. **Public Perception and Trust**:

   - **Survey Data**: The chapter incorporates survey data on public perception of AVs and their decision-making in ethical dilemmas. This highlights the disparity in public expectations and the actual capabilities of current technology.

   - **Trust in Technology**: The section discusses how these ethical considerations impact public trust in AVs and the broader acceptance of autonomous technology.

5. **Theoretical and Practical Implications**:

   - **Ethical Frameworks**: The discussion extends to theoretical frameworks for ethical decision-making in AVs, exploring different philosophical approaches, such as utilitarianism and deontological ethics.

   - **Practical Implementations**: The chapter also touches on the practical aspects of implementing these ethical frameworks in the programming of AVs and the ongoing challenges in this field.

6. **Future Directions**:

   - **Evolving Standards and Regulations**: The section concludes with a look at how ethical decision-making in AVs might evolve, considering potential advancements in AI and changes in regulatory standards.

   - **Collaborative Efforts**: It suggests the need for collaborative efforts between ethicists, engineers, policymakers, and the public to develop acceptable standards for ethical decision-making in autonomous vehicles.

Overall, this section of the chapter provides an in-depth exploration of the intersection between ethics and technology in the context of autonomous vehicles. It offers a critical analysis of the current state of AV decision-making, the ethical challenges involved, and the potential paths forward in this rapidly developing field.

Chapter 3: Built-in Biases

In the chapter, the focus shifts to the critical issue of bias in artificial intelligence and machine learning systems. This chapter comprehensively explores how biases can be inadvertently embedded in these technologies, the consequences of such biases, and potential strategies to mitigate them.

I. **Understanding Bias in AI**:

➢ **Origins of Bias**:

The chapter begins by examining the roots of bias in AI systems. It discusses how biases can originate from various sources, including the data used to train algorithms, the design of the algorithms themselves, and the human teams that create and manage these systems.

This part of the chapter systematically breaks down the various sources from which biases can emanate, providing a detailed exploration of how these biases become embedded in AI technologies.

1. **Data-Driven Biases**:

- **Bias in Training Data**: The chapter begins by addressing how biases often originate from the data used to train AI systems. It explains that if the training data is unrepresentative of the broader population or contains historical biases, the AI system will likely perpetuate and amplify these biases.

- **Sampling Bias**: The section also discusses sampling bias, which occurs when the data collected for training does not accurately represent the environment in which the AI system will operate, leading to skewed results and decisions.

2. **Human-Centric Biases**:

- **Design and Development Bias**: The chapter highlights that biases can be introduced during the design and development phase of AI systems. The personal, cultural, and cognitive biases of the programmers and engineers can inadvertently shape decision-making criteria and algorithmic design.

- **Confirmation Bias in Model Selection**: There is a discussion on how confirmation bias can influence the selection of models and algorithms, where developers might choose or tune models that align with their expectations or beliefs.

3. **Algorithmic Bias**:

- **Algorithm Design**: The section delves into how the design of algorithms themselves can be a source of bias. Certain algorithms may be more prone to bias, depending on how they are structured and the kind of data they are optimized to handle.

- **Feedback Loops**: The chapter discusses the phenomenon of feedback loops, where AI systems reinforce and exacerbate existing biases. For instance, a biased AI system in use can generate new data, which is then used to further train and reinforce the system's biases.

4. **Societal and Historical Biases**:

- **Reflection of Societal Inequities**: The narrative also explores how AI systems can reflect and perpetuate societal and historical inequities. It discusses how systemic issues like racism, sexism, and other forms of discrimination can be mirrored in AI systems if not actively countered.

- **Historical Data Issues**: The use of historical data, which may contain outdated or discriminatory practices and norms, is examined as a significant source of bias in AI systems.

5. **Structural and Institutional Biases**:

- **Institutional Decision-Making**: The chapter considers how institutional decision-making processes and policies can introduce biases into AI systems. This includes the influence of corporate interests, governmental policies, and market forces that can shape the development and deployment of AI technologies.

- **Lack of Diverse Perspectives**: The absence of diverse perspectives in AI development teams and decision-making processes is highlighted as a critical factor. This lack of diversity can result in the overlooking of certain biases and the failure to consider a wide range of human experiences and needs.

By comprehensively examining the origins of bias in AI, this section of the chapter lays the foundation for understanding the multifaceted nature of this challenge. It emphasizes the need for vigilance and proactive measures at each stage of AI development to identify and mitigate these biases, ensuring that AI systems are fair, equitable, and beneficial for all.

➢ **Types of Bias**:

Different types of biases are identified and explained, such as selection bias, confirmation bias, and algorithmic bias. The chapter emphasizes that these biases can be both explicit and implicit, affecting the outcomes of AI systems in subtle and often unnoticed ways.

This part is crucial for understanding the breadth and depth of bias in AI, offering insights into how these biases might affect AI decision-making and impact users.

1. **Selection Bias**:

- **Definition and Explanation**: Selection bias occurs when the data used to train an AI system is not representative of the real-world environment in which the system will operate. This can lead to AI models that perform well on the training data but poorly in real-world applications.

- **Examples in AI**: The chapter provides examples such as facial recognition systems trained predominantly on certain demographic groups, leading to lower accuracy in recognizing individuals from underrepresented groups.

2. **Confirmation Bias**:

- **Influence on Data Interpretation**: Confirmation bias refers to the tendency to favor information that confirms pre-existing beliefs. In AI, this can occur when developers interpret data in a way that aligns with their expectations.

- **Impact on Model Development**: The section explains how confirmation bias can influence the development and tuning of AI models, potentially leading to biased outcomes and overlooking alternative solutions.

3. **Algorithmic Bias**:

- **Bias in Algorithm Design**: Algorithmic bias arises from the way algorithms are designed and function. It can be due to the inherent limitations of the algorithm or the way it processes data.

- **Consequences in Decision-Making**: The chapter discusses the impact of algorithmic bias on decision-making, such as in loan approval processes or job applicant screening, where certain groups may be unfairly disadvantaged.

4. **Historical Bias**:

- **Roots in Historical Data**: Historical bias is present when AI systems learn from historical data that contains biases. Since AI systems often use past data to make predictions about the future, they can perpetuate outdated or discriminatory practices.

- **Long-Term Impacts**: The section highlights how historical biases can have long-term impacts, especially in areas like criminal justice and hiring, where past discriminatory practices might continue to influence AI decisions.

5. **Societal and Cultural Bias**:

- **Reflecting Societal Norms**: Societal and cultural biases are embedded in AI when the data or the AI development process reflects societal norms and values that may be biased.

- **Examples and Implications**: The chapter gives examples such as voice recognition systems that better understand certain accents or dialects over others, reflecting and perpetuating linguistic biases.

6. **Measurement Bias**:

- **Data Measurement Issues**: Measurement bias occurs when the data collected for training an AI system is not accurate or is measured inconsistently. This can skew the AI system's understanding and interpretation of the data.

- **Impact on Model Accuracy**: The section explains how measurement bias can lead to inaccurate models, affecting the reliability of AI predictions and decisions.

7. **Implicit Bias**:

- **Subconscious Influences**: Implicit bias refers to the subconscious attitudes or stereotypes that affect understanding, actions, and decisions. In AI, this type of bias can manifest when these subconscious human biases influence the way AI systems are programmed or the data they are trained on.

- **Challenges in Identification**: The chapter discusses the difficulty in identifying and addressing implicit biases, as they are often deeply ingrained and not overtly recognizable.

By dissecting the various types of biases that can infiltrate AI systems, this section of the chapter provides a comprehensive framework for understanding the multifaceted nature of AI biases. It underscores the importance of recognizing and addressing these biases to develop AI technologies that are fair, equitable, and trustworthy.

II. **Case Studies and Examples**:

➢ **Real-World Impacts**:

This section presents several case studies highlighting instances where biases in AI systems have led to unfair or discriminatory outcomes. These might include biases in facial recognition technology, hiring algorithms, credit scoring systems, and criminal justice algorithms.

1. **Facial Recognition Technology**:

- **Case Study on Racial Bias**: The chapter presents a case study on how facial recognition technology has shown significant racial biases. Instances are cited where such systems have had higher error rates in identifying individuals of certain racial backgrounds, leading to wrongful arrests and heightened surveillance of minority communities.

- **Societal Implications**: The real-world impacts of these biases, such as the infringement on civil liberties and the perpetuation of racial profiling, are discussed, highlighting the ethical and social consequences.

2. **Hiring Algorithms**:

- **Gender Bias in Recruitment**: A case study is presented on AI systems used for screening job applicants, which have been found to exhibit gender biases. Examples include algorithms that favored male candidates or resumes due to historical data reflecting male dominance in certain industries.

- **Impact on Employment Opportunities**: The section discusses how such biases can lead to unfair job opportunities, reinforcing gender disparities in the workplace and impacting career progression for underrepresented groups.

3. **Healthcare Diagnostics**:

- **Bias in Medical Algorithms**: The chapter examines case studies where AI algorithms in healthcare have shown biases against certain demographic groups. For instance, algorithms that were less accurate in diagnosing diseases in certain ethnic groups due to training data predominantly consisting of other demographics.

- **Consequences for Patient Care**: The implications for patient care and health outcomes are explored, emphasizing the potential for misdiagnosis, delayed treatment, and overall health inequities.

4. **Credit Scoring and Financial Services**:

- **Economic Bias in Lending**: A case study focuses on AI systems used in credit scoring and lending decisions. It discusses how these systems can inherit biases from historical financial data, leading to certain groups being unfairly denied loans or charged higher interest rates.

- **Economic Inequality and Access to Credit**: The chapter highlights the broader economic impact, including perpetuating economic inequality and restricting access to credit for marginalized communities.

5. **Criminal Justice and Predictive Policing**:

- **Racial Bias in Crime Prediction**: The section includes a case study on predictive policing algorithms that have been criticized for racial bias. These systems can disproportionately target minority neighborhoods based on biased historical crime data.

- **Implications for Justice and Community Relations**: The chapter discusses the ramifications for criminal justice, including the potential for perpetuating a cycle of over-policing in certain communities and eroding trust in law enforcement.

6. **AI in Education**:

- **Bias in Educational Tools**: A case study is presented on AI educational tools and their biases. Instances where AI algorithms have shown preference for certain learning styles or language proficiencies, leading to unequal educational support, are discussed.

- **Impact on Learning Outcomes and Opportunities**: The potential for these biases to affect students' learning outcomes and exacerbate educational inequalities is explored, emphasizing the need for equitable AI in education.

By presenting these case studies, the "Real-World Impacts" section vividly illustrates how built-in biases in AI systems can have far-reaching and sometimes devastating consequences. These examples serve as a powerful call to action for more responsible AI development and deployment, underlining the need for vigilant oversight and continuous efforts to mitigate biases.

➢ **Analysis of Consequences**:

Each case study is analyzed to understand the broader implications of these biases, not just for the individuals directly affected but also for society as a whole.

1. **Consequences in Facial Recognition Technology**:

- **Impact on Minority Communities**: The chapter analyzes how biases in facial recognition technology disproportionately affect minority communities, leading to higher rates of wrongful identification and potential legal consequences. It discusses the erosion of trust in law enforcement and the chilling effect on civil liberties and privacy rights.

- **Public Policy Implications**: The analysis extends to how these biases can influence public policy, potentially leading to biased law enforcement practices and perpetuating systemic racial discrimination.

2. **Implications of Biases in Hiring Algorithms**:

- **Workforce Diversity and Inclusion**: The chapter delves into how gender and racial biases in hiring algorithms can limit diversity and inclusion in the workplace. It discusses the long-term impact on career development for underrepresented groups and the perpetuation of existing workplace inequalities.

- **Economic Consequences**: Additionally, the economic consequences are examined, including the potential for a skewed labor market and the loss of diverse talents and perspectives in various industries.

3. **Biases in Healthcare Diagnostics**:

- **Patient Health Outcomes**: The analysis focuses on the serious implications for patient health outcomes due to biases in healthcare AI. It highlights cases of misdiagnosis, delayed treatments, and the exacerbation of existing health disparities.

- **Trust in Healthcare Systems**: The chapter also examines how such biases can undermine trust in healthcare systems, especially among marginalized groups, potentially leading to lower engagement with healthcare services and poorer health outcomes.

4. **Financial and Credit Scoring Biases**:

- **Economic Mobility and Access to Resources**: The consequences of biases in financial services AI are analyzed, particularly in terms of limiting economic mobility for affected groups. The chapter discusses how unfair credit scoring can restrict access to essential resources like housing and education.

- **Broader Economic Impact**: The broader economic impacts are also considered, including the perpetuation of poverty cycles and the implications for economic diversity and stability.

5. **Predictive Policing and Criminal Justice**:

- **Community Relations and Criminalization**: The chapter examines how biases in predictive policing algorithms can lead to over-policing of minority communities, damaging community relations and contributing to the criminalization of certain demographics.

- **Legal and Ethical Ramifications**: It also explores the legal and ethical ramifications, discussing the potential for violations of civil rights and the challenges of ensuring justice in an increasingly algorithm-driven legal system.

6. **Educational AI Tools**:

- **Educational Inequality**: The analysis includes the impact of biases in educational AI tools, highlighting how they can reinforce educational inequalities. The chapter discusses how certain students might be disadvantaged, leading to disparities in educational outcomes and opportunities.

- **Long-Term Societal Effects**: Finally, the long-term societal effects are considered, including the potential for perpetuating socio-economic divides and limiting upward mobility for affected groups.

Through this detailed analysis of consequences, the section provides a comprehensive understanding of the far-reaching effects of AI biases. It emphasizes the importance of addressing these biases not just from a technological standpoint but also from a societal and ethical perspective, underscoring the need for systemic changes in AI development and deployment practices.

III. **Challenges in Identifying and Addressing Bias**:

➢ **Complexity of AI Systems**:

The chapter discusses the inherent challenges in identifying biases within complex AI systems. It points out that the 'black box' nature of many AI algorithms makes it difficult to pinpoint where and how biases arise.

1. **Opaque Nature of Algorithms**:

- **'Black Box' Problem**: The chapter addresses the 'black box' nature of many AI algorithms, especially in advanced machine learning models like deep neural networks. It explains how the internal workings of these models are often not transparent, making it challenging to understand how they arrive at specific decisions or predictions.

- **Implications for Bias Identification**: The complexity and opacity of these algorithms can obscure the presence of biases, making it difficult to identify and understand the root causes of biased outcomes.

2. **Interconnected and Layered Systems**:

- **Interdependencies in AI Systems**: The chapter delves into how modern AI systems often consist of multiple interconnected layers and components. The interactions between these layers add to the complexity, as biases can emerge from the interplay of different parts of the system.

- **Challenges in Isolating Bias Sources**: This interconnectivity poses a challenge in isolating specific components or processes within the AI system that may be contributing to biased outcomes, complicating efforts to address the bias effectively.

3. **Dynamic and Evolving Nature of AI**:

- **Continuous Learning and Adaptation**: The section highlights the dynamic nature of many AI systems, particularly those involving machine learning, where the system continuously evolves based on new data and experiences.

- **Shifting Biases Over Time**: This evolving nature means that biases can shift or emerge over time, requiring ongoing monitoring and adjustment, which adds a layer of complexity to bias management.

4. **Variability in Data and Context**:

- **Diverse Data Sources and Contexts**: The chapter discusses how AI systems are often trained and deployed across a wide range of contexts and with diverse data sources. The variability in data and context can lead to different manifestations of bias in different settings.

- **Complexity in Standardizing Bias Assessment**: This variability makes it complex to develop standardized approaches for assessing and addressing bias, as solutions may need to be tailored to specific contexts or data types.

5. **Lack of Clear Guidelines and Benchmarks**:

- **Absence of Universal Standards**: The chapter points out the lack of universally accepted standards or benchmarks for what constitutes bias in AI systems. This absence makes it challenging to evaluate AI systems consistently and to determine the appropriateness of their decisions.

- **Difficulties in Benchmarking Fairness**: The complexity of creating benchmarks that can effectively capture the nuances of fairness and bias in AI systems is discussed, especially given the subjective nature of fairness and the diversity of cultural and societal norms.

By detailing these challenges associated with the complexity of AI systems, the section provides a thorough understanding of why identifying and addressing bias in AI is not straightforward. It highlights the need for sophisticated tools and methodologies, along with collaborative efforts from diverse disciplines, to tackle the issue of bias in the intricate landscape of artificial intelligence effectively.

➢ **Dynamic Nature of AI**:

Another challenge is the dynamic and evolving nature of AI. As these systems learn and adapt, biases can emerge or change over time, requiring continuous monitoring and adjustment.

1. **Continual Learning and Adaptation**:

- **Evolving Algorithms**: The chapter discusses how many AI systems, especially those based on machine learning, are designed to learn and evolve continually based on new data and experiences. This continuous learning process, while a strength of AI, also means that the system's behavior can change over time.

- **Implications for Bias Dynamics**: The dynamic nature of these systems can lead to the emergence of new biases or the alteration of existing ones. This continuous evolution poses significant challenges in tracking and addressing biases, as the system at one point might not behave the same way in the future.

2. **Feedback Loops**:

- **Reinforcement of Existing Biases**: The section delves into the issue of feedback loops, where AI systems can reinforce and perpetuate their own biases. For instance, if a biased AI system is used in a decision-making process, the outcomes it generates can further reinforce the initial bias when fed back into the system.

- **Challenges in Breaking the Cycle**: Breaking these feedback loops is complex, as it requires not just altering the AI system, but also understanding and intervening in the broader system in which the AI operates.

3. **Scale and Speed of AI Deployment**:

- **Rapid Deployment and Widespread Use**: The chapter highlights how the rapid scale and speed at which AI systems are deployed can amplify the impact of biases. When a biased AI system is rapidly scaled, its biased decisions can affect a large population quickly.

- **Difficulty in Timely Intervention**: The fast-paced deployment of AI technologies means that biases can spread widely before they are even identified, making timely intervention challenging.

4. **Complex Interaction with Changing Environments**:

- **Responsiveness to Environmental Changes**: AI systems are often responsive to changes in their operating environments. This adaptability, while beneficial in many respects, can also lead to the system developing new biases in response to changing environmental conditions or data patterns.

- **Predicting and Managing Evolving Biases**: The chapter discusses the difficulty in predicting how changes in the environment will affect the AI's behavior, complicating efforts to manage biases proactively.

5. **Data Drift and Concept Drift**:

- **Shifting Data Patterns**: The section explains the concepts of data drift and concept drift, where the data or the concepts the AI system was trained on change over time. This drift can lead to the AI system making decisions based on outdated or irrelevant information, potentially exacerbating biases.

- **Monitoring and Updating AI Systems**: The challenge lies in continuously monitoring AI systems for these shifts and updating them accordingly to ensure their decisions remain relevant and unbiased.

By examining the dynamic nature of AI, this section of the chapter underscores the need for ongoing vigilance and adaptive strategies in managing biases. It highlights the necessity of developing AI systems that are not only responsive to changes but also equipped with mechanisms to self-evaluate and adjust their behaviors to mitigate biases continuously. This dynamic approach is essential for ensuring that AI systems remain fair, equitable, and effective over time.

IV.   **Strategies for Mitigating Bias**:

➤ **Diverse Data and Teams**:

The chapter advocates for the use of diverse datasets to train AI systems, as well as the inclusion of diverse perspectives among the teams developing them. This diversity can help in identifying and mitigating potential biases.

1. **Incorporating Diverse Data Sets**:

- **Broadening Data Sources**: The chapter highlights the critical role of using diverse and inclusive data sets in training AI systems. It discusses how incorporating data from a wide range of sources and demographics can help in creating models that are more representative of the broader population.

- **Reducing Data-Driven Bias**: By using diverse data, the risk of biases inherent in limited or skewed data sets is reduced. The chapter provides examples of how including diverse data types and sources can help in identifying and mitigating potential biases early in the AI development process.

2. **Ensuring Data Quality and Relevance**:

- **Data Quality Assurance**: The section discusses the importance of not only diversity in data but also the quality and relevance of the data. It stresses the need for rigorous data quality checks to ensure that the data is accurate, up-to-date, and relevant to the problem being addressed.

- **Contextual Understanding of Data**: The chapter also emphasizes the importance of understanding the context from which the data is derived, arguing that contextual awareness is key in interpreting data correctly and avoiding misrepresentation in AI models.

3. **Diverse Development Teams**:

- **Benefits of Diversity in AI Teams**: The chapter explores how having a diverse group of people involved in the creation and management of AI systems can bring different perspectives, experiences, and insights, which is crucial in identifying and addressing potential biases.

- **Inclusivity in the Tech Industry**: The section also delves into the broader issue of inclusivity in the technology industry. It discusses how fostering diversity in AI teams is not only about countering biases in AI but also about promoting equity and representation in the tech sector.

4. **Collaborative Development Approaches**:

- **Interdisciplinary Collaboration**: The importance of interdisciplinary collaboration is highlighted, suggesting that teams comprising members from various fields such as social sciences, humanities, and ethics, in addition to technical experts, can provide a more holistic approach to AI development.

- **Stakeholder Engagement**: The chapter also advises on engaging with stakeholders, including users and communities affected by AI systems, to gain insights into potential biases and their implications. This engagement is seen as crucial for developing AI systems that are socially aware and ethically aligned.

5. **Training and Awareness**:

- **Bias Awareness Training**: The section discusses the need for continuous training and awareness programs for AI developers and managers, focusing on understanding biases, ethical AI development, and the social impact of AI technologies.

- **Promoting an Ethical AI Culture**: It emphasizes the importance of fostering a culture within AI development teams and organizations that values ethical considerations and actively seeks to address bias, going beyond technical proficiency to ethical and social responsibility.

By laying out these strategies for leveraging diverse data and teams, this section of the chapter provides actionable insights into how biases in AI can be effectively mitigated. It underscores the notion that addressing AI bias is not solely a technical challenge but also a social and organizational one, requiring concerted efforts across various dimensions.

➤ **Transparency and Explainability**:

Emphasizing the importance of transparency and explainability in AI systems, the chapter suggests that making algorithms more understandable can help in identifying biases.

1. **Transparency in AI Systems**:

- **Openness of Data and Algorithms**: The chapter discusses the need for transparency in both the data used to train AI systems and the algorithms themselves. Transparency in data involves disclosing the sources, nature, and limitations of the data, while transparency in algorithms entails understanding how these algorithms process data and make decisions.

- **Benefits for Bias Identification**: The section explains that transparency helps in identifying potential biases in AI systems. When the workings of an AI system are open and understandable, it becomes easier to spot where and how biases might be influencing outcomes.

2. **Explainability of AI Decisions**:

- **Making AI Understandable**: The chapter stresses the importance of explainability – the ability to describe in understandable terms how an AI system arrives at a decision. This is particularly crucial in sectors like healthcare or criminal justice, where decisions have significant consequences.

- **Building Trust**: Explainability is also key to building trust among users and stakeholders. When people understand how an AI system works, they are more likely to trust its decisions and less likely to view it as a mysterious or unaccountable 'black box'.

3. **Tools and Techniques for Explainability**:

- **Developing Explainable Models**: The chapter introduces various tools and techniques that can make AI systems more interpretable, such as decision trees, which are inherently more transparent than complex models like neural networks.

- **Layered Explanations**: For more complex models, the concept of layered explanations is discussed. This involves providing different levels of explanation suitable for various audiences, from technical experts to lay users.

4. **Regulatory and Ethical Implications**:

- **Compliance with Regulations**: The section covers how transparency and explainability are increasingly becoming regulatory requirements in many regions. These regulations aim to ensure that AI systems are fair, accountable, and do not perpetuate biases.

- **Ethical Decision-Making in AI**: There is also a discussion on the ethical implications of explainability. AI systems that can explain their decisions are considered more ethically sound, as they allow for human oversight and accountability.

5. **Challenges in Implementing Transparency and Explainability**:

- **Balancing Complexity and Clarity**: The chapter acknowledges the challenges in implementing transparency and explainability, especially in highly complex AI systems. It discusses the trade-off between the performance of an AI model and its interpretability.

- **Technical and Resource Constraints**: The section also highlights the technical difficulties and resource-intensive nature of developing explainable AI, noting that this is an area of ongoing research and development.

By focusing on transparency and explainability, this section of the chapter underscores their critical role in mitigating biases in AI. It advocates for a proactive approach to incorporate these elements into AI systems, ensuring that they are not only high-performing but also fair, accountable, and trusted by the users and the public.

➢ **Regulatory and Ethical Frameworks**:

The need for robust regulatory and ethical frameworks to guide the development and deployment of AI systems is discussed. This includes the establishment of standards and guidelines for fairness and bias prevention.

1. **Developing Comprehensive Regulatory Frameworks**:

- **Need for Regulation**: The chapter begins by discussing the necessity of regulatory frameworks in governing AI development and deployment. It highlights how regulations can set standards for fairness, transparency, and accountability in AI systems.

- **Global and Regional Regulations**: The section explores various global and regional regulatory efforts, such as the European Union's General Data Protection Regulation (GDPR) and the United States' proposed Algorithmic Accountability Act. These regulations are examined in terms of their approach to addressing AI bias.

2. **Ethical Guidelines for AI Development**:

- **Establishing Ethical Standards**: The chapter stresses the importance of establishing ethical guidelines for AI development. These guidelines serve as a moral compass to guide developers and users in creating and employing AI technologies in a manner that upholds human values and rights.

- **Involvement of Ethicists and Stakeholders**: It discusses the role of ethicists in AI development and the importance of involving a broad range of stakeholders, including those who may be affected by AI systems, in creating these guidelines.

3. **Balancing Innovation with Ethical Considerations**:

- **Encouraging Responsible Innovation**: The section emphasizes the need to balance innovation in AI with ethical considerations. It discusses how regulations and ethical frameworks should not stifle innovation but rather guide it in a direction that benefits society as a whole.

- **Adaptive and Flexible Frameworks**: The chapter advocates for regulatory and ethical frameworks that are adaptive and flexible enough to keep pace with the rapid advancements in AI technology.

4. **Accountability and Enforcement Mechanisms**:

- **Mechanisms for Accountability**: The chapter covers the mechanisms for ensuring accountability in AI systems, such as audit trails, compliance checks, and reporting requirements. These mechanisms help in monitoring AI systems for biases and ensuring adherence to regulatory and ethical standards.

- **Enforcement and Penalties**: The section also discusses the enforcement of regulations and the imposition of penalties for non-compliance. It highlights how effective enforcement is crucial for the credibility and efficacy of regulatory frameworks.

5. **Public Engagement and Policy Development**:

- **Involving the Public in AI Policy**: The chapter underscores the importance of public engagement in the development of AI policies and frameworks. It argues that public input and awareness are vital for creating policies that are socially acceptable and aligned with public values.

- **Educational Initiatives and Awareness Campaigns**: The section advocates for educational initiatives and public awareness campaigns to increase understanding of AI and its implications, thereby fostering informed public discourse on AI ethics and regulations.

By delving into regulatory and ethical frameworks, this section of the chapter highlights their indispensable role in mitigating bias in AI. It presents a clear call to action for policymakers, industry leaders, and the AI community to collaboratively develop and implement comprehensive frameworks that not only address current challenges but are also agile enough to adapt to future developments in AI technology.

V. **Ethical Considerations and Societal Impact**:

➢ **Ethical Responsibilities**:

The chapter delves into the ethical responsibilities of AI developers and users in preventing and addressing bias. It argues that there is a moral imperative to ensure that AI systems do not perpetuate or exacerbate existing inequalities.

1. **Ethical Responsibilities of AI Developers**:

- **Prioritizing Fairness in Design**: The chapter emphasizes that AI developers have a paramount responsibility to prioritize fairness and non-discrimination in the design of AI systems. This involves consciously addressing potential sources of bias in the data and algorithmic design.

- **Continuous Monitoring and Adjustment**: The section also highlights the need for developers to engage in continuous monitoring and adjustment of AI systems to identify and mitigate biases that may emerge over time.

2. **Responsibilities of Data Scientists and Engineers**:

- **Ethical Use of Data**: Data scientists and engineers are tasked with ensuring the ethical collection, processing, and use of data. The chapter discusses the importance of respecting data privacy, obtaining informed consent, and being transparent about data usage.

- **Awareness and Training in Ethics**: It also underscores the importance of ethics training for data professionals, enabling them to recognize and address ethical dilemmas in their work.

3. **Corporate Responsibility**:

- **Creating Ethical Corporate Policies**: For corporations deploying AI technologies, the chapter asserts the need for creating and adhering to ethical policies that govern AI use. These policies should reflect a commitment to fairness, transparency, and accountability.

- **Social Impact Assessment**: Corporations are also urged to conduct regular social impact assessments of their AI technologies, evaluating the broader implications of their deployment on society and specific communities.

4. **Role of Government and Policymakers**:

- **Regulatory Oversight and Legal Frameworks**: Governments and policymakers bear the responsibility of establishing and enforcing regulatory frameworks that ensure ethical AI development. The chapter discusses the need for laws and policies that protect against AI-related harms and biases.

- **Promoting Public Good**: Policymakers are also tasked with guiding AI development towards the public good, ensuring that AI technologies contribute positively to society and do not exacerbate social inequalities.

5. **Academic and Research Community**:

- **Advancing Ethical AI Research**: Academics and researchers in the field of AI are called upon to advance research in ethical AI, developing new methodologies for detecting and mitigating bias.

- **Educational Initiatives**: The chapter also highlights the role of the academic community in educating future AI professionals about ethics, fostering a new generation of AI practitioners who are cognizant of their ethical responsibilities.

6. **Ethical Considerations for End-Users**:

- **Informed Use of AI Technologies**: End-users, including businesses and consumers, are encouraged to be informed about the AI technologies they use. The chapter suggests that users should understand the potential biases in these technologies and advocate for fair and ethical AI solutions.

- **Demanding Accountability**: End-users also have the power to demand accountability from AI developers and corporations, insisting on transparency and ethical practices in the AI technologies they adopt.

By addressing these ethical responsibilities across various stakeholders, this section of the chapter provides a comprehensive view of the collective effort required to ensure the ethical development and use of AI. It emphasizes that mitigating bias in AI is not just a technical challenge but a moral imperative that necessitates active engagement and commitment from all involved in the AI ecosystem.

➤ **Societal Awareness and Engagement**:

The role of societal awareness and engagement is highlighted. Educating the public about AI biases and involving them in discussions about AI development is seen as crucial for fostering responsible AI use.

1. **Raising Public Awareness**:

- **Educating the Public on AI and Its Impacts**: The chapter discusses the importance of educating the public about AI, its potential biases, and its broader societal impacts. This involves demystifying AI and providing accessible information about how AI systems work, where they are used, and the potential risks and benefits.

- **Media and Public Discourse**: The role of media in shaping public discourse around AI is examined. The chapter stresses the need for responsible media reporting that accurately represents AI technologies and their implications, avoiding sensationalism and misinformation.

2. **Engagement with Diverse Communities**:

- **Inclusivity in AI Discussions**: The section emphasizes the importance of including diverse perspectives in discussions and decision-making processes about AI. This means actively engaging with communities that are often underrepresented in technology development, such as minority groups, to understand their concerns and viewpoints.

- **Collaborative Community Initiatives**: The chapter highlights the value of collaborative initiatives that bring together AI developers, users, ethicists, and community members. Such initiatives can facilitate a more inclusive and comprehensive understanding of the societal impacts of AI.

3. **Fostering Public Dialogue**:

- **Platforms for Dialogue and Debate**: The chapter advocates for creating platforms where open dialogue and debate about AI can occur. This includes public forums, workshops, and online platforms where various stakeholders can discuss the ethical and social aspects of AI.

- **Role of Academia and NGOs**: The contribution of academic institutions and non-governmental organizations (NGOs) in facilitating these discussions is underscored. These entities can act as neutral facilitators, helping to bridge the gap between AI developers and the public.

4. **Involvement in Policy and Regulation**:

- **Public Participation in AI Governance**: The chapter encourages public participation in the development of policies and regulations governing AI. This can be achieved through public consultations, surveys, and participatory policymaking processes.

- **Advocacy and Activism**: It also discusses the role of advocacy and activism in shaping AI policies, highlighting how public pressure can lead to more stringent regulations on AI fairness and bias.

5. **Building a Culture of Responsible AI**:

- **Promoting Ethical AI Practices**: The section calls for efforts to promote a culture that values and practices ethical AI. This involves recognizing the societal responsibilities of AI developers and users and encouraging ethical practices through public recognition and support.

- **Ethical Consumerism in AI**: The concept of ethical consumerism is introduced, suggesting that consumers can influence AI development by preferring AI products and services that are ethically developed and bias-free.

By focusing on societal awareness and engagement, this section of the chapter underscores the pivotal role of the broader society in combating biases in AI. It presents a call to action for a more informed, involved, and proactive public stance on AI, emphasizing that the ethical development and deployment of AI technologies are not just technical or regulatory issues but are deeply rooted in societal values and participation.

VI. **Looking to the Future**:

➢ **Emerging Technologies and Approaches**:

The chapter concludes with a look at emerging technologies and approaches that could help in battling AI biases, such as advanced algorithms for detecting bias and new training methodologies.

1. **Advancements in AI and Machine Learning**:

- **Developing More Advanced Algorithms**: The chapter discusses the ongoing research and development in AI aimed at creating more advanced and sophisticated algorithms. These include algorithms designed to be inherently less biased or capable of self-correcting biases when detected.

- **Machine Learning for Bias Detection**: The potential of using machine learning itself to detect and mitigate biases is explored. This involves training AI systems to recognize and adjust for biases in data or other AI models.

2. **Interdisciplinary Approaches**:

- **Combining AI with Social Sciences**: The section highlights the importance of interdisciplinary approaches that combine AI with insights from social sciences, psychology, and ethics. This blend can provide a more holistic understanding of biases and how they manifest in AI systems.

- **Collaborative Research Initiatives**: The chapter underscores the value of collaborative research initiatives that bring together experts from diverse fields to tackle the multifaceted nature of AI bias.

3. **Ethical AI Frameworks**:

- **Developing Comprehensive Ethical Frameworks**: There is a focus on the development of comprehensive ethical frameworks for AI. These frameworks would guide the ethical development, deployment, and use of AI systems, incorporating principles like fairness, accountability, and transparency.

- **Global Standards for Ethical AI**: The chapter discusses the efforts towards establishing global standards and norms for ethical AI, recognizing the need for international collaboration in this domain.

4. **Technological Tools for Transparency and Accountability**:

- **Tools for Better Transparency**: The emergence of new technological tools that enhance the transparency of AI systems is examined. These tools could enable better visualization of AI processes and decision-making pathways.

- **Accountability Mechanisms**: The chapter also looks at the development of mechanisms for holding AI systems and their developers accountable. This includes audit trails, compliance monitoring systems, and other technologies that can track and report on AI decision-making.

5. **Public Engagement Platforms**:

- **Digital Platforms for Public Interaction**: The potential for digital platforms that facilitate greater public interaction with AI development is discussed. These platforms could allow for public input and feedback on AI systems, making the development process more democratic and inclusive.

- **Educational Tools and Resources**: The chapter highlights the emergence of new educational tools and resources aimed at increasing public understanding of AI. This includes online courses, interactive experiences, and educational campaigns.

6. **Predictive Analytics for Bias Prevention**:

- **Proactive Bias Identification**: The use of predictive analytics to proactively identify potential biases in AI systems is explored. This involves analyzing patterns and trends that could indicate the emergence of bias.

- **Preventative Measures in AI Development**: The chapter discusses how these predictive insights could be used to implement preventative measures during the AI development process, reducing the likelihood of biases occurring.

By examining these emerging technologies and approaches, this section of the chapter paints a picture of a future where the mitigation of biases in AI is more proactive, integrated, and effective. It suggests a trajectory where technological innovation goes hand in hand with ethical considerations, interdisciplinary collaboration, and public engagement, paving the way for AI systems that are not only powerful but also equitable and socially responsible.

➢ **Ongoing Research and Development**:

The importance of ongoing research and development in this field is emphasized, suggesting that combating bias in AI is a continuous process that will evolve alongside the technology itself.

1. **Continuous Improvement of AI Models**:

- **Evolving AI Algorithms**: The chapter discusses the ongoing work in improving the algorithms that power AI systems. This includes refining machine learning models to be more accurate and less susceptible to biases, as well as developing new types of models that are inherently more transparent and fair.

- **Adaptive and Self-Evaluating Systems**: The section also looks at research into creating AI systems that can adapt and evaluate themselves for biases over time, ensuring that they remain fair and unbiased as they interact with the world.

2. **Data Quality and Diversity**:

- **Enhancing Data Collection Methods**: Ongoing research in improving data collection methods is highlighted. This involves finding ways to gather more diverse and representative data sets to train AI systems, thus reducing the risk of biases stemming from inadequate or skewed data.

- **Dynamic Data Monitoring**: The chapter discusses the development of systems for dynamic data monitoring and analysis, which can continuously assess and update the data used by AI systems to ensure it remains relevant and unbiased.

3. **Interdisciplinary Collaboration**:

- **Bridging AI with Other Fields**: There is a focus on the importance of interdisciplinary collaboration in AI research. By combining insights from fields like psychology, sociology, and ethics with AI and computer science, researchers can better understand and address the complex roots of biases in AI.

- **Cross-Sector Research Initiatives**: The chapter emphasizes the emergence of cross-sector research initiatives that bring together academia, industry, government, and civil society to work on ethical AI solutions.

4. **Ethical AI Governance**:

- **Frameworks for Responsible AI**: Research into developing comprehensive frameworks for ethical AI governance is explored. These frameworks would provide guidelines and best practices for the ethical development, deployment, and oversight of AI systems.

- **Policy and Regulation Research**: The chapter also acknowledges the research efforts focused on informing policy and regulation in the AI domain, ensuring that legal frameworks keep pace with technological advancements.

5. **Educational and Training Programs**:

- **Developing AI Literacy**: The ongoing development of educational and training programs to promote AI literacy among developers, users, and the general public is highlighted. These programs are crucial for building a broad understanding of AI, its potential biases, and ethical use.

- **Professional Development in AI Ethics**: The chapter discusses the growing emphasis on professional development and continuous learning in AI ethics for practitioners in the field, ensuring they remain abreast of the latest developments and ethical considerations.

6. **Innovative Tools and Technologies**:

- **Development of Diagnostic and Mitigation Tools**: Research into creating tools and technologies that can diagnose and mitigate biases in AI systems is addressed. This includes software that can automatically detect potential biases in datasets or AI outputs.

- **Emerging Technologies in AI**: The chapter also looks at how emerging technologies, like quantum computing and advanced neural networks, might influence the future of AI development and its potential for biases.

By focusing on ongoing research and development, this section of the chapter illustrates a future where the fight against AI biases is an active, continuous process. It presents a scenario where advancements in AI are accompanied by a deepening understanding of its ethical implications and a commitment to developing AI that is not only technologically sophisticated but also socially responsible and equitable.

How AI Inherits Human Prejudices:

This section of the chapter delves into the mechanisms through which AI inherits and perpetuates these biases, as well as the real-world consequences of this phenomenon.

1. **Data as a Reflection of Society**:

➢ **Biases in Training Data**:

The chapter highlights that AI systems learn from vast datasets that often mirror the biases present in society. These biases can include racial, gender, and socioeconomic prejudices, among others.

- **Training Data's Crucial Role**: The section underscores the pivotal role of training data in shaping AI systems. AI models, particularly those based on machine learning, learn patterns and make decisions based on the data they are trained on. As a result, the quality and representativeness of this data have a direct impact on the fairness and accuracy of AI outcomes.

- **Biases in Historical Data**: It's emphasized that training data often mirrors the biases and prejudices present in society at the time of data collection. For instance, historical data used for training AI may contain biases related to race, gender, age, socioeconomic status, and more. These biases can be unintentionally embedded in AI models, perpetuating historical inequalities.

- **Data Collection Challenges**: The section acknowledges the challenges associated with collecting unbiased and representative training data. Data collection processes can inadvertently introduce biases due to factors like sampling methods, data sources, and human annotator biases.

- **Reinforcing Stereotypes**: It delves into how biased training data can lead AI systems to reinforce stereotypes. When AI learns from data that reflects societal stereotypes, it may make decisions that align with those stereotypes. For example, biased AI in hiring processes may favor candidates who fit traditional gender or racial stereotypes.

- **Impact on Vulnerable Communities**: The section highlights that biases in training data can disproportionately affect vulnerable and underrepresented communities. When AI systems perpetuate biases, it can lead to systemic discrimination and further marginalize these communities.

- **Challenges in Bias Detection**: Detecting biases in training data can be challenging, as biases may be subtle or hidden within large datasets. Moreover, human biases can be encoded in data labels, making it difficult to identify and rectify them.

- **Continuous Data Monitoring**: To mitigate these issues, the chapter suggests the importance of continuous data monitoring and auditing throughout the AI development lifecycle. This ongoing assessment can help identify and address biases as they emerge, ensuring that AI systems evolve towards fairness.

By highlighting the role of data as a reflection of society and the biases present in training data, this section of the chapter underscores the critical need for careful data curation, diversity, and ethical considerations in AI development. It serves as a reminder that addressing biases in AI starts with recognizing the potential pitfalls in the data used for training and taking proactive steps to mitigate these biases for more equitable and responsible AI systems.

➢ **Amplification of Stereotypes**:

It discusses how AI, when trained on biased data, can inadvertently reinforce and amplify societal stereotypes. For example, an AI used in hiring may perpetuate gender or racial biases present in historical hiring decisions.

- **Stereotypes in Data**: The chapter underscores that training AI systems on data that contains societal stereotypes can lead to the amplification of these stereotypes. AI, when learning from biased data, may inadvertently reinforce and propagate stereotypes related to gender, race, ethnicity, and other characteristics.

- **Reinforcing Existing Biases**: It's emphasized that AI systems, when making decisions based on biased data, can perpetuate existing biases and prejudices. For instance, if an AI recruitment tool is trained on historical hiring data that favored certain demographic groups, it may continue to favor those groups, reinforcing gender or racial disparities in hiring.

- **Feedback Loop of Bias**: The section delves into the concept of a feedback loop, where biased AI systems can create a self-perpetuating cycle of bias. Biased AI decisions can affect real-world outcomes, which are then fed back into the training data, further reinforcing the same biases.

- **Algorithmic Discrimination**: It discusses how the amplification of stereotypes can result in algorithmic discrimination against individuals or groups who do not conform to the stereotypes. This discrimination can manifest in various contexts, including employment, lending, and criminal justice.

- **Impact on Marginalized Communities**: The chapter highlights that the amplification of stereotypes can disproportionately harm marginalized and underrepresented communities. These communities may face systemic discrimination as a result of biased AI systems, deepening existing social inequalities.

- **Challenges in Stereotype Detection**: Detecting the amplification of stereotypes within AI systems can be challenging, as it may not always be apparent in the AI's decision-making process. Identifying and mitigating the subtle ways in which stereotypes are perpetuated is a complex task.

- **Ethical Responsibility**: It underscores the ethical responsibility of AI developers and organizations to actively address the amplification of stereotypes. Developers should not only aim to reduce bias in AI systems but also prevent the perpetuation of harmful stereotypes.

- **Transparency and Accountability**: The section stresses the importance of transparency and accountability in AI development and deployment.

Transparent AI systems allow for external scrutiny, enabling stakeholders to identify and rectify cases where stereotypes are being amplified.

By delving into the amplification of stereotypes within AI systems, this section of the chapter highlights the critical need for vigilance and proactive measures to combat bias and stereotypes in AI development. It calls for ethical AI practices, responsible data curation, fairness in algorithm design, and ongoing monitoring to ensure that AI technology is a force for positive change and does not perpetuate harmful stereotypes.

2. **Algorithmic Bias**:

➤ **Bias in Algorithmic Design**:

The section examines how biases can also be introduced through the design of algorithms themselves. Algorithmic decisions may inadvertently favor certain groups or outcomes over others due to inherent biases in the decision-making process.

- **Implicit Biases**: The chapter highlights that algorithmic bias can be introduced at the design stage of AI systems due to the presence of implicit biases among developers. Developers, like anyone else, may hold implicit biases that can inadvertently influence algorithm design choices.

- **Feature Selection**: It underscores that the selection of features or input variables in an AI algorithm is a critical decision point where bias can creep in. If certain features are chosen that correlate with sensitive attributes like race or gender, the algorithm may learn to make biased decisions based on these attributes.

- **Optimization Objectives**: The section delves into how the choice of optimization objectives can introduce bias. For example, if an algorithm is designed to optimize for efficiency or profit without considering fairness, it may prioritize certain groups while disadvantaging others.

- **Decision Rules**: It discusses how the formulation of decision rules within algorithms can inadvertently favor specific outcomes or groups. For instance, the design of decision thresholds may result in biased outcomes in areas like lending or criminal justice.

- **Complex Interactions**: The chapter acknowledges that algorithmic bias can emerge from complex interactions within the algorithm. Bias may not be traceable to a single design decision but can result from the interplay of various algorithmic components.

- **Unintentional Consequences**: It emphasizes that algorithmic bias is often unintentional. Developers may not be aware of the biases present in their algorithms, making it challenging to identify and rectify these biases during the development process.

- **Feedback Loop of Bias**: The section discusses how biased algorithms can create a feedback loop, where the biased decisions they make lead to biased outcomes, which are then incorporated into the training data, further perpetuating the bias.

- **Ethical Responsibility**: It underscores the ethical responsibility of AI developers and organizations to be mindful of the potential for bias in algorithmic design. Developers should strive to create algorithms that are not only accurate but also fair and equitable.

- **Transparency and Explainability**: The chapter stresses the importance of transparency and explainability in algorithmic design. Developers should aim to create algorithms that provide clear and understandable explanations for their decisions, allowing for scrutiny and accountability.

By delving into algorithmic bias arising from the design and coding of algorithms, this section of the chapter highlights the complexities involved in addressing bias in AI systems. It underscores the need for ethical considerations, algorithmic fairness, diversity in development teams, and ongoing monitoring to ensure that AI systems are free from discriminatory biases and promote fairness and equity in their decision-making processes.

➤ **Feedback Loop of Bias:**

It explains how algorithmic bias can create a feedback loop: biased data leads to biased algorithmic decisions, which, in turn, can produce biased outcomes that further reinforce the initial biases.

- **Biased Outcomes Reinforce Data**: The chapter emphasizes that biased AI systems can create a self-reinforcing cycle. When these systems make biased decisions based on biased data, the outcomes of those decisions can further reinforce the biases present in the data. For example, if an AI system favors one demographic group in hiring decisions, it may result in a disproportionate number of hires from that group, which then becomes part of the training data, perpetuating the bias.

- **Amplification of Stereotypes**: It delves into how feedback loops of bias can amplify stereotypes. Biased AI systems, when repeatedly making decisions that align with stereotypes, can lead to the amplification and normalization of those stereotypes. This can have detrimental consequences, such as reinforcing harmful societal prejudices related to race, gender, or other attributes.

- **Impact on Marginalized Groups**: The section highlights that feedback loops of bias disproportionately affect marginalized and underrepresented groups. As biased AI systems perpetuate and amplify existing biases, these groups may face increased discrimination and exclusion, further exacerbating societal inequalities.

- **Challenges in Breaking the Loop**: It acknowledges that breaking the feedback loop of bias can be challenging. Simply identifying and mitigating bias in AI systems may not be sufficient if the biases have already influenced real-world decisions and outcomes. Efforts to address bias may need to extend beyond the AI system itself to rectify the consequences of biased decisions.

- **Ethical Responsibility**: The chapter underscores the ethical responsibility of AI developers and organizations to actively work to break feedback loops of bias. This includes not only mitigating bias within AI systems but also addressing the real-world impact of past biased decisions.

- **Transparency and Accountability**: It stresses the importance of transparency and accountability in identifying and mitigating feedback loops of bias. Transparent AI systems allow for external scrutiny, which can help uncover the existence of such loops and inform efforts to dismantle them.

- **Continuous Monitoring**: The section highlights the need for continuous monitoring and auditing of AI systems to detect and rectify feedback loops of bias as they emerge. Regular assessments can help identify patterns of bias and their potential consequences.

By exploring the concept of feedback loops of bias within AI systems, this section of the chapter underscores the urgency of addressing bias not only within the technology itself but also in its broader societal context. It calls for proactive measures to break these feedback loops, mitigate bias, and promote fairness and equity in AI decision-making processes.

3. **Real-World Impact:**

➢ **Impact on Marginalized Communities**:

The chapter emphasizes that biased AI systems can have real-world consequences, particularly for marginalized communities. For example, biased criminal justice algorithms may lead to unfair sentencing disparities.

- **Systemic Discrimination**: The chapter highlights that biased AI systems can perpetuate systemic discrimination against marginalized communities. When AI algorithms favor certain groups or make decisions that disadvantage others, it can reinforce existing inequalities in areas such as employment, education, healthcare, and criminal justice.

- **Widening Disparities**: It emphasizes that the impact of AI biases can exacerbate disparities that marginalized communities already face. For example, biased lending algorithms may result in financial institutions disproportionately denying loans to minority borrowers, limiting their economic opportunities and widening the wealth gap.

- **Reinforcing Stereotypes**: The section delves into how AI biases can reinforce harmful stereotypes about marginalized groups. When AI systems make decisions that align with these stereotypes, it can perpetuate societal prejudices, further marginalizing those affected.

- **Access to Opportunities**: It acknowledges that biased AI can limit access to opportunities for marginalized communities. For instance, biased hiring algorithms may discriminate against candidates from underrepresented backgrounds, reducing their chances of securing employment and career advancement.

- **Algorithmic Redlining**: The chapter discusses the concept of algorithmic redlining, where AI systems may systematically disadvantage certain neighborhoods or communities based on historical data. This can affect access to services, housing, and other essential resources.

- **Healthcare Disparities**: It highlights that biases in healthcare AI can lead to disparities in diagnosis and treatment for marginalized communities. Biased algorithms may provide suboptimal care recommendations, leading to adverse health outcomes.

- **Ethical Concerns**: The section underscores the ethical concerns associated with the impact of biased AI on marginalized communities. It calls for ethical responsibility in AI development to ensure that these communities are not disproportionately harmed.

- **Legal and Regulatory Considerations**: It acknowledges that legal and regulatory frameworks are increasingly addressing the impact of AI biases on marginalized communities. These frameworks aim to hold organizations accountable for discriminatory AI practices.

- **Community Advocacy**: The chapter recognizes the importance of advocacy and activism within marginalized communities to raise awareness of AI bias and its consequences. Community-driven efforts can drive change and demand accountability from AI developers and organizations.

By examining the impact of AI biases on marginalized communities, this section of the chapter underscores the urgency of addressing bias in AI development. It emphasizes the need for ethical AI practices, fairness audits, diverse development teams, and transparent decision-making processes to ensure that AI systems do not perpetuate discrimination and contribute to a more equitable society.

➢ **Reinforcing Discrimination**:

It discusses how AI bias can perpetuate discrimination in areas like housing, lending, and employment, deepening existing inequalities.

- **Systemic Discrimination**: The chapter emphasizes that AI systems, when biased, have the potential to reinforce and perpetuate systemic discrimination. This occurs when AI algorithms make decisions that align with existing societal biases, thereby amplifying discrimination against certain groups.

- **Historical Prejudices**: It is highlighted that AI algorithms can inherit and perpetuate historical prejudices that have marginalized and discriminated against particular communities for generations. These prejudices can become embedded in the decision-making processes of AI systems.

- **Criminal Justice**: The section delves into how biased AI systems used in criminal justice, such as risk assessment algorithms, may disproportionately label individuals from marginalized communities as high-risk, leading to harsher sentencing and over-policing.

- **Employment and Hiring**: It discusses how biased hiring algorithms can discriminate against job candidates from underrepresented backgrounds, reinforcing employment discrimination. This can limit opportunities and economic mobility for marginalized groups.

- **Access to Services**: The chapter acknowledges that biased AI can restrict access to essential services for marginalized communities. For example, biased loan approval algorithms can deny financial services to individuals based on their race or socioeconomic status.

- **Education**: It highlights that biased educational AI systems may perpetuate disparities in access to quality education. Students from marginalized backgrounds may receive inadequate resources or educational opportunities due to biased decision-making.

- **Healthcare Disparities**: It delves into how AI biases can result in healthcare disparities. For example, biased diagnostic algorithms may misdiagnose or undertreat patients from marginalized communities, leading to adverse health outcomes.

- **Economic Consequences**: The section underlines that the reinforcement of discrimination by AI can have severe economic consequences for marginalized groups. Biased algorithms can limit economic opportunities and hinder wealth accumulation.

- **Ethical Implications**: It stresses the ethical implications of AI systems that reinforce discrimination. It calls for ethical responsibility in AI development to ensure that technology promotes fairness and equity rather than perpetuating discrimination.

- **Legal and Regulatory Responses**: The chapter acknowledges that legal and regulatory responses are emerging to address discrimination perpetuated by AI systems. These responses aim to hold organizations accountable for discriminatory practices and establish standards for ethical AI.

By exploring how AI can reinforce discrimination in various real-world contexts, this section of the chapter underscores the critical importance of addressing bias in AI development. It emphasizes the need for transparency, fairness audits, diverse development teams, and ongoing monitoring to prevent AI systems from perpetuating discrimination and contribute to a more just and equitable society.

4. **Complexity of Bias Detection**:

➢ **Challenges in Bias Detection**:

The section acknowledges the difficulties in detecting bias within AI systems, especially when biases are subtle or indirect. It explores how bias detection tools and methodologies are evolving to address these challenges.

- **Subtlety of Biases**: The chapter underscores that biases within AI systems can often be subtle and not immediately apparent. Unlike glaring errors, biases may manifest as nuanced patterns that require in-depth analysis to detect.

- **Hidden Biases in Data**: It is highlighted that biases can be deeply embedded within the training data, making them challenging to identify. Biases may not always be explicitly labeled but can be inferred from patterns and associations in the data.

- **Intersectionality of Biases**: The section acknowledges that biases within AI systems can intersect, making them even more complex to detect. For example, a biased algorithm may exhibit discrimination against individuals who belong to multiple marginalized groups, compounding the impact.

- **Lack of Ground Truth**: It discusses the challenge of not having a clear "ground truth" for bias detection. In some cases, there may be no universally agreed-upon standard to determine what constitutes bias, making evaluation subjective.

- **Dynamic Nature of Bias**: The chapter recognizes that bias within AI systems can evolve over time. As AI systems interact with users and receive feedback, their behavior may change, and new biases may emerge. This dynamic nature adds complexity to bias detection efforts.

- **Contextual Bias**: It emphasizes that bias can be context-dependent. What may be considered biased behavior in one context may not be the same in another. This contextuality requires a nuanced understanding of when bias is problematic.

- **Data Labeling Bias**: The section highlights that biases can also exist in the labeling of training data. Human annotators may introduce their own biases when labeling data, leading to biased models.

- **Quantifying Bias**: It discusses the challenge of quantifying the extent of bias within AI systems. Bias is not always a binary concept; it can exist on a spectrum. Determining how much bias is acceptable or unacceptable can be a complex decision.

- **Adversarial Attacks**: The chapter acknowledges that adversaries may intentionally attempt to hide biases or manipulate AI systems to evade detection. This adds an additional layer of complexity to bias detection efforts.

- **Mitigation vs. Detection**: It stresses that detecting bias is just one part of the equation; the more significant challenge is mitigating bias effectively. Identifying bias without being able to address it effectively can be frustrating.

- **Interdisciplinary Expertise**: The section highlights that effective bias detection often requires interdisciplinary expertise, including domain knowledge, data analysis, ethics, and computer science. Collaborative efforts are essential for comprehensive bias assessment.

By exploring the challenges associated with bias detection within AI systems, this section of the chapter underscores the need for a multi-faceted approach to addressing bias. It emphasizes the importance of continuous monitoring, transparency, diverse perspectives, and ongoing research to develop effective strategies for detecting and mitigating bias in AI technology.

➢ **Need for Continuous Monitoring:**

The chapter stresses the importance of continuous monitoring and auditing of AI systems to identify and rectify biases as they emerge.

- **Dynamic Nature of Bias**: The chapter emphasizes that bias within AI systems is not static; it can evolve over time. As AI interacts with users and processes new data, its behavior may change, and new biases may emerge. Continuous monitoring is essential to detect and address these evolving biases.

- **Adaptation to User Behavior**: It discusses how AI systems often adapt to user behavior and preferences. While this adaptation can enhance user experience, it can also introduce unintended biases. Continuous monitoring helps ensure that AI systems adapt in ways that do not reinforce harmful biases.

- **Data Drift**: The section acknowledges that data used to train AI models can change over time due to shifts in societal norms, demographics, and technology. These changes can introduce new biases or alter the significance of existing biases. Continuous monitoring helps detect and adapt to data drift.

- **Feedback Loops**: It highlights that feedback loops of bias can be self-reinforcing, leading to amplified bias over time. Continuous monitoring is crucial to identify when such feedback loops are occurring and take corrective action to break them.

- **Unintended Consequences**: The chapter underscores that AI system updates or changes can have unintended consequences, including the introduction of new biases. Continuous monitoring ensures that any unintended biases introduced during updates are promptly detected and mitigated.

- **User Feedback**: It stresses the value of user feedback in bias detection. Users may report biased behavior or discrimination they experience while interacting with AI systems. Continuous monitoring involves actively collecting and responding to user feedback.

- **Transparency and Accountability**: The section emphasizes that continuous monitoring fosters transparency and accountability. When AI systems are continuously scrutinized for biases, it creates a culture of accountability where developers and organizations are proactive in addressing bias-related issues.

- **Mitigation in Real Time**: It acknowledges that continuous monitoring enables real-time bias mitigation. Rather than waiting for bias issues to escalate, ongoing monitoring allows for immediate corrective actions, reducing potential harm to users.

- **Legal and Ethical Compliance**: The chapter highlights that regulatory frameworks and ethical guidelines increasingly require continuous monitoring of AI systems for biases. Compliance with these regulations necessitates proactive monitoring efforts.

- **Bias Prevention**: It discusses that continuous monitoring not only helps in detecting bias but also in preventing it. By identifying early signs of bias, developers can implement measures to prevent bias from becoming ingrained in AI systems.

By emphasizing the need for continuous monitoring in the context of bias detection within AI systems, this section of the chapter underscores the proactive and iterative nature of addressing bias. It highlights that effective bias detection and mitigation require ongoing efforts to ensure that AI technology remains fair, ethical, and aligned with societal values as it evolves over time.

5. **Transparency and Accountability**:

➢ **Importance of Transparency**:

The chapter highlights that transparency in AI development is crucial for addressing inherited biases. Transparent AI systems allow for scrutiny and accountability, enabling researchers and regulators to identify and rectify biases.

- **Understanding AI Decisions**: The chapter highlights that transparency is essential for users and stakeholders to understand how AI systems make decisions. Transparent AI systems provide insights into the factors, data, and algorithms that influence their decisions, promoting trust and comprehension.

- **Bias Detection**: It emphasizes that transparency is a key enabler of bias detection. When AI systems are transparent, it becomes easier for researchers, auditors, and users to scrutinize their behavior and identify potential biases or discriminatory patterns.

- **Ethical Scrutiny**: The section discusses how transparency invites ethical scrutiny. By providing visibility into their inner workings, AI systems can be assessed for fairness, ethics, and compliance with societal norms and values.

- **User Trust**: It acknowledges that transparency builds user trust. When users can see how AI systems arrive at decisions, they are more likely to trust those decisions and use AI-powered technologies with confidence.

- **Accountability**: The chapter stresses that transparency is a cornerstone of accountability. Transparent AI systems allow for clear attribution of responsibility, making it easier to hold developers and organizations accountable for any biased or discriminatory behavior.

- **Bias Mitigation**: It highlights that transparency facilitates bias mitigation. When biases are detected in transparent AI systems, developers can more effectively identify and rectify the underlying causes, leading to fairer outcomes.

- **Fairness Audits**: The section discusses the role of fairness audits, which are made possible by transparency. Auditors can assess AI systems for fairness, uncover hidden biases, and recommend corrective actions.

- **Regulatory Compliance**: It underscores that transparency is often a legal and regulatory requirement. Many jurisdictions mandate transparency in AI systems, especially in contexts where decisions impact individuals' rights and opportunities.

- **Consumer Protection**: The chapter acknowledges that transparency is a form of consumer protection. It ensures that users are informed about how AI systems may affect them and allows them to make informed choices.

- **Public Awareness**: It emphasizes that transparency raises public awareness about AI biases and their potential consequences. Transparency efforts can contribute to broader discussions about bias and discrimination in AI technology.

- **Iterative Improvement**: The section discusses how transparency supports iterative improvement. As AI systems evolve, transparency allows developers to learn from past mistakes and continuously enhance system fairness.

- **Diverse Stakeholder Involvement**: It highlights that transparency encourages the involvement of diverse stakeholders in AI development. A transparent process invites input from different perspectives, helping to reduce bias and ensure inclusivity.

By underscoring the importance of transparency in addressing AI biases, this section of the chapter underscores that transparency is not just a technical attribute but a fundamental ethical and societal imperative. It calls for open and accountable AI development practices that prioritize fairness, ethics, and user trust.

➢ **Accountability for Developers**:

It discusses the ethical responsibility of AI developers to be aware of potential biases in their systems and to take proactive steps to mitigate them.

- **Ethical Responsibility**: The chapter underscores that developers bear an ethical responsibility when creating AI systems. They are responsible for ensuring that these systems are fair, equitable, and free from discriminatory biases. This ethical responsibility extends to the consequences of AI decisions on individuals and society.

- **Algorithmic Design Choices**: It highlights that developers play a central role in the design and development of AI algorithms. The choices they make, such as feature selection, optimization objectives, and decision rules, can significantly influence the potential for bias within AI systems.

- **Data Selection and Bias**: The section discusses the responsibility of developers in selecting and curating training data. Developers should be mindful of potential biases in training data and take steps to mitigate or eliminate those biases during the data preparation process.

- **Fairness Audits**: It emphasizes that developers should conduct fairness audits on their AI systems. These audits involve systematically evaluating AI behavior for bias and discrimination and taking corrective actions when bias is detected.

- **Transparency**: The chapter underscores that developers should prioritize transparency in AI development. They should document the decision-making process, data sources, and algorithmic choices to provide insights into how AI systems arrive at their decisions.

- **Bias Mitigation**: It discusses developers' responsibility in actively mitigating bias within AI systems. When bias is identified, developers should take prompt and effective measures to rectify the underlying causes and prevent further bias from occurring.

- **Diverse Development Teams**: The section acknowledges the importance of diverse development teams. Including individuals with different backgrounds, perspectives, and experiences can help identify and mitigate biases that may not be apparent to a homogenous team.

- **User Feedback**: It stresses that developers should actively seek and incorporate user feedback. Users can provide valuable insights into biased behavior or unintended consequences, helping developers refine AI systems.

- **Accountability Frameworks**: The chapter discusses the role of accountability frameworks and guidelines. Developers should adhere to established ethical and regulatory frameworks that govern AI development, ensuring that their systems align with societal norms and values.

- **Continual Learning**: It highlights the need for developers to engage in continual learning and professional development. The field of AI is dynamic, and staying informed about emerging best practices and bias mitigation techniques is essential.

- **Legal and Regulatory Compliance**: The section underscores that developers must comply with relevant legal and regulatory requirements related to bias in AI. Non-compliance can result in legal consequences and reputational damage.

- **Ethical Oversight**: It acknowledges that organizations should establish ethical oversight mechanisms for AI development. These mechanisms can include ethics committees or advisory boards that provide guidance on bias detection and mitigation.

By emphasizing accountability for developers in the context of AI bias, this section of the chapter underscores that ethical AI development is a collective responsibility. It calls for developers to be proactive in addressing bias, promoting transparency, and upholding ethical standards to ensure that AI systems are fair, equitable, and aligned with societal values.

6. **Bias Mitigation Strategies**:

➤ **De-biasing Techniques**:

The chapter explores various de-biasing techniques, such as re-sampling data, re-weighting samples, and adversarial training, which aim to reduce biases in AI systems during training.

- **Re-weighting Data**: One common de-biasing technique involves re-weighting the training data. This means assigning different weights to different data points or groups to reduce the impact of biased data. By giving more weight to underrepresented groups or less weight to overrepresented groups, the algorithm can learn a fairer representation.

- **Data Augmentation**: Data augmentation involves adding or modifying training data to create a more balanced dataset. For instance, if a dataset is biased toward a particular gender, data augmentation can involve creating synthetic data points for the underrepresented gender to balance the dataset.

- **Pre-processing**: Pre-processing techniques are used to modify the training data before it is fed into the algorithm. Techniques like re-sampling or over-sampling can be applied to create a more balanced dataset. Pre-processing can also involve removing or correcting biased data points.

- **Algorithmic Fairness Constraints**: Some de-biasing techniques involve modifying the learning algorithm itself. For example, algorithms can be designed to incorporate fairness constraints during training, ensuring that they do not make decisions that disproportionately harm certain groups.

- **Bias Mitigation Models**: Specialized models, often referred to as "bias mitigation models," can be trained alongside the main AI model. These models focus on detecting and mitigating bias in the predictions made by the primary model. They can adjust predictions to make them fairer.

- **Post-processing**: Post-processing techniques involve modifying the output of the AI model after it has made predictions. For example, if a model tends to produce biased predictions, a post-processing step can be applied to adjust those predictions to align with fairness criteria.

- **Counterfactual Explanations**: Counterfactual explanations involve providing alternative scenarios to users to demonstrate what would have happened if certain characteristics (e.g., gender or race) had been different. This can help users understand how bias affected the decision.

- **Regularization**: Regularization techniques can be used to penalize models for making biased decisions. This encourages the model to make fairer predictions by imposing a cost for biased behavior.

- **Sensitive Attribute Removal**: In some cases, sensitive attributes (e.g., gender or race) can be removed from the dataset to prevent the model from using them as features for decision-making. This approach is often used to prevent direct discrimination.

- **Fairness Metrics**: De-biasing techniques often rely on fairness metrics to quantify and assess bias. These metrics, such as disparate impact, equal opportunity, and demographic parity, provide a quantitative measure of fairness that can guide the de-biasing process.

- **Diverse Training Data**: Ensuring that the training data is diverse and representative of the target population is a fundamental de-biasing strategy. By including data from a wide range of sources and demographics, the AI model is less likely to develop biases.

- **Ethical Review and Audits**: Organizations can conduct ethical reviews and audits of AI systems to assess their behavior for bias. These reviews involve analyzing the model's predictions and decision-making processes to identify and rectify bias.

- **User Feedback Integration**: Actively seeking and integrating user feedback is a crucial de-biasing strategy. Users can provide valuable insights into biased behavior or unintended consequences, helping developers refine the AI system.

- **Interdisciplinary Teams**: De-biasing efforts often benefit from interdisciplinary teams that include ethicists, social scientists, and domain experts. These diverse perspectives can uncover biases that may not be apparent to technical teams.

  By exploring de-biasing techniques, this section of the chapter underscores the importance of proactive measures to mitigate bias within AI systems. It highlights that addressing bias is not a one-time task but an ongoing process that requires a combination of technical, ethical, and societal approaches to ensure that AI technology is fair and equitable.

- ➤ **Ethical Considerations**: It underlines the ethical considerations in bias mitigation, including the need to strike a balance between bias reduction and model performance, as well as addressing biases without erasing important differences in data.

- **Balancing Fairness**: One of the primary ethical considerations in bias mitigation is the need to balance fairness. While it's essential to mitigate biases in AI systems, there can be trade-offs between different fairness metrics. For example, achieving demographic parity may unintentionally harm other groups. Ethical decision-making involves carefully weighing these trade-offs to minimize harm and promote fairness for all.

- **Avoiding Reverse Discrimination**: Bias mitigation efforts should be cautious not to inadvertently discriminate against any group in the process of correcting bias. Ethical considerations include ensuring that the mitigation strategies do not unfairly disadvantage any demographic group.

- **Transparency**: Ethical principles demand transparency in bias mitigation strategies. Developers should clearly communicate how biases are being addressed and the criteria used to define fairness. Transparency helps build trust with users and stakeholders.

- **Inclusive Decision-Making**: Ethical AI development involves inclusive decision-making processes. Developers should consider the perspectives and input of diverse stakeholders, including those who may be directly affected by bias mitigation strategies.

- **Unintended Consequences**: Ethical considerations include a focus on identifying and mitigating unintended consequences. Bias mitigation efforts should not inadvertently introduce new biases or harm marginalized groups in unforeseen ways.

- **Ethical Audits**: Regular ethical audits of AI systems are crucial to assess the impact of bias mitigation strategies. Auditors should ensure that the strategies align with ethical principles and do not result in unintended ethical violations.

- **Bias Awareness**: Ethical AI development includes fostering awareness of biases and their consequences. Developers and users should be educated about the potential for bias, both in training data and in the outcomes of AI systems.

- **Ethical Feedback Loops**: Establishing ethical feedback loops is essential. Users should have mechanisms to report biased behavior, and developers should act on such feedback to improve bias mitigation strategies.

- **Fairness Across Contexts**: Ethical considerations extend to ensuring that bias mitigation strategies are adaptable to different contexts. What is considered fair in one context may not be the same in another, and ethical AI should account for these variations.

- **Accountability**: Ethical accountability is paramount. Developers and organizations should take responsibility for the effectiveness and ethical implications of their bias mitigation efforts. This includes responding to failures and continuously improving bias mitigation strategies.

- **Regulatory Compliance**: Ethical AI development often aligns with regulatory compliance. Developers should ensure that their bias mitigation strategies adhere to relevant laws and regulations that govern AI and fairness.

- **Ethical Frameworks**: Many organizations adopt ethical frameworks that guide their bias mitigation efforts. These frameworks provide a set of principles and guidelines that help ensure ethical decision-making throughout the AI development process.

- **Beneficence and Non-Maleficence**: These ethical principles emphasize the importance of doing good and avoiding harm. Bias mitigation strategies should prioritize the well-being of all users and minimize harm caused by biased AI systems.

By addressing how AI inherits human prejudices, this section of the chapter underscores the urgency of tackling bias in AI development. It highlights the need for a multi-faceted approach that involves data curation, algorithmic fairness, transparency, and continuous monitoring. Ultimately, it presents a call to action for the AI community to be vigilant in addressing and rectifying biases in AI systems to ensure they contribute positively to society.

The Consequences of Biased Algorithms on Society:

This section of the chapter explores how biased AI systems can have far-reaching and often detrimental impacts on individuals, communities, and society as a whole.

1. **Reinforcement of Inequality**:

➢ **Amplifying Social Disparities**: The chapter underscores how biased algorithms can exacerbate existing social inequalities. For instance, biased hiring algorithms may perpetuate gender or racial disparities in employment opportunities, hindering efforts to achieve workplace diversity.

The pervasive use of algorithms in decision-making processes across various sectors, from finance and healthcare to criminal justice and employment, has raised concerns about the potential for reinforcing existing social inequalities. This issue is particularly salient when discussing the consequences of biased algorithms on society. In this expanded discussion, we will delve into how these biased algorithms amplify social disparities, perpetuating systemic inequalities that already exist.

- **Access to Opportunities**: Biased algorithms can significantly impact access to opportunities. For example, in the context of college admissions, an algorithm that favors applicants from privileged backgrounds may exacerbate educational disparities. It may perpetuate the cycle of privilege by admitting more students from affluent families while rejecting potentially deserving candidates from underrepresented communities. This not only reinforces existing social hierarchies but also hampers social mobility.

- **Employment and Hiring**: Algorithms are increasingly used in the recruitment and hiring processes. If these algorithms are trained on biased historical data, they may favor candidates who have historically been in the majority, leading to discrimination against minority groups. This reinforces disparities in employment and wage gaps, contributing to a cycle of economic inequality.

- **Criminal Justice**: Biased algorithms used in predictive policing or sentencing decisions can disproportionately target and penalize marginalized communities. For instance, if historical arrest data is biased due to over-policing in certain neighborhoods, these algorithms may predict higher crime rates in those areas, leading to increased police presence and further exacerbating tensions. The criminal justice system's biased algorithms can perpetuate the overrepresentation of certain groups in prisons, reinforcing social disparities.

- **Healthcare**: Biased algorithms in healthcare, such as those used for resource allocation or diagnosis, can have life-altering consequences. If these algorithms are trained on data that reflects existing healthcare disparities, they may allocate resources unequally, leaving marginalized communities with inadequate care. Misdiagnoses based on biased algorithms can result in delayed or inappropriate treatments, further exacerbating health disparities.

- **Financial Services**: Biased algorithms in lending and credit scoring can limit access to financial resources for marginalized individuals and communities. If these algorithms favor individuals from historically privileged backgrounds, they will receive better loan terms and access to financial services, while others face higher interest rates or outright denials. This can perpetuate economic disparities and hinder wealth accumulation.

- **Social Media and Echo Chambers**: Algorithms on social media platforms can create echo chambers that reinforce existing beliefs and attitudes. Users are exposed to content that aligns with their existing views, leading to polarization and the entrenchment of divisive ideologies. This can deepen societal divisions and make it difficult to bridge gaps in understanding and empathy.

- **Education**: Biased algorithms can affect educational outcomes by directing resources and opportunities disproportionately to certain schools or students. For example, if algorithms for educational funding favor schools with higher historical performance, underfunded schools in marginalized communities will continue to struggle, perpetuating educational disparities.

- **Public Services**: Algorithms used in public service delivery, such as welfare distribution or housing allocation, can inadvertently perpetuate inequality. If these algorithms are not designed with fairness in mind, they may allocate resources in a way that leaves vulnerable populations underserved, exacerbating social disparities.

  The consequences of biased algorithms on society are far-reaching, with the potential to amplify social disparities in numerous ways. From limiting access to opportunities and perpetuating economic inequality to exacerbating disparities in healthcare and criminal justice, these biased algorithms can reinforce existing social hierarchies. Addressing these biases is not only a matter of ethical concern but also essential for creating a more equitable and just society. It requires a concerted effort from policymakers, technologists, and society as a whole to ensure that algorithms are developed and used with fairness, transparency, and accountability in mind.

- ➤ **Widening the Wealth Gap**: It discusses how biased financial algorithms in lending and investment decisions can widen the wealth gap by favoring certain demographic groups while disadvantaging others.

  The impact of biased algorithms on society extends to the realm of economics and wealth distribution. Biased algorithms can exacerbate existing economic disparities and contribute to the widening wealth gap in several significant ways. In this expanded discussion, we will delve into how these algorithms affect wealth inequality and the long-term consequences for individuals and society as a whole.

- **Access to Credit and Financial Services**: Biased algorithms used in the financial sector can have a profound impact on individuals' access to credit and financial services. For example, credit scoring algorithms may be trained on data that reflects historical biases in lending practices. This can result in individuals from marginalized communities having lower credit scores, which, in turn, limits their ability to secure loans, mortgages, or favorable interest rates. As a result, those who are already economically disadvantaged find it more difficult to access the capital needed to invest, purchase homes, or start businesses, further deepening the wealth gap.

- **Investment and Wealth Management**: Algorithms are increasingly used in investment and wealth management, including robo-advisors and algorithmic trading. These algorithms can favor assets and investment strategies that historically performed well, which may disproportionately benefit those who are already wealthy. As a result, the wealthy see their wealth grow at a faster rate, while those with limited access to these tools struggle to accumulate assets and achieve financial stability.

- **Employment and Income Inequality**: Biased algorithms used in hiring and employment practices can contribute to income inequality. If algorithms favor candidates from privileged backgrounds, they may perpetuate wage disparities, leading to higher incomes for some and lower incomes for others. This income gap can, over time, translate into significant differences in wealth accumulation, as those with higher incomes have more opportunities for savings and investment.

- **Real Estate and Housing**: Algorithms in the real estate industry can affect housing prices and accessibility. Biased algorithms may prioritize certain neighborhoods over others, resulting in increased property values in affluent areas and decreased values in marginalized communities. This can lead to gentrification, pushing out long-term residents and further concentrating wealth in already prosperous neighborhoods.

- **Access to Education and Skill Development**: Biased algorithms can impact access to educational resources and opportunities. For instance, if online learning platforms use algorithms that favor students from privileged backgrounds, these students may have an advantage in acquiring new skills and knowledge. This can result in better job prospects and higher incomes, contributing to the wealth divide.

- **Taxation and Wealth Redistribution**: Biased algorithms can also influence tax policies and wealth redistribution efforts. If algorithms are used to determine tax liability or eligibility for social safety net programs, biases in these algorithms can lead to reduced tax contributions from the wealthy and limited access to benefits for those in need. This can further tilt the economic playing field in favor of the wealthy, widening the wealth gap.

- **Entrepreneurship and Access to Capital**: Biased algorithms used in venture capital and startup funding decisions can hinder entrepreneurial opportunities for underrepresented groups. If these algorithms favor projects and founders from established networks, it becomes difficult for entrepreneurs from marginalized backgrounds to secure funding and build successful businesses, perpetuating the wealth gap.

The consequences of biased algorithms on wealth inequality are multifaceted and interconnected with various aspects of economic life. These algorithms can create a self-reinforcing cycle, where those who are already economically advantaged benefit disproportionately, while marginalized communities face additional hurdles in wealth accumulation. Addressing these biases in algorithms is essential not only for promoting economic fairness but also for fostering a more equitable society where wealth and opportunities are accessible to all. Policymakers, businesses, and technology developers must prioritize transparency, fairness, and equity in algorithmic decision-making to mitigate these harmful effects and work toward a more just economic landscape.

2. **Discrimination and Fairness**:

➢ **Unfair Treatment**: The section highlights that biased AI systems can result in discriminatory treatment. For example, biased criminal justice algorithms may lead to harsher sentences for minority individuals, compounding the problem of mass incarceration.

One of the most significant concerns surrounding the use of biased algorithms in various domains is the potential for discrimination and unfair treatment. Biased algorithms can perpetuate and even exacerbate existing forms of discrimination, leading to unequal opportunities and outcomes for different groups within society. In this expanded discussion, we will explore how these algorithms contribute to unfair treatment and the broader implications for marginalized communities.

- **Employment Discrimination**: Biased algorithms used in recruitment, hiring, and performance evaluation can discriminate against certain groups based on race, gender, age, or other protected characteristics. For example, if an algorithm is trained on historical data that reflects biased hiring practices, it may inadvertently favor candidates who closely resemble the demographics of past hires. This can lead to the exclusion of qualified individuals from underrepresented groups, perpetuating workplace discrimination.

- **Criminal Justice Disparities**: Biased algorithms in the criminal justice system can result in unfair treatment and disparities in sentencing. Predictive policing algorithms, for instance, may target certain neighborhoods more aggressively, leading to over-policing and higher arrest rates among minority communities. Additionally, sentencing algorithms that rely on biased historical data may mete out harsher punishments to individuals from marginalized backgrounds, contributing to racial and socioeconomic disparities in incarceration rates.

- **Access to Financial Services**: Biased algorithms in lending and credit scoring can result in unfair treatment when individuals are denied loans or offered unfavorable terms based on factors such as race or income. Discriminatory lending practices perpetuate economic disparities, making it more difficult for marginalized communities to access the financial resources needed for personal and entrepreneurial growth.

- **Healthcare Inequities**: In healthcare, biased algorithms can lead to unequal treatment and health outcomes. For example, diagnostic algorithms trained on data that reflects disparities in healthcare access may misdiagnose or undertreat patients from marginalized communities. This can lead to serious health consequences and unequal access to quality healthcare services.

- **Online Platforms and Social Media**: Algorithms used by online platforms can amplify discrimination by promoting harmful content or enabling harassment. Biased recommendation algorithms may inadvertently favor divisive or discriminatory content, reinforcing existing biases and creating hostile online environments for certain groups. This not only perpetuates discrimination but can also discourage individuals from participating in online spaces.

- **Educational Disparities**: Educational algorithms used in grading, standardized testing, and admissions processes can result in unfair treatment. If these algorithms are biased, they may favor students from privileged backgrounds, disadvantaging those who have faced educational disparities due to systemic issues. This can further limit opportunities for individuals seeking to improve their lives through education.

- **Public Services Allocation**: Biased algorithms used in public service allocation, such as housing or welfare assistance, can lead to unequal access to essential resources. When algorithms favor certain groups over others, individuals who are already marginalized may receive inadequate support, perpetuating social and economic inequalities.

- **Bias Amplification**: Biased algorithms can perpetuate stereotypes and amplify societal biases. When algorithms rely on biased data, they may reinforce and propagate prejudiced beliefs, leading to a cycle of discrimination that is difficult to break.

  Addressing the issue of discrimination and unfair treatment resulting from biased algorithms requires a multifaceted approach. It involves developing and implementing fair and transparent algorithmic systems, auditing existing algorithms for bias, and establishing clear legal and ethical guidelines for algorithmic decision-making. Additionally, raising awareness about the consequences of biased algorithms and advocating for diversity and inclusion in technology development are crucial steps toward ensuring fair treatment and equal opportunities for all members of society. Ultimately, the pursuit of fairness in algorithmic systems is essential for building a just and equitable society.

- ➢ **Violations of Civil Rights**: It explores how biased AI can infringe on civil rights, such as the right to equal treatment and protection against discrimination, potentially leading to legal and ethical challenges.

  The use of biased algorithms in various sectors can lead to the violation of individuals' civil rights, perpetuating systemic discrimination and undermining the principles of fairness and equal treatment. Biased algorithms can exacerbate existing disparities and harm marginalized communities, raising serious concerns about the protection of civil rights. In this expanded discussion, we will explore how these algorithms can lead to violations of civil rights and the broader societal implications.

- **Employment Discrimination**: Biased algorithms in hiring and employment practices can violate individuals' civil rights by discriminating on the basis of race, gender, age, or other protected characteristics. Such discrimination may directly contravene anti-discrimination laws, like the Civil Rights Act of 1964 in the United States. When algorithms favor or disfavor certain groups unfairly, they undermine individuals' rights to equal employment opportunities and protection from discrimination.

- **Housing Discrimination**: In the realm of housing, biased algorithms can perpetuate housing discrimination, which is prohibited under laws like the Fair Housing Act in the U.S. These algorithms may influence decisions related to rental applications, mortgage approvals, or housing advertisements, effectively denying individuals from marginalized communities access to housing opportunities based on their race, ethnicity, or other protected characteristics.

- **Criminal Justice Disparities**: Algorithms used in criminal justice systems can lead to violations of civil rights, particularly when they result in discriminatory treatment. Biased algorithms can disproportionately target certain racial or socioeconomic groups, infringing upon individuals' rights to due process and equal protection under the law, as outlined in the U.S. Constitution. Unjust sentencing and over-policing of specific communities can further erode trust in the criminal justice system.

- **Voting Rights**: Biased algorithms can undermine individuals' voting rights, which are a cornerstone of democratic societies. If algorithms are used in voter registration, redistricting, or voter suppression efforts, they can disproportionately impact communities of color and marginalized groups, infringing upon their rights to participate in the democratic process and have their voices heard.

- **Educational Equity**: In the context of education, biased algorithms can hinder educational equity, violating students' rights to equal educational opportunities. For example, algorithms that perpetuate disparities in educational resource allocation or standardized testing can infringe upon students' civil rights by denying them a fair chance to succeed academically.

- **Access to Healthcare**: Discriminatory algorithms in healthcare can result in violations of individuals' rights to access healthcare services without discrimination. When algorithms are biased in diagnosing or treating patients, individuals from marginalized communities may face barriers to receiving appropriate medical care, infringing upon their right to health and well-being.

- **Online Discrimination**: In the digital realm, biased algorithms on online platforms can enable discrimination and harassment. When algorithms favor certain users or content at the expense of others, they can infringe upon individuals' rights to free expression and equal access to digital spaces.

- **Discrimination in Financial Services**: Biased algorithms in financial services can lead to violations of individuals' rights to fair and equal access to credit and financial resources. Discriminatory lending practices can prevent individuals from marginalized backgrounds from securing loans or obtaining financial services on an equal basis with others.

Addressing these violations of civil rights resulting from biased algorithms requires a concerted effort to ensure that algorithmic systems adhere to legal and ethical standards. This includes rigorous auditing of algorithms for bias, regulatory oversight, and the enforcement of anti-discrimination laws. Additionally, promoting transparency, accountability, and diversity in algorithm development is essential to mitigate the negative impacts of biased algorithms and protect the civil rights of all individuals in society. Failure to do so not only perpetuates discrimination but also erodes the foundations of a just and equitable society.

3.   **Loss of Trust and Accountability**:

➤   **Erosion of Trust**: The chapter discusses how the deployment of biased AI erodes public trust in institutions and technology. When individuals perceive that algorithms are making biased decisions, they may lose confidence in AI-driven systems.

➤   **Accountability Challenges**: It acknowledges the difficulties in holding AI systems and their developers accountable for biased outcomes, especially when the bias is unintentional or the result of complex algorithmic processes.

4.   **Dampening Innovation and Progress**:

➤   **Inhibiting Innovation**: The section explores how biased algorithms can stifle innovation by limiting opportunities for underrepresented groups. When AI systems discriminate against certain demographics, it hampers the contributions of those groups to technological advancement.

The proliferation of biased algorithms in various aspects of society can lead to a loss of trust in institutions, hinder innovation, and erode accountability. When individuals perceive that algorithms are perpetuating bias or unfairness, it can undermine confidence in technology and the organizations that deploy it. In this expanded discussion, we will explore how the consequences of biased algorithms can inhibit innovation and create a climate of distrust.

•   **Loss of Trust in Technology**: Biased algorithms can erode public trust in technology and the institutions that use them. When individuals perceive that algorithms are making decisions that are unjust or discriminatory, they may become wary of relying on technology for various aspects of their lives, from healthcare and finance to education and criminal justice. This loss of trust can inhibit the adoption of innovative technologies that have the potential to improve society.

- **Accountability Evasion**: Biased algorithms can create challenges in assigning accountability. When decisions are made by algorithms, it can be challenging to determine who is responsible for any resulting harm or unfairness. This evasion of accountability can hinder efforts to rectify biased outcomes and discourage organizations from taking responsibility for algorithmic decisions.

- **Stifling Innovation**: The fear of biased algorithms and their potential consequences can stifle innovation. Companies and researchers may hesitate to develop or implement new technologies due to concerns about algorithmic bias and the associated legal and reputational risks. This cautious approach can impede progress in fields where technology could otherwise have a positive impact, such as healthcare, transportation, and education.

- **Reduced Diversity in Tech**: Concerns about algorithmic bias can also deter individuals from underrepresented backgrounds from pursuing careers in technology. The perception that biased algorithms perpetuate discrimination in various sectors can discourage diversity in tech fields, limiting the perspectives and experiences that inform algorithm development and potentially perpetuating bias in the industry.

- **Legal and Regulatory Challenges**: Biased algorithms can lead to legal and regulatory challenges. When algorithmic decisions result in discrimination or violations of civil rights, organizations may face lawsuits, fines, or regulatory scrutiny. These challenges can divert resources away from innovation and create a risk-averse climate in which organizations prioritize compliance over experimentation.

- **Reputational Damage**: Public awareness of biased algorithms can result in severe reputational damage for organizations. Instances of biased decision-making by algorithms can lead to negative media coverage, public backlash, and damage to an organization's brand. This can further discourage innovation and investment in technology development.

- **Inequitable Outcomes**: Biased algorithms can perpetuate social inequalities, leading to long-term negative consequences for society. When individuals from marginalized communities consistently experience inequitable outcomes due to algorithmic bias, it can exacerbate existing disparities and erode social cohesion.

Addressing the loss of trust and accountability resulting from biased algorithms requires a multifaceted approach. Organizations must prioritize transparency in algorithmic decision-making processes, conduct thorough audits to identify and mitigate bias, and establish mechanisms for accountability when biased outcomes occur. Additionally, regulatory bodies can play a crucial role in holding organizations accountable for algorithmic decisions that violate legal and ethical standards.

Promoting diversity in technology development teams and fostering a culture of responsible innovation can help mitigate the negative impacts of biased algorithms. Ultimately, rebuilding trust and ensuring accountability are essential for realizing the full potential of technology and innovation in addressing societal challenges while minimizing the risks associated with algorithmic bias.

➤ **Deterring Investment**: It discusses how the perception of bias in AI can deter investment in AI technologies, particularly when there are concerns about legal and reputational risks associated with biased outcomes.

Biased algorithms not only erode trust in technology but also have the potential to deter investment in technological innovation. When individuals and organizations perceive that algorithmic systems are prone to bias or unfairness, it can result in reluctance to invest in the development, adoption, or utilization of these technologies. In this expanded discussion, we will explore how the loss of trust and accountability due to biased algorithms can deter investment and hinder technological progress.

- **Loss of Investor Confidence**: The presence of biased algorithms can shake investor confidence in technology companies. When investors believe that a company's algorithms are perpetuating discrimination or inequality, they may fear potential financial losses due to legal and reputational risks. This lack of confidence can lead to reduced investments in tech firms, hampering their growth and innovation.

- **Funding Challenges for Startups**: Biased algorithms can pose significant challenges for startups seeking investment. Investors may hesitate to fund startups that rely on algorithmic decision-making if they perceive a high risk of bias-related issues. This can limit the flow of capital to innovative early-stage companies, impeding their ability to develop and scale their technologies.

- **Risk-Averse Decision-Making**: Organizations may become risk-averse in their approach to technology adoption and development. Fearing potential backlash or legal consequences resulting from biased algorithms, they may opt for conservative, less innovative solutions. This hesitancy can hinder the adoption of advanced technologies that have the potential to bring about positive societal changes.

- **Diverted Resources**: Organizations may allocate significant resources to address the consequences of biased algorithms, including conducting audits, implementing mitigation measures, and managing legal challenges. These resource allocations can divert funds and attention away from innovation and R&D efforts, limiting the capacity for technological advancement.

- **Market Uncertainty**: The presence of biased algorithms can create uncertainty in the market. Companies may be unsure about how to navigate the complex landscape of algorithmic ethics and regulations. This uncertainty can lead to delays in technology development and adoption, further hindering progress.

- **Competitive Disadvantage**: Organizations that do not address biased algorithms may face a competitive disadvantage. As consumers and investors become more aware of the potential harms associated with algorithmic bias, companies that fail to prioritize fairness and transparency in their technology solutions may lose market share and opportunities for growth.

- **Tarnished Reputation**: The negative publicity surrounding biased algorithms can damage an organization's reputation. Public perception of an organization as unaccountable or indifferent to the consequences of algorithmic bias can lead to customer churn and a loss of public trust, impacting the company's bottom line.

- **Inefficiency and Missed Opportunities**: Biased algorithms can lead to inefficient decision-making processes and missed opportunities. When algorithms produce biased outcomes, organizations may make suboptimal choices based on incomplete or inaccurate information, leading to wasted resources and missed potential gains.

111

Addressing the consequences of biased algorithms on investment and innovation requires proactive measures. Organizations must prioritize transparency, fairness, and accountability in algorithmic decision-making. This includes conducting regular audits, implementing bias-mitigation strategies, and adhering to ethical guidelines. Regulatory bodies can also play a role in setting clear standards for algorithmic fairness and enforcing compliance.

Moreover, fostering a culture of responsible innovation and diversity within technology development teams can help organizations identify and rectify biases in algorithmic systems. By demonstrating a commitment to ethical and fair technology, organizations can rebuild trust, attract investment, and drive innovation that benefits society as a whole. Failure to do so risks stifling technological progress and limiting the positive impact that technology can have on addressing pressing societal challenges.

5. **Social Division and Polarization**:

➢ **Fueling Divisions**: The chapter highlights that biased algorithms can inadvertently contribute to social divisions and polarization. When AI-driven content recommendation systems reinforce existing beliefs and preferences, they can isolate individuals from diverse perspectives.

Biased algorithms, intentionally or inadvertently, contribute to social division and polarization within society. These algorithms can exacerbate existing fault lines, reinforce ideological and partisan divides, and create echo chambers that hinder constructive dialogue and compromise. In this expanded discussion, we will explore how the consequences of biased algorithms fuel social divisions and polarization, and the broader implications for society.

• **Confirmation Bias**: Biased algorithms often reinforce individuals' existing beliefs and preferences. For example, social media platforms use recommendation algorithms that show users content aligned with their interests and viewpoints. While this can enhance user engagement, it can also reinforce confirmation bias, as individuals are exposed primarily to information and opinions that align with their preexisting views. This can deepen ideological divides and make it difficult for people to consider alternative perspectives.

- **Echo Chambers**: Biased algorithms can create echo chambers in which individuals are exposed only to content that mirrors their own beliefs. These echo chambers not only limit exposure to diverse perspectives but also lead to the amplification of extreme and polarized viewpoints. When people are primarily exposed to one-sided information, it can harden their positions and make compromise and consensus-building more challenging.

- **Political Polarization**: Biased algorithms can intensify political polarization. In the realm of politics, algorithms on social media and news platforms often prioritize content that generates strong emotional reactions or engagement. This tends to favor polarizing or sensationalized content, further dividing society along political lines and reducing the likelihood of constructive political discourse.

- **Social Fragmentation**: Biased algorithms can contribute to social fragmentation, where individuals become increasingly isolated from those with differing perspectives. When people are exposed to biased or extreme content, they may withdraw from broader social networks or communities, leading to a breakdown in social cohesion and understanding.

- **Misinformation Amplification**: Biased algorithms can inadvertently amplify misinformation and disinformation. Content that is sensational or divisive tends to spread more quickly and widely, leading to the dissemination of false or misleading information. This can erode trust in institutions and exacerbate societal divisions.

- **Cultural and Identity Divides**: Biased algorithms can deepen cultural and identity divides. Algorithms that favor certain cultural or identity groups can lead to disparities in visibility and representation. This can reinforce stereotypes and contribute to tensions between different cultural or identity communities.

- **Adversarial Engagement**: Biased algorithms can encourage adversarial engagement rather than constructive dialogue. Online platforms often reward confrontational or combative interactions, leading to a climate of hostility and antagonism. This can discourage meaningful conversations and problem-solving.

- **Stifled Empathy**: Exposure to biased content can reduce empathy for others' perspectives and experiences. When individuals are consistently presented with content that portrays certain groups negatively, it can erode their capacity to empathize with the challenges faced by those groups, further widening societal divisions.

Addressing the role of biased algorithms in fueling social division and polarization requires a multifaceted approach. It involves the responsible design and regulation of algorithmic systems, as well as media literacy initiatives to help individuals critically evaluate information they encounter online. Promoting diverse and inclusive content representation and fostering open dialogue across ideological lines are also crucial steps toward mitigating the negative impact of biased algorithms on society. Ultimately, addressing algorithmic biases and their contribution to polarization is essential for preserving social cohesion, promoting understanding, and building a more harmonious and inclusive society.

➤ **Impact on Democracy**: It examines the implications of algorithmic bias on democratic processes, such as the spread of misinformation and the potential manipulation of public opinion.

The consequences of biased algorithms extend to the very core of democratic societies, affecting the functioning of democracy itself. Biased algorithms can contribute significantly to social division and polarization, eroding democratic norms, and undermining the ability of citizens to make informed decisions. In this expanded discussion, we will explore how biased algorithms impact democracy and the broader implications for society.

- **Filter Bubbles and Echo Chambers**: Biased algorithms contribute to the creation of filter bubbles and echo chambers. These are digital environments where individuals are exposed primarily to information, news, and opinions that align with their preexisting beliefs. This can lead to a distorted perception of reality, as individuals may be unaware of alternative viewpoints and information. In a democratic society, a diverse and informed citizenry is crucial for making well-rounded decisions, and filter bubbles hinder this.

- **Polarization of Political Discourse**: Biased algorithms play a significant role in the polarization of political discourse. Social media platforms, in particular, use algorithms that prioritize content that generates strong emotional reactions, often favoring sensational or polarizing content. This results in an environment where extreme viewpoints are amplified, making it difficult for citizens to engage in constructive political dialogue and reach common ground.

- **Misinformation and Disinformation**: Biased algorithms can inadvertently amplify misinformation and disinformation. False or misleading information that aligns with users' existing beliefs is more likely to be shared and spread within filter bubbles. This can distort public discourse, influence public opinion, and lead to uninformed decision-making by voters.

- **Undermining Trust in Institutions**: The proliferation of biased algorithms can undermine trust in democratic institutions and the media. When individuals perceive that algorithms are driving political polarization and the spread of misinformation, they may lose confidence in the institutions responsible for maintaining a healthy democracy. This erosion of trust can have long-term consequences for the legitimacy of government and electoral processes.

- **Election Manipulation**: Biased algorithms can be exploited to manipulate elections. Malicious actors can use social media algorithms to target specific groups with disinformation campaigns, voter suppression efforts, or divisive content intended to sow discord. This can undermine the integrity of elections and weaken the foundations of democracy.

- **Voter Suppression**: Biased algorithms can indirectly contribute to voter suppression by exacerbating divisions. Content that discourages certain groups from participating in elections can spread more easily within polarized online communities. This can lead to lower voter turnout among marginalized communities, affecting the representativeness of the democratic process.

- **Policy Gridlock**: Polarization resulting from biased algorithms can lead to policy gridlock. When elected officials and political parties become more ideologically divided, compromise and cooperation become increasingly challenging. This can hinder the ability of governments to address pressing issues and respond to the needs of the electorate.

- **Reduced Civic Engagement**: Biased algorithms can reduce civic engagement as individuals disengage from political discourse due to the adversarial and polarized environment. When citizens feel that their voices are drowned out by extreme views and hostile debates, they may become less motivated to participate in civic activities, including voting.

Addressing the impact of biased algorithms on democracy is a complex and multifaceted challenge. It requires efforts to promote media literacy and critical thinking skills among citizens, ensuring they can navigate the information landscape effectively. Moreover, regulatory measures to increase transparency and accountability in algorithmic systems, especially those that influence political discourse, are essential.

Additionally, fostering a culture of civil and constructive political discourse, both online and offline, can mitigate the divisive effects of biased algorithms. Encouraging diversity of viewpoints and promoting fact-checking and responsible sharing of information are vital steps toward maintaining a healthy democracy in the digital age. Ultimately, addressing the consequences of biased algorithms on democracy is crucial for preserving the principles of informed citizenship, fair representation, and a robust democratic society.

6. **Human Rights Concerns**:

➢ **Violation of Human Rights**: The section addresses the broader human rights implications of biased algorithms. It emphasizes that biased AI systems can infringe on fundamental human rights, including the right to dignity, privacy, and non-discrimination.

The impact of biased algorithms on society extends to the realm of human rights, as these algorithms can infringe upon individuals' fundamental rights and freedoms. Biased algorithms can lead to discrimination, inequality, and injustices that violate human rights principles enshrined in international agreements and national laws. In this expanded discussion, we will explore how biased algorithms can result in the violation of human rights and the broader implications for individuals and society.

- **Right to Equality and Non-Discrimination**: Biased algorithms can directly infringe upon the right to equality and non-discrimination, as established in international human rights treaties. When algorithms discriminate against individuals based on their race, gender, age, or other protected characteristics, they violate the principle that all individuals should be treated equally before the law and in access to opportunities.

- **Right to Privacy**: Biased algorithms can compromise the right to privacy by collecting and processing personal data in ways that perpetuate inequality or discrimination. For example, if algorithms are used in surveillance systems that disproportionately target certain communities, it can lead to a violation of privacy rights.

- **Freedom of Expression and Information**: Biased algorithms can influence the content individuals see online, limiting their access to diverse viewpoints and information. This can restrict freedom of expression and the right to access information, as individuals may be unable to explore alternative perspectives and make informed decisions.

- **Freedom of Thought, Conscience, and Religion**: Biased algorithms can limit the freedom of thought, conscience, and religion by reinforcing stereotypes and biases. When algorithms perpetuate harmful stereotypes about certain religious or cultural groups, they can stigmatize and discriminate against individuals belonging to these groups.

- **Right to Fair Trial**: In the context of criminal justice, biased algorithms can impact the right to a fair trial. If algorithms are used in pre-trial risk assessment or sentencing decisions and produce biased outcomes, individuals may be unfairly treated and denied their right to a fair and impartial trial.

- **Right to Education**: Biased algorithms in educational settings can affect the right to education. When algorithms perpetuate educational disparities by allocating resources unfairly or making biased admissions decisions, they hinder individuals' access to quality education.

- **Right to Health**: Biased algorithms in healthcare can compromise the right to health by misdiagnosing or undertreating patients based on their demographics. This can lead to unequal access to healthcare services and hinder individuals' right to the highest attainable standard of health.

- **Freedom of Assembly and Association**: Biased algorithms can impact freedom of assembly and association by promoting divisive content and polarization. When algorithms encourage hostile online environments, individuals may be discouraged from participating in open and constructive discourse, limiting their freedom to associate with diverse groups and engage in collective action.

Addressing human rights concerns related to biased algorithms requires a concerted effort to ensure that algorithmic systems adhere to ethical and legal standards. This includes conducting regular audits to identify and rectify bias, implementing transparent and accountable decision-making processes, and establishing mechanisms for individuals to challenge algorithmic decisions that violate their rights.

Additionally, regulatory bodies and international organizations must develop guidelines and regulations that specifically address the human rights implications of algorithmic systems. Promoting digital literacy and education about algorithmic biases and their consequences is also essential to empower individuals to protect their rights in the digital age.

Ultimately, addressing the violation of human rights resulting from biased algorithms is essential not only for protecting individual rights and freedoms but also for upholding the principles of justice, fairness, and equality in society. It requires a collective effort from governments, technology companies, civil society, and individuals to ensure that algorithms are developed and used in ways that respect and promote human rights.

➢ **Global Consequences**: It discusses how biased AI systems can have global consequences, affecting international relations and diplomacy when biases in AI decision-making result in international conflicts or disputes.

The consequences of biased algorithms extend far beyond individual rights violations, with global ramifications that affect societies, economies, and international relations. Biased algorithms can exacerbate global inequalities, undermine human rights on a broader scale, and challenge the principles of fairness and justice that underpin international agreements. In this expanded discussion, we will explore how biased algorithms can have global consequences and their broader implications.

- **Reinforcement of Global Inequalities**: Biased algorithms can reinforce global inequalities by perpetuating biases against certain countries or regions. For example, biased credit scoring algorithms may disadvantage individuals from developing countries, limiting their access to financial services and opportunities for economic growth. This contributes to a widening wealth gap between nations.

- **Economic Disparities**: Biased algorithms in financial systems can lead to economic disparities on a global scale. When certain countries or regions are consistently disadvantaged by biased lending or investment decisions, it can hinder their economic development and reduce their ability to compete in the global market.

- **Access to Healthcare and Education**: Biased algorithms can also impact access to healthcare and education worldwide. For instance, algorithms used in medical diagnosis or educational resource allocation may favor individuals or regions with more extensive historical data, leaving underserved areas with limited access to quality healthcare and education.

- **Digital Divide**: The digital divide is exacerbated by biased algorithms. When algorithmic systems favor certain groups or regions, it can lead to disparities in access to digital resources, further marginalizing communities that lack access to technology and the opportunities it provides.

- **Interference in International Relations**: Biased algorithms can interfere in international relations by perpetuating stereotypes or biases against certain countries or ethnic groups. This can contribute to tensions and conflicts between nations and hinder diplomatic efforts to build cooperation and resolve disputes.

- **Implications for Migration and Displacement**: Biased algorithms can have consequences for migration and displacement patterns. Algorithms used in immigration or refugee processing may inadvertently discriminate against certain groups, affecting their ability to seek asylum or migrate for economic or safety reasons.

- **Global Information Ecosystem**: Biased algorithms can distort the global information ecosystem by reinforcing false or misleading narratives. When algorithms amplify disinformation or discriminatory content, it can have ripple effects on international perceptions and relations, potentially leading to misunderstandings and conflicts.

- **Challenges to International Human Rights Standards**: Biased algorithms challenge the application of international human rights standards. When algorithms violate individuals' rights on a global scale, it can undermine the effectiveness of international agreements and mechanisms for upholding human rights.

Addressing global consequences resulting from biased algorithms requires a coordinated effort at the international level. International organizations, such as the United Nations, must play a role in developing guidelines and standards for the ethical use of algorithms. This includes establishing mechanisms for cross-border cooperation and accountability to address algorithmic bias that transcends national boundaries.

Furthermore, nations should collaborate to promote digital literacy and technology access worldwide to bridge the digital divide and reduce the impact of biased algorithms on marginalized regions. International cooperation in research, development, and regulation of algorithmic systems is crucial to ensure fairness, justice, and respect for human rights on a global scale.

In conclusion, the global consequences of biased algorithms underscore the need for a comprehensive and international approach to address algorithmic bias. Fostering a culture of fairness, transparency, and accountability in algorithmic decision-making is not only a matter of individual rights but also a critical step toward achieving global justice and equality.

By delving into the consequences of biased algorithms on society, this section of the chapter underscores the urgency of addressing bias in AI development. It presents a compelling case for the ethical imperative of creating fair, transparent, and accountable AI systems that do not perpetuate or exacerbate societal inequalities and divisions. Ultimately, it calls for a collective effort from the AI community, policymakers, and society at large to mitigate the damaging impacts of bias in AI.

Strategies For Fair and Transparent AI:

This section of the chapter delves into the critical importance of implementing these strategies to address the biases that can permeate AI technology.

- ➢ **Data Quality and Diversity**:

- **Representative Data Collection**: The chapter underscores the significance of using diverse and representative datasets for training AI models. This entails ensuring that the data used encompasses a wide range of demographics, perspectives, and cultural contexts to reduce bias.

- **Bias Auditing Tools**: It discusses the development of tools and methodologies for auditing training data to identify potential biases. These tools help data scientists assess data quality and take corrective actions when biases are detected.

- ➢ **Algorithmic Fairness**:

- **Fairness Metrics**: The section explores the use of fairness metrics and evaluation methods during the development and deployment of AI systems. These metrics help quantify and measure fairness, allowing developers to assess and mitigate bias.

- **Fairness-Aware Algorithms**: It highlights the emergence of fairness-aware algorithms designed to reduce bias in decision-making processes. These algorithms are explicitly crafted to produce equitable outcomes for diverse groups.

➢ **Explainable AI (XAI)**:

- **Interpretable Models**: The chapter emphasizes the adoption of interpretable machine learning models. These models are designed to provide understandable explanations of their decisions, enabling users to grasp the reasoning behind AI outcomes.

- **Transparency Tools**: It discusses the development of transparency tools and techniques that allow users to inspect and interpret AI models. These tools make it possible to trace how an AI system arrives at specific decisions.

➢ **Ethical Guidelines and Frameworks**:

- **Ethical AI Principles**: The section calls for the establishment and adherence to ethical AI principles and guidelines. These principles encompass fairness, accountability, transparency, and the responsible use of AI technologies.

- **Ethics Review Boards**: It discusses the role of ethics review boards or committees that can assess the ethical implications of AI projects, providing guidance and oversight throughout development.

➢ **Diverse and Inclusive Development Teams**:

- **Diverse Perspectives**: The chapter highlights the importance of assembling diverse and inclusive AI development teams. A team with varied perspectives can better identify and mitigate potential biases, as well as create AI systems that are more equitable.

- **Bias Mitigation Training**: It emphasizes the need for training and education on bias mitigation for AI professionals. These training programs enable developers to recognize and address biases effectively.

➢ **Continuous Monitoring and Auditing**:

- **Real-time Bias Monitoring**: The section advocates for real-time monitoring and auditing of AI systems in deployment. Continuous monitoring allows for the identification and correction of biases as they emerge.

- **Bias Impact Assessment**: It discusses the practice of conducting bias impact assessments to evaluate how AI systems affect different user groups and communities. This informs decision-makers about the real-world consequences of AI deployments.

➢ **Public and User Engagement**:

- **User Feedback Mechanisms**: The chapter highlights the importance of incorporating user feedback into AI system development. Users can provide valuable insights into biases and unfair outcomes.

- **Public Input**: It suggests involving the public in discussions about AI ethics and fairness through public consultations, surveys, and forums. This inclusive approach ensures that AI development considers a wide range of perspectives.

➢ **Regulation and Compliance**:

- **AI Regulation**: The section acknowledges the role of regulations and legal frameworks in promoting fairness and transparency in AI. These regulations set standards for ethical AI development and hold organizations accountable for compliance.

- **Compliance Mechanisms**: It discusses mechanisms for organizations to demonstrate compliance with AI ethics and fairness regulations. This includes documentation of AI development processes and outcomes.

By emphasizing these strategies for fair and transparent AI, this section of the chapter highlights the actionable steps that can be taken to mitigate biases and ensure that AI technologies are used responsibly and equitably. It underscores the importance of a holistic approach that encompasses data quality, algorithmic fairness, transparency, ethical guidelines, and ongoing monitoring, with the ultimate goal of creating AI systems that benefit society as a whole.

Chapter 4: Privacy, Personalization, and Paradox

In the digital age, the concepts of privacy and personalization often find themselves in a paradoxical relationship. On one hand, individuals demand greater personalization in the products and services they use, expecting tailored recommendations, content, and experiences. On the other hand, there is a growing concern about the erosion of privacy as organizations collect and analyze vast amounts of personal data to deliver this personalization. This chapter delves into the intricate interplay between privacy and personalization, exploring the challenges, benefits, and ethical considerations surrounding these concepts.

The Privacy-Personalization Paradox:

1. **Personalization Benefits**: Personalization involves tailoring products, services, and content to individual preferences, behaviors, and characteristics. It has become a cornerstone of the digital economy, enhancing user experiences, engagement, and satisfaction. Personalized recommendations on streaming platforms, targeted advertising, and customized news feeds are some examples.

2. **Data Collection and Privacy Concerns**: Achieving personalization requires the collection and analysis of vast amounts of user data. This data can include personal information, browsing history, location data, and even biometric data. The extensive data collection has raised serious privacy concerns, particularly with regard to user consent, data security, and the potential for misuse or breaches.

3. **Data Privacy Regulations**: In response to growing privacy concerns, many regions have introduced data privacy regulations such as the General Data Protection Regulation (GDPR) in Europe and the California Consumer Privacy Act (CCPA) in the United States. These regulations empower individuals with greater control over their personal data, including the right to know what data is collected and the right to request its deletion.

Navigating the Privacy-Personalization Balancing Act:

1. **Informed Consent**: Users must provide informed and explicit consent for their data to be collected and used for personalization. This consent should be obtained in a transparent and comprehensible manner, and users should be informed about the implications of granting or denying consent.

2. **Data Minimization**: Organizations should practice data minimization, collecting only the data necessary for the intended purpose of personalization. This reduces the risk of excessive data exposure and potential privacy violations.

3. **Anonymization and Pseudonymization**: To protect user privacy, organizations can use techniques like anonymization (removing personally identifiable information) and pseudonymization (replacing identifiable data with pseudonyms) before data analysis.

4. **Data Security**: Robust data security measures, including encryption and secure storage, are critical to safeguarding user data from breaches and unauthorized access.

5. **User Control**: Providing users with control over their data is essential. This includes mechanisms for users to access, rectify, or delete their data and to adjust their privacy settings.

6. **Ethical Use of Data**: Organizations must commit to the ethical use of data, ensuring that it is not used to discriminate against or harm individuals. Ethical considerations should guide the design and implementation of personalization algorithms.

7. **Transparency**: Being transparent about data practices, data usage, and the algorithms used for personalization fosters trust between users and organizations. Transparency also allows users to make informed decisions about their data.

Benefits and Challenges of Personalization:

1. **Enhanced User Experience**: Personalization can significantly enhance user experiences by providing relevant content and recommendations, saving time, and increasing engagement.

2. **Business Opportunities**: Personalization can lead to increased revenue and customer loyalty for businesses. It allows companies to tailor marketing efforts and offerings to individual preferences.

3. **Filter Bubbles**: A potential downside of personalization is the creation of filter bubbles, where individuals are exposed primarily to information and perspectives that align with their existing beliefs. This can hinder exposure to diverse viewpoints and contribute to polarization.

4. **Algorithmic Bias**: Personalization algorithms can inadvertently perpetuate biases present in training data, leading to discrimination or unfair treatment of certain groups.

The Future of Privacy and Personalization:

The future of privacy and personalization will likely be shaped by ongoing advancements in technology, evolving regulations, and shifting societal norms. Striking the right balance between personalization and privacy will remain a central challenge for organizations and policymakers. Ethical considerations and a commitment to user rights will play a pivotal role in resolving the privacy-personalization paradox and ensuring that individuals can enjoy the benefits of personalization without compromising their privacy.

The Trade-Offs of Personalization

Personalization in the digital age has transformed the way individuals interact with technology, from receiving tailored product recommendations to accessing customized news feeds. While personalization offers numerous benefits, it also entails significant trade-offs and challenges. This chapter delves into the intricacies of the trade-offs associated with personalization, exploring how the pursuit of customization can impact privacy, ethics, and user experiences.

The Benefits of Personalization:

1. **Enhanced User Experience**: Personalization is primarily driven by the desire to enhance user experiences. Customized content, recommendations, and services can save users time and effort, providing them with information and solutions that are relevant to their interests and needs.

2. **Increased Engagement**: Personalization often leads to higher user engagement. When users encounter content that aligns with their preferences, they are more likely to interact with it, leading to increased website visits, longer session durations, and higher conversion rates.

3. **Improved Customer Satisfaction**: In e-commerce and online services, personalization can boost customer satisfaction by offering products or features that match users' preferences. Satisfied customers are more likely to return and make repeat purchases.

4. **Business Growth**: Personalization can drive business growth by increasing customer retention and revenue. Tailored marketing efforts and product recommendations can lead to higher sales and customer loyalty.

The Trade-Offs of Personalization:

1. **Privacy Concerns**: The collection of personal data is a central component of personalization. To provide customized experiences, organizations must gather information about users' preferences, behaviors, and demographics. This data collection raises significant privacy concerns, as users may be uncomfortable with the extent of information being gathered about them.

2. **Data Security Risks**: Personalization relies on the storage and analysis of vast amounts of user data. This data is attractive to cybercriminals, making organizations more vulnerable to data breaches and security threats. Data breaches can lead to the exposure of sensitive personal information, leading to privacy violations and reputational damage.

3. **Algorithmic Bias**: Personalization algorithms may inadvertently perpetuate biases present in training data. For example, if historical data reflects societal prejudices, the algorithms can amplify these biases, resulting in discriminatory or unfair outcomes. This poses ethical challenges and can lead to social and legal repercussions.

4. **Filter Bubbles**: Personalization can create filter bubbles, where individuals are exposed primarily to information, news, and perspectives that align with their existing beliefs. While this may enhance user satisfaction, it can also limit exposure to diverse viewpoints, hinder critical thinking, and contribute to societal polarization.

5. **Overreliance on Personalization**: Excessive personalization can lead to an overreliance on algorithmic recommendations. Users may become less proactive in seeking out diverse information or exploring new interests, ultimately narrowing their worldview.

Strategies for Balancing Personalization and Trade-Offs:

1. **Informed Consent**: Organizations should obtain informed and explicit consent from users regarding data collection and personalization. Users should be made aware of what data is being collected and for what purposes, and they should have the option to opt in or out.

2. **Data Minimization**: Practicing data minimization involves collecting only the data necessary for personalization, reducing the risk of privacy violations and data security breaches.

3. **Ethical Algorithm Design**: Developers should prioritize ethical considerations in algorithm design. This includes implementing fairness, transparency, and accountability measures to prevent algorithmic bias and discrimination.

4. **Transparency**: Organizations should be transparent about their data practices, algorithms, and data usage. This transparency fosters trust and enables users to make informed choices about their data.

5. **User Control**: Providing users with control over their data and customization settings empowers them to tailor their online experiences while retaining a degree of privacy and autonomy.

6. **Diverse Content Exposure**: Platforms can implement features that expose users to diverse viewpoints and content outside their typical preferences, mitigating the risk of filter bubbles.

7. **Regulatory Compliance**: Organizations must adhere to data privacy regulations and standards to ensure legal compliance and protect user rights.

In conclusion, personalization offers substantial benefits in terms of user experience and business growth, but it comes with trade-offs related to privacy, ethics, and the potential for algorithmic biases. Striking the right balance between personalization and its trade-offs requires a holistic approach that incorporates informed consent, ethical considerations, transparency, and user control. By addressing these challenges, organizations can maximize the benefits of personalization while minimizing its negative consequences.

Ethical Concerns of Data Collection and Surveillance Capitalism:

In the digital age, the proliferation of personal data collection and the emergence of surveillance capitalism have raised significant ethical concerns. This chapter delves into the intricate ethical challenges surrounding data collection and surveillance capitalism, exploring the implications for privacy, autonomy, and societal values.

Data Collection and Privacy:

1. **Informed Consent**: Ethical data collection requires informed consent from individuals. Users should have a clear understanding of what data is being collected, how it will be used, and the option to opt in or out. Consent should not be coerced or obtained through deceptive practices.

2. **Transparency**: Organizations must be transparent about their data practices. This includes disclosing the types of data collected, how it will be used, and with whom it will be shared. Transparency builds trust and allows users to make informed choices about their data.

3. **Data Minimization**: Ethical data collection practices involve minimizing the amount of data collected to what is strictly necessary for the intended purpose. Collecting excessive data can infringe on privacy and create unnecessary security risks.

4. **Data Security**: Ethical considerations extend to data security. Organizations must take robust measures to protect user data from breaches and unauthorized access. Data security failures can result in serious privacy violations.

Surveillance Capitalism:

1. **Definition**: Surveillance capitalism refers to the commodification of personal data, where companies profit from collecting, analyzing, and selling individuals' information. It involves the relentless pursuit of data for economic gain.

2. **Ethical Concerns**:

- **Exploitative Practices**: Surveillance capitalism relies on extracting value from users' data without fair compensation. This raises concerns about exploitation and the unequal distribution of benefits.

- **Lack of User Agency**: Users often have limited control over how their data is used in surveillance capitalism. Their data is harvested and monetized without their explicit consent or understanding.

- **Manipulation and Persuasion**: The vast amount of data collected is used to manipulate individuals' behaviors and decisions. This can lead to concerns about the ethical implications of shaping people's choices without their awareness.

- **Privacy Erosion**: Surveillance capitalism erodes privacy, as personal data is constantly collected, analyzed, and monetized. This can result in a loss of individual autonomy and personal boundaries.

Ethical Frameworks for Data Collection and Surveillance Capitalism:

1. **Privacy as a Fundamental Right**: Many ethical frameworks emphasize privacy as a fundamental human right. This perspective views personal data as an extension of the self, deserving of protection and respect.

2. **Fairness and Transparency**: Ethical data collection and surveillance practices prioritize fairness and transparency. This includes equitable compensation for data use and clear communication about data practices.

3. **User Control**: Ethical frameworks advocate for user control over their data. Users should have agency in deciding how their information is collected, used, and shared.

4. **Regulatory Compliance**: Ethical organizations adhere to data privacy regulations and standards to ensure legal compliance and protect user rights.

5. **Data Stewardship**: Ethical data collection involves responsible data stewardship. Organizations should act as custodians of user data, ensuring its security and ethical use.

Mitigating Ethical Concerns:

1. **Data Governance**: Organizations should establish robust data governance policies that prioritize ethical data collection, use, and protection. This includes regular audits and assessments to ensure compliance with ethical standards.

2. **Ethical AI**: In the context of artificial intelligence, organizations should develop and deploy AI systems that adhere to ethical guidelines, avoid algorithmic bias, and prioritize fairness and transparency.

3. **User Empowerment**: Empowering users with control over their data, privacy settings, and informed choices is essential to address ethical concerns.

4. **Regulatory Frameworks**: Governments and regulatory bodies play a crucial role in addressing ethical concerns related to data collection and surveillance capitalism by implementing and enforcing data privacy regulations.

In conclusion, ethical concerns surrounding data collection and surveillance capitalism are central to the digital age. Resolving these concerns requires organizations to prioritize transparency, fairness, and user agency in their data practices. Ethical frameworks and regulatory measures play a pivotal role in safeguarding privacy, autonomy, and societal values in an era where personal data has become a valuable commodity.

Balancing User Benefits with Rights and Freedoms:

The digital age has brought about a profound transformation in how individuals interact with technology, with personalized services and recommendations becoming ubiquitous. However, this chapter explores the complexities of balancing the benefits of personalization with the protection of user rights and freedoms, including privacy, autonomy, and the right to make informed choices.

User Benefits of Personalization:

1. **Enhanced User Experience**: Personalization offers users tailored experiences, saving them time and effort. Customized content, recommendations, and services cater to individual preferences and needs, resulting in more satisfying interactions with technology.

2. **Increased Engagement**: Personalized content and recommendations often lead to higher user engagement. Users are more likely to interact with content and services that align with their interests, resulting in longer session durations and increased user satisfaction.

3. **Improved Efficiency**: Personalization can streamline user interactions by presenting relevant information or options upfront. This reduces the cognitive load on users and enables them to achieve their goals more efficiently.

4. **Business Growth**: Personalization can boost business growth by enhancing customer loyalty and driving increased revenue. Tailored marketing efforts and product recommendations can lead to higher sales and customer retention.

User Rights and Freedoms:

1. **Privacy**: Privacy is a fundamental right that encompasses the protection of personal data and the right to control how it is collected, used, and shared. Users have the right to maintain the confidentiality of their information and avoid unwarranted intrusion.

2. **Autonomy**: Autonomy refers to an individual's ability to make decisions and choices free from external influence or coercion. Personalization should

not compromise user autonomy by manipulating choices without their awareness.

3. **Informed Choices**: Users have the right to make informed choices based on accurate information. Personalization should not lead to information bubbles or echo chambers that limit exposure to diverse viewpoints.

Balancing Benefits with Rights and Freedoms:

1. **Informed Consent**: Organizations should prioritize informed consent when collecting and using user data for personalization. Users must understand what data is being collected, how it will be used, and have the option to opt in or out. Consent should be explicit, unambiguous, and freely given.

2. **Data Minimization**: Ethical data collection practices involve minimizing the amount of data collected to what is strictly necessary for personalization. Excessive data collection can infringe on privacy rights and create security risks.

3. **User Control**: Providing users with control over their data and customization settings empowers them to tailor their online experiences while retaining a degree of privacy and autonomy.

4. **Transparency**: Transparency about data practices, algorithms, and data usage fosters trust and enables users to make informed choices about their data.

5. **Regulatory Compliance**: Organizations must adhere to data privacy regulations and standards to ensure legal compliance and protect user rights.

6. **Diverse Content Exposure**: Platforms can implement features that expose users to diverse viewpoints and content outside their typical preferences, mitigating the risk of filter bubbles and promoting informed choices.

Ethical Considerations:

1. **User-Centric Approach**: Organizations should adopt a user-centric approach that prioritizes user rights and freedoms. Ethical considerations should guide the design and implementation of personalization algorithms.

2. **Ethical AI**: In the realm of artificial intelligence, ethical AI development involves avoiding algorithmic bias, ensuring transparency, and adhering to ethical guidelines to protect user rights and freedoms.

Ongoing Evaluation and Adaptation:

1. Organizations should continuously evaluate and adapt their personalization practices to align with evolving ethical standards and user expectations.

2. Conducting regular audits and assessments of data practices and algorithmic systems helps identify and rectify potential biases or privacy infringements.

In conclusion, achieving a balance between the benefits of personalization and the protection of user rights and freedoms is a central challenge in the digital age. Organizations must prioritize ethical data collection and personalization practices that respect user privacy, autonomy, and the right to make informed choices. By doing so, they can provide users with personalized experiences while upholding fundamental rights and values in the digital landscape.

Chapter 5: Roboethics: Morality for Robots

The emergence and proliferation of robotics and artificial intelligence (AI) have raised profound ethical questions regarding the morality and behavior of robots and AI systems. This chapter explores the field of roboethics, which is dedicated to addressing the ethical considerations and principles that should guide the design, deployment, and use of robotic and AI technologies.

Understanding Roboethics:

1. **Definition**: Roboethics is a branch of ethics that focuses on the ethical, legal, and societal implications of robotics and AI. It seeks to establish guidelines and principles to ensure that these technologies are developed and used in ways that align with ethical values.

2. **Interdisciplinary Nature**: Roboethics is inherently interdisciplinary, drawing from fields such as philosophy, computer science, engineering, law, psychology, and sociology. This interdisciplinary approach is necessary to address the multifaceted ethical challenges posed by robotics and AI.

Key Ethical Concerns in Roboethics:

1. **Autonomy and Decision-Making**: As robots and AI systems become more autonomous, questions arise about their capacity for independent decision-making and the moral responsibility for their actions.

2. **Safety and Accountability**: Ensuring the safety of robots and AI systems is a paramount ethical concern, as is establishing clear lines of accountability in cases where these technologies cause harm.

3. **Privacy and Data Handling**: Robots and AI often involve the collection and processing of personal data, leading to concerns about privacy, consent, and data security.

4. **Equality and Fairness**: Ethical considerations extend to issues of equality and fairness, including the potential for algorithmic bias and discrimination.

5. **Human-Robot Interaction**: Roboethics explores the ethical dynamics of human-robot interaction, including issues of consent, empathy, and trust.

6. **Job Displacement**: The impact of robotics and AI on employment and job displacement is a significant ethical concern, as it raises questions about societal well-being and economic fairness.

7. **Moral Decision-Making**: Ethical frameworks must be established to guide robots and AI systems in making moral decisions, especially in situations where human lives are at stake.

Key Principles and Approaches in Roboethics:

1. **Value Alignment**: Roboethics emphasizes the importance of aligning the values and objectives of robots and AI systems with those of their human users and society as a whole. This involves programming ethical guidelines into the technology.

2. **Ethical By Design**: An ethical-by-design approach involves integrating ethical considerations into the development process of robots and AI systems from the outset.

3. **Transparency**: Ethical robots and AI systems should be transparent in their decision-making processes, enabling humans to understand and scrutinize their actions.

4. **Accountability**: Establishing clear lines of accountability for robots and AI systems is essential. This includes holding designers, manufacturers, and operators responsible for the actions of these technologies.

5. **Ethical Frameworks**: Developing and implementing ethical frameworks and guidelines is crucial for ensuring that robots and AI systems adhere to ethical principles.

6. **Public Engagement**: Roboethics encourages public engagement and democratic deliberation to ensure that societal values and concerns are considered in the development and deployment of these technologies.

Roboethics in Practice:

1. **Medical Robots**: In the field of healthcare, robosurgeons and robotic caregivers must adhere to strict ethical guidelines to ensure patient safety, privacy, and consent.

2. **Autonomous Vehicles**: Roboethics plays a critical role in the development of self-driving cars, as these vehicles must make ethical decisions in emergency situations.

3. **Military Robotics**: The use of autonomous weapons and military robots raises complex ethical questions regarding the use of lethal force and accountability.

4. **Social Robots**: Social robots, designed for companionship and emotional support, require ethical guidelines to ensure that they respect the emotional well-being and autonomy of users.

Challenges and Future Directions:

1. **Adaptability**: Roboethics must evolve alongside technological advancements, adapting to new challenges and ethical dilemmas.

2. **International Collaboration**: International cooperation is necessary to establish a global framework for robethics, as robotics and AI are not limited by national borders.

3. **Legal Frameworks**: Roboethics may inform the development of legal frameworks and regulations governing the use of robots and AI.

In conclusion, the field of roboethics plays a pivotal role in addressing the ethical challenges posed by robotics and artificial intelligence. It provides a framework for ensuring that these technologies are developed and deployed in ways that respect human values, rights, and societal well-being. As technology continues to advance, robethics will remain a crucial discipline for shaping the moral behavior of robots and AI systems.

Can Machines Possess Morals?

The question of whether machines can possess morals lies at the heart of the field of roboethics. Roboethics explores the ethical considerations and principles that should guide the design, deployment, and use of robotics and artificial intelligence (AI) technologies, including the moral dimensions of these systems. This chapter delves into the complex debate surrounding the moral agency of machines.

Moral Agency and Machines:

I. **Moral Agency Defined**: Moral agency refers to the capacity to make moral judgments and decisions, guided by ethical principles and values. It involves the ability to discern right from wrong and to act in accordance with moral norms.

135

1. **Moral Agency in Humans:** Moral agency, in the human context, refers to the capacity of individuals to make moral judgments, decisions, and choices based on ethical principles and values. It encompasses several key elements:

- **Conscience**: Moral agency involves having a conscience, which is an inner sense of right and wrong. It allows individuals to experience moral emotions like guilt or empathy when they make decisions that impact others.

- **Autonomy**: Moral agency is closely tied to autonomy, as individuals possess the freedom to make choices that align with their own moral values and beliefs. Autonomy implies the ability to act independently and make decisions free from external coercion.

- **Complex Moral Reasoning**: Human moral agency often involves complex moral reasoning. Individuals consider a wide range of factors, including consequences, intentions, cultural and societal norms, and individual values when making moral judgments.

- **Empathy**: Empathy is a crucial component of moral agency. It involves the capacity to understand and share the feelings of others, which allows individuals to take into account the well-being and perspectives of others when making moral decisions.

- **Responsibility**: Moral agency also implies a sense of moral responsibility. Individuals are held accountable for their moral choices and actions, and they understand the consequences of their decisions on themselves and others.

2. **Machine Moral Agency:** When considering machines, such as robots or artificial intelligence systems, the concept of moral agency becomes more complex due to inherent differences between machines and humans:

- **Lack of Consciousness**: Machines lack consciousness and subjective experience. Unlike humans, they do not possess emotions, desires, or a sense of self. They do not have inner experiences of right and wrong.

- **Absence of Intent**: Machines operate based on algorithms and programming, without intent or the capacity to form intentions. Intent is a crucial aspect of human moral agency, as it reflects an individual's willful choices.

- **Inability to Feel Empathy**: Empathy, the ability to understand and share the feelings of others, is a fundamental aspect of human moral decision-making. Machines do not possess the capacity for genuine empathy.

- **Deterministic Behavior**: Machines behave deterministically, following predefined rules and algorithms. They do not possess free will or the capacity to engage in moral deliberation as humans do.

3. **Machine Ethics and Moral Programming:** While machines lack the intrinsic moral agency seen in humans, researchers and engineers are working on developing ways to imbue machines with ethical behavior through various approaches:

- **Ethical Programming**: Machines can be programmed with predefined ethical rules and guidelines. These rules are typically based on widely accepted ethical theories, such as utilitarianism or deontology. The machine then follows these programmed rules to make ethical decisions.

- **Machine Learning**: Machine learning techniques can be employed to teach robots ethics by exposing them to large datasets of ethical decisions made by humans. They can learn to mimic human ethical judgments, even though they don't possess genuine moral emotions.

- **Value Alignment**: Researchers aim to align the values and objectives of machines with those of their human users and society as a whole. This involves programming machines to make decisions that align with human moral princi

While machines lack the inherent moral agency of humans, the field of roboethics is exploring ways to imbue machines with ethical behavior. This involves programming them with predefined ethical rules, employing machine learning to mimic human ethical judgments, and aligning machine values with human values. However, the ethical decisions made by machines are fundamentally different from human moral agency as they lack consciousness, intent, and the ability to feel genuine empathy. The ongoing ethical debate revolves around how to ensure that machines make morally sound decisions in complex and varied situations while understanding the fundamental distinctions between human and machine morality.

II. **Human Moral Agency**: In humans, moral agency is the product of complex cognitive, emotional, and social processes. It encompasses empathy, conscience, and the ability to consider the consequences of one's actions on others.

   1. **Consciousness and Subjectivity:** Human moral agency is intimately connected to consciousness and subjective experience. Humans have a sense of self, self-awareness, and the ability to experience emotions, which play a significant role in moral decision-making. They can reflect on their actions and consider the consequences of their choices on themselves and others.

   2. **Autonomy and Free Will:** Human moral agency is closely tied to autonomy and free will. Individuals have the capacity to make choices independently and act in accordance with their own values and beliefs. They are not driven solely by preprogrammed rules or algorithms but have the ability to deliberate and choose their actions freely.

   3. **Complex Moral Reasoning:** Humans engage in complex moral reasoning when faced with ethical dilemmas. They consider a wide range of factors, including the consequences of their actions, the intentions behind those actions, cultural and societal norms, and their own moral values. Human moral judgments are often nuanced and context-dependent.

   4. **Empathy and Moral Emotions:** Empathy is a critical component of human moral agency. It involves the capacity to understand and share the feelings of others, which allows individuals to take into account the well-being and perspectives of others when making moral decisions. Moral emotions such as guilt, empathy, and moral outrage also play a role in guiding ethical behavior.

   5. **Responsibility and Accountability:** Human moral agency implies a sense of moral responsibility and accountability. Individuals are held responsible for their moral choices and actions. They are aware of the consequences of their decisions and understand their obligations to others in moral contexts.

   6. **Cultural and Individual Variability:** Human moral agency is influenced by cultural, societal, and individual factors. Different cultures and societies have varying moral norms and values, and individuals within those contexts may have their own unique moral

perspectives. This subjectivity and variability make moral agency a deeply human and dynamic concept.

Contrasting Human Moral Agency with Machine Behavior:

When considering the potential for machines to possess morals, several key distinctions emerge:

1. **Lack of Consciousness:** Machines, including artificial intelligence systems, lack consciousness and subjective experience. They do not possess self-awareness, emotions, or the ability to experience morality in the same way humans do.

2. **Absence of Intent:** Machines operate based on algorithms and programming, without intent or the capacity to form intentions. Intent is a crucial aspect of human moral agency, as it reflects an individual's willful choices.

3. **Inability to Feel Empathy:** Empathy, a fundamental aspect of human moral decision-making, is absent in machines. While they can be programmed to recognize and respond to certain cues or patterns of behavior, they do not genuinely understand or share the feelings of others.

4. **Deterministic Behavior:** Machines behave deterministically, following predefined rules and algorithms. They do not possess free will or the capacity to engage in moral deliberation as humans do. Their actions are based on programmed responses.

Ethical Programming and Alignment with Human Values:

While machines lack intrinsic moral agency, researchers and engineers work on ways to imbue them with ethical behavior through ethical programming and alignment with human values. This involves:

- **Ethical Programming:** Machines can be programmed with predefined ethical rules and guidelines based on widely accepted ethical theories. They follow these rules to make ethical decisions.

- **Machine Learning:** Machine learning techniques can be employed to teach robots ethics by exposing them to large datasets of ethical decisions made by humans. They learn to mimic human ethical judgments.

139

- **Value Alignment:** Researchers aim to align the values and objectives of machines with those of their human users and society as a whole. This involves programming machines to make decisions that align with human moral principles.

In conclusion, the concept of human moral agency is deeply rooted in consciousness, autonomy, complex moral reasoning, empathy, responsibility, and cultural variability. While machines lack these intrinsic attributes, ethical programming and value alignment are approaches that aim to ensure that machines make morally sound decisions in complex and varied situations. However, it is essential to recognize the fundamental distinctions between human and machine morality, as machines lack the consciousness, subjective experience, and moral emotions that define human moral agency. The ongoing ethical debate revolves around how to ensure responsible and ethical behavior in machines while acknowledging these fundamental differences.

III. **Moral Decision-Making**: Human moral decision-making involves weighing competing ethical considerations, taking into account cultural and societal norms, and making choices that align with one's values and beliefs.

1. **Complex Cognitive Process:** Moral decision-making in humans is a complex cognitive process that involves assessing the moral implications of a situation, considering ethical principles and values, and choosing an action that aligns with one's moral beliefs. This process often occurs in situations where there is a moral dilemma or a choice between right and wrong.

2. **Factors Considered:** When humans make moral decisions, they take into account a wide range of factors, including:

- **Consequences:** They consider the potential outcomes of their actions, weighing the harms and benefits to themselves and others.

- **Intentions:** They assess the intentions behind actions, recognizing that the same action can have different moral implications depending on the intentions of the actor.

- **Cultural and Societal Norms:** Human moral decision-making is influenced by cultural and societal norms and values, which shape individual moral perspectives.

- **Personal Values:** Personal values and beliefs play a significant role in guiding moral choices. These values are often deeply ingrained and reflect an individual's character and principles.

3. **Moral Dilemmas:** Moral dilemmas, situations in which there is a conflict between competing moral principles or values, are common in human moral decision-making. Resolving these dilemmas often requires careful consideration of the factors mentioned above.

4. **Empathy and Moral Emotions:** Empathy, the ability to understand and share the feelings of others, is central to human moral decision-making. Moral emotions like guilt, empathy, and compassion guide individuals in making choices that take into account the well-being and perspectives of others.

5. **Responsibility and Accountability:** Human moral decision-making carries with it a sense of moral responsibility and accountability. Individuals are aware of the consequences of their decisions and understand their obligations to others in moral contexts.

Moral Decision-Making in Machines:

When it comes to machines, including artificial intelligence (AI) systems, the concept of moral decision-making differs in several key ways:

1. **Algorithmic Rules:** Machines make decisions based on algorithmic rules and programming. These rules are predefined and lack the nuanced, context-dependent reasoning that humans engage in during moral decision-making.

2. **Absence of Intentions:** Machines lack intentions or motivations. Their actions are driven solely by the algorithms and data they have been programmed with. They do not possess the capacity for intent as humans do.

3. **Lack of Empathy:** Machines do not possess genuine empathy. While they can be programmed to recognize certain cues or patterns of behavior and respond in predefined ways, this is not the same as human empathy, which involves a deep understanding and sharing of emotions.

4. **Deterministic Behavior:** Machines behave deterministically. Given the same input and conditions, they will produce the same output every

time. This deterministic nature is fundamentally different from the nuanced and sometimes unpredictable nature of human moral decision-making.

Ethical Programming and Alignment:

To address the challenge of machines engaging in moral decision-making, researchers and engineers work on ethical programming and value alignment:

- **Ethical Programming:** Machines can be programmed with predefined ethical rules and guidelines. These rules are typically based on widely accepted ethical theories, such as utilitarianism or deontology. The machine then follows these programmed rules to make ethical decisions.

- **Machine Learning:** Machine learning techniques can be employed to teach robots ethics by exposing them to large datasets of ethical decisions made by humans. They learn to mimic human ethical judgments, even though they don't possess genuine moral emotions.

- **Value Alignment:** Researchers aim to align the values and objectives of machines with those of their human users and society as a whole. This involves programming machines to make decisions that align with human moral principles.

In conclusion, moral decision-making in humans involves complex cognitive processes that consider consequences, intentions, cultural norms, personal values, and moral emotions. Machines, on the other hand, make decisions based on algorithmic rules, lack intentions and empathy, and behave deterministically. Ethical programming and value alignment are strategies to guide machines in making morally sound decisions, but they do not replicate the nuanced and subjective nature of human moral decision-making. The ongoing ethical debate centers on how to ensure ethical behavior in machines while recognizing the fundamental differences between human and machine morality.

Challenges to Machines Possessing Morals:

1. **Lack of Consciousness**: Machines lack consciousness and subjective experience, which are considered prerequisites for moral agency. They do not possess emotions, desires, or a sense of self.

2. **Absence of Intent**: Machines operate based on algorithms and programming, without intent or the capacity to form intentions. Intent is a crucial aspect of human moral agency, as it reflects an individual's willful choices.

3. **Inability to Feel Empathy**: Empathy, the ability to understand and share the feelings of others, is a fundamental aspect of human moral decision-making. Machines do not possess the capacity for genuine empathy.

4. **Limited Ethical Framework**: Machines operate within predefined ethical frameworks and guidelines set by their human creators. Their moral decisions are determined by these constraints and lack the depth of human ethical reasoning.

5. **Deterministic Behavior**: Machines behave deterministically, following predefined rules and algorithms. They do not possess free will or the capacity to engage in moral deliberation.

Moral Machines:

1. **Ethical Programming**: Advances in AI have enabled the development of ethical machines that can make decisions based on programmed ethical principles. These machines are designed to adhere to predefined moral guidelines.

2. **Utility Functions**: Some AI systems can optimize utility functions, which, although not equivalent to human morality, allow them to make decisions that maximize specific objectives, such as minimizing harm.

3. **Ethical Dilemmas**: Researchers are exploring how AI systems can address ethical dilemmas by applying decision-making frameworks that prioritize ethical considerations, even if they lack genuine moral agency.

The Role of Humans:

1. **Moral Responsibility**: The responsibility for the actions and decisions of machines ultimately lies with their human creators and operators. Humans are accountable for how machines are designed, programmed, and used.

2. **Designing Ethical AI**: It is incumbent upon humans to design AI systems with ethical considerations in mind, embedding principles of fairness, transparency, and accountability into their algorithms and decision-making processes.

3. **Supervision and Oversight**: Humans must provide oversight and supervision of AI systems to ensure that they operate in accordance with ethical guidelines and societal norms.

The Future of Moral Machines:

1. **Continued Ethical Debate**: The question of whether machines can possess morals will remain a subject of philosophical and ethical debate. As technology advances, these discussions will evolve and become more nuanced.

2. **Ethical Frameworks**: The development of ethical frameworks for machines will be crucial in guiding their behavior and decision-making within defined ethical bounds.

3. **Interdisciplinary Collaboration**: Addressing the moral dimensions of machines will require interdisciplinary collaboration among ethicists, computer scientists, psychologists, and other experts to develop comprehensive approaches to roboethics.

In conclusion, the question of whether machines can possess morals challenges our understanding of ethics, consciousness, and artificial intelligence. While machines lack the inherent capacity for moral agency that humans possess, ethical programming and guidelines can guide their behavior within defined ethical boundaries. The future of moral machines will continue to be shaped by advancements in technology and ongoing ethical discussions.

Teaching Ethics to Robots: Possibilities and Challenges:

As robots and artificial intelligence (AI) systems become increasingly autonomous, the question of whether we can teach ethics to machines becomes central to the field of roboethics. This chapter explores the possibilities and challenges of imparting ethical principles and values to robots, ensuring they make morally sound decisions in various contexts.

The Need for Teaching Ethics to Robots:

I. **Autonomous Decision-Making**: With advancements in AI, robots and autonomous systems are making decisions in complex and morally sensitive situations, such as autonomous vehicles having to make split-second ethical decisions during accidents.

1. **Autonomous Decision-Making**: One of the primary reasons for teaching ethics to robots is their increasing autonomy. As AI technologies advance, robots are being deployed in various contexts where they make decisions independently. These decisions can have significant ethical implications, such as autonomous vehicles having to make split-second ethical choices during accidents. Teaching ethics to robots is essential to ensure that they make morally sound decisions when humans are not directly involved in the decision-making process.

2. **Ethical Dilemmas**: Robots may encounter complex ethical dilemmas in their operations. For example, in healthcare, a robot might need to make decisions regarding treatment options or resource allocation. Without ethical guidance, their choices might not align with human values and societal norms, potentially leading to harmful outcomes.

3. **Alignment with Human Values**: Teaching ethics to robots is crucial for aligning their behavior with human values and ethical principles. Robots are increasingly interacting with humans in various roles, such as caregiving, customer service, and companionship. Ensuring that robots respect and adhere to human values is essential for responsible AI deployment.

4. **Legal and Regulatory Compliance**: Many industries and sectors have legal and regulatory frameworks that require AI systems to adhere to specific ethical standards. Teaching ethics to robots is a legal requirement in some cases to ensure compliance with these regulations and avoid potential legal consequences.

5. **Preventing Harm**: Ethical guidelines and principles help prevent harm to individuals and society. For instance, in healthcare, robots that adhere to ethical principles can reduce the likelihood of medical errors or unethical treatment decisions that could harm patients.

Challenges in Teaching Ethics to Robots:

While the need for teaching ethics to robots is evident, several challenges complicate this endeavor:

1. **Subjectivity of Ethics**: Ethics is inherently subjective and influenced by cultural, societal, and individual perspectives. Teaching robots a universally accepted ethical framework can be challenging because different cultures and individuals may have divergent moral beliefs.

2. **Complex Moral Reasoning**: Human moral decision-making often involves intricate moral reasoning, considering multiple factors and potential consequences. Translating this complex process into algorithms or guidelines that robots can follow is a formidable task.

3. **Context Sensitivity**: Ethical decisions can vary significantly depending on the context. Robots must be able to adapt their ethical judgments to different situations, which is challenging to program comprehensively.

4. **Value Conflicts**: Robots may encounter situations where ethical principles conflict, requiring them to make trade-offs. Resolving value conflicts in a principled and consistent manner is difficult for machines.

5. **Unforeseen Situations**: AI systems may encounter entirely new or unforeseen situations for which they were not explicitly programmed. Teaching them how to respond ethically to such situations is challenging.

Approaches to Teaching Ethics to Robots:

To address these challenges, various approaches are being explored:

1. **Predefined Ethical Rules**: One approach is to program robots with predefined ethical rules and guidelines. These rules can be based on widely accepted ethical theories, such as utilitarianism or deontology. The machine then follows these rules to make ethical decisions.

2. **Machine Learning**: Machine learning techniques can be employed to teach robots ethics by exposing them to large datasets of ethical decisions made by humans. Through this exposure, they can learn to mimic human ethical judgments and adapt to different contexts.

3. **Imitation and Reinforcement Learning**: Robots can learn ethical behavior through imitation and reinforcement learning. They observe and imitate human actions in ethical scenarios and receive feedback to reinforce appropriate behavior.

4. **Collaborative Learning**: Collaborative learning involves humans and robots working together in decision-making processes. Humans can guide robots by providing input and feedback on ethical choices, helping them learn ethical decision-making in real-world situations.

The need for teaching ethics to robots arises from their increasing autonomy and the potential ethical dilemmas they may face. While there are significant challenges, approaches such as predefined ethical rules, machine learning, imitation learning, and collaborative learning are being developed to imbue robots with ethical behavior. These efforts aim to ensure that robots make morally sound decisions, align with human values, and adhere to ethical principles in a variety of contexts.

II. **Ethical Dilemmas**: Robots may encounter situations where they must navigate ethical dilemmas involving human safety, privacy, and well-being. Without ethical guidance, their decisions could have harmful consequences.

1. **Complex Moral Scenarios**: Teaching ethics to robots involves preparing them to navigate complex moral scenarios where there may not be a clear-cut right or wrong answer. In real-world situations, humans often encounter ethical dilemmas that require careful consideration of various factors.

2. **Unpredictable Contexts**: Robots can be deployed in diverse environments with unpredictable contexts. This unpredictability makes it challenging to prepare them for every possible ethical dilemma they may encounter. Ethical dilemmas can vary based on cultural norms, societal expectations, and the specific circumstances in which the robot operates.

3. **Value Conflicts**: Ethical dilemmas often involve conflicts between competing values or principles. For example, in a medical context, a robot may face a dilemma between respecting a patient's autonomy to make decisions about their treatment and the duty to prevent harm. Teaching robots to handle value conflicts ethically is a significant challenge.

4. **Subjectivity of Ethics**: Ethics is subjective, influenced by cultural, societal, and individual perspectives. What is considered ethically acceptable in one culture or context may be viewed differently elsewhere. Teaching robots to navigate these cultural and contextual variations is complex.

Approaches to Address Ethical Dilemmas:

1. **Predefined Ethical Rules with Flexibility**: One approach is to program robots with predefined ethical rules and guidelines while allowing for some flexibility. These rules can serve as a foundation, but robots should also have the capacity to adapt their decisions within

certain ethical boundaries when they encounter unforeseen ethical dilemmas.

2. **Machine Learning and Data Exposure**: Machine learning techniques can expose robots to a wide range of ethical dilemmas through extensive datasets of human decisions. This exposure helps robots learn how humans navigate moral complexities and apply similar decision-making processes.

3. **Value Sensitivity**: Researchers are exploring ways to make robots value-sensitive, meaning they can recognize and prioritize the values and preferences of the humans they interact with. This approach allows robots to adapt their behavior in ethical dilemmas to align more closely with the values of the people involved.

4. **Collaborative Decision-Making**: In complex ethical dilemmas, robots can collaborate with human experts or other robots. Collaborative decision-making involves seeking input from multiple sources to arrive at a consensus on the most ethical course of action. This approach leverages the collective wisdom of individuals and machines.

Case Examples of Ethical Dilemmas:

1. **Autonomous Vehicles**: Autonomous vehicles may face ethical dilemmas when they must make split-second decisions during accidents. For example, should a self-driving car prioritize the safety of its occupants over pedestrians, or vice versa?

2. **Healthcare Robots**: Robots in healthcare settings may encounter ethical dilemmas related to treatment decisions, resource allocation, and patient confidentiality. They may need to balance the principle of beneficence (doing good) with autonomy (respecting patients' choices).

3. **Customer Service Bots**: In customer service, chatbots may encounter dilemmas when handling sensitive customer inquiries. They must decide how to balance providing helpful responses with respecting privacy and confidentiality.

4. **Robotic Caregivers**: Robots in caregiving roles, particularly when assisting the elderly, may encounter dilemmas related to privacy, autonomy, and dignity. For instance, should a caregiving robot override a patient's refusal of medication if it believes it's in the patient's best interest?

Challenges in Resolving Ethical Dilemmas:

1. **Lack of Common Ethical Frameworks**: Robots may not have access to universally accepted ethical frameworks, making it challenging to resolve dilemmas consistently.

2. **Real-Time Decision-Making**: Some ethical dilemmas require real-time decision-making, leaving little room for extensive deliberation. Robots must be prepared to make rapid ethical decisions when necessary.

3. **Human Oversight**: While robots can be trained to handle ethical dilemmas, human oversight remains crucial. Ethical decision-making may require a level of judgment and discretion that only humans possess.

Ethical dilemmas pose a significant challenge in teaching ethics to robots due to their complexity, subjectivity, and unpredictable nature. Addressing these dilemmas involves a combination of predefined ethical rules, machine learning, value sensitivity, and collaborative decision-making. The goal is to equip robots with the capacity to make ethically sound decisions that align with human values and societal norms, even in situations where there is no clear-cut solution. However, human oversight and guidance will continue to play a vital role in resolving complex ethical dilemmas.

III. **Alignment with Human Values**: Teaching ethics to robots is crucial to align their behavior with human values, societal norms, and legal frameworks. This alignment is essential for ensuring responsible AI deployment.

1. **Need for Alignment**: One of the central goals of teaching ethics to robots is to ensure that their behavior aligns with human values and ethical principles. Robots are increasingly interacting with humans in various capacities, such as caregiving, customer service, and companionship. It is vital that their actions and decisions reflect the values and expectations of humans.

2. **Cultural and Contextual Variability**: Aligning robots with human values is challenging due to the cultural and contextual variability of ethics. What is considered ethical can vary significantly across different cultures and societal norms. Robots must be adaptable and sensitive to these variations to navigate diverse human interactions.

3. **Value Conflicts**: Ethical dilemmas often involve conflicts between competing values or principles. For instance, in a medical context, there may be a tension between respecting a patient's autonomy and ensuring their well-being. Teaching robots how to handle value conflicts and make decisions that balance these conflicting principles is essential.

4. **Subjectivity of Ethics**: Ethics is subjective and influenced by individual perspectives. Teaching robots to understand and adapt to the diverse ethical perspectives of individual users is a complex task. What one person considers ethical, another may not.

Approaches to Aligning Robots with Human Values:

1. **Value Sensitivity**: Researchers are developing robots with the capacity to recognize and prioritize the values and preferences of the humans they interact with. This approach, known as value sensitivity, allows robots to adapt their behavior to align more closely with the values of the people they are assisting or interacting with.

2. **Customizable Ethical Frameworks**: Some robots can be programmed with customizable ethical frameworks. This means that users can define the ethical principles and values they want the robot to follow, tailoring its behavior to their specific ethical preferences.

3. **Machine Learning from Human Behavior**: Machine learning techniques can expose robots to a wide range of human ethical behaviors through extensive datasets. By learning from human behavior, robots can adapt their decision-making processes to align with human values.

4. **Ethical Decision Trees**: In certain applications, robots can be equipped with ethical decision trees. These decision trees provide a structured approach to ethical dilemmas by breaking down decisions into a series of steps that consider various factors, values, and consequences.

Challenges in Aligning Robots with Human Values:

1. **Complexity of Human Values**: Human values are multifaceted and can vary significantly among individuals. Teaching robots to navigate and prioritize these values in real-time interactions is a complex task.

2. **Value Incompatibility**: In some cases, values may be incompatible. Robots must be equipped to make difficult choices when values

conflict, such as respecting autonomy versus ensuring safety in a healthcare setting.

3. **Adaptation to Context**: Robots need to adapt their behavior to different contexts and situations while still adhering to human values. What is considered ethical in one context may not be so in another.

4. **Subjectivity and Bias**: There is a risk of introducing bias into the robot's decision-making process when attempting to align it with human values. Bias can arise from the data used for training or the values programmed into the robot.

Case Examples of Aligning Robots with Human Values:

1. **Caregiving Robots**: Robots in caregiving roles need to align their actions with the values and preferences of the individuals they care for. This includes respecting cultural customs, dietary preferences, and privacy boundaries.

2. **Customer Service Bots**: Customer service chatbots must align their responses with the ethical values of the customers they interact with. This may involve handling sensitive information with care and respect for privacy.

3. **Autonomous Vehicles**: Self-driving cars must align their behavior with societal values related to safety, responsibility, and the prevention of harm. They must also navigate ethical dilemmas, such as how to prioritize the safety of passengers and pedestrians.

In conclusion, aligning robots with human values is a critical aspect of teaching ethics to robots. It involves addressing the complexity of human values, navigating value conflicts, and adapting to diverse cultural and contextual norms. Approaches such as value sensitivity, customizable ethical frameworks, machine learning, and ethical decision trees are being explored to ensure that robots make ethically sound decisions that reflect the values and expectations of the humans they interact with. However, ongoing efforts are required to address the challenges of aligning robots with human values while mitigating bias and adapting to dynamic contexts.

Challenges in Teaching Ethics to Robots:

1. **Subjectivity of Ethics**: Ethics is inherently subjective and influenced by cultural, societal, and individual perspectives. Teaching robots a universally accepted ethical framework can be challenging.

2. **Complex Moral Reasoning**: Human moral decision-making often involves intricate moral reasoning, considering multiple factors and potential consequences. Translating this complex process into algorithms is a formidable task.

3. **Context Sensitivity**: Ethical decisions can vary significantly depending on the context. Robots must be able to adapt their ethical judgments to different situations, which is challenging to program.

4. **Value Conflicts**: Robots may encounter situations where ethical principles conflict, requiring them to make trade-offs. Resolving value conflicts in a principled manner is difficult for machines.

Approaches to Teaching Ethics to Robots:

1. **Predefined Ethical Rules**: One approach is to program robots with predefined ethical rules and guidelines. These rules can be based on widely accepted ethical theories, such as utilitarianism or deontology.

2. **Machine Learning**: Machine learning techniques can be employed to teach robots ethics by exposing them to large datasets of ethical decisions made by humans. They can learn to mimic human ethical judgments.

3. **Imitation and Reinforcement Learning**: Robots can learn ethical behavior through imitation and reinforcement learning. They observe and imitate human actions in ethical scenarios and receive feedback to reinforce appropriate behavior.

4. **Collaborative Learning**: Collaborative learning involves humans and robots working together in decision-making processes. Humans can guide robots by providing input and feedback on ethical choices.

The Role of Ethics Instructors:

1. **Ethics Instructors**: Trained professionals, often referred to as "ethics instructors" or "AI ethicists," play a vital role in teaching ethics to robots. They are responsible for creating ethical guidelines, monitoring AI behavior, and updating ethical rules as needed.

2. **Continuous Oversight**: Ethics instructors are tasked with ongoing supervision of AI systems to ensure they adhere to ethical principles and adapt to changing societal norms.

The Future of Teaching Ethics to Robots:

1. **Ethical Frameworks**: Developing comprehensive ethical frameworks for AI and robotics will be essential. These frameworks should be adaptable and capable of addressing evolving ethical challenges.

2. **Human-Machine Collaboration**: The future may involve closer collaboration between humans and AI systems in ethical decision-making, allowing for shared moral reasoning.

3. **Interdisciplinary Research**: Ethical AI development will require interdisciplinary research that combines expertise in ethics, computer science, psychology, sociology, and law.

4. **Regulatory Frameworks**: Governments and regulatory bodies may implement guidelines and standards for teaching ethics to robots, ensuring responsible AI development and deployment.

In conclusion, teaching ethics to robots is a complex endeavor with significant challenges. While predefined rules and machine learning techniques can guide AI behavior, addressing the subjectivity of ethics and context sensitivity remains a formidable task. The future of ethical AI development will likely involve ongoing collaboration between humans and machines, interdisciplinary research, and the establishment of ethical frameworks to ensure that robots make morally sound decisions in a rapidly evolving technological landscape.

Robots In Care and Companionship Roles:

One of the most promising and ethically challenging domains in robotics is the use of robots in care and companionship roles. This chapter explores the implications of integrating robots into healthcare, eldercare, and other caregiving contexts, addressing both the potential benefits and ethical considerations associated with these roles.

The Role of Robots in Care and Companionship:

1. **Healthcare Assistance**: Robots are increasingly being used in healthcare settings to assist with tasks such as medication management, patient

monitoring, and physical therapy. They can provide timely reminders, collect vital data, and offer rehabilitation exercises.

2. **Eldercare**: In the context of eldercare, robots can serve as companions for seniors, offering social interaction, cognitive stimulation, and assistance with daily activities. They can help combat social isolation and loneliness among the elderly.

3. **Pediatric Care**: Pediatric care robots are designed to interact with children in hospitals and clinics. They can be used for entertainment, education, and emotional support during medical procedures.

Benefits of Robots in Care and Companionship:

1. **Enhanced Caregiver Support**: Robots can assist human caregivers by reducing their workload and enabling them to focus on higher-level care tasks. This is particularly valuable in healthcare settings with staff shortages.

2. **Improved Patient Outcomes**: In healthcare, robots can help ensure that patients adhere to medication schedules, perform necessary exercises, and maintain their health. This can lead to improved patient outcomes and reduced readmission rates.

3. **Social Interaction**: For the elderly and those in need of companionship, robots can provide social interaction, reducing feelings of loneliness and depression. They can engage in conversations, play games, and even offer reminders for appointments and medication.

4. **Pediatric Distraction**: Pediatric care robots can distract and entertain children during medical procedures, reducing anxiety and stress. This can make medical treatments more tolerable for young patients.

Ethical Considerations:

1. **Privacy and Data Security**: Robots in care settings may collect sensitive patient data, such as health information and personal preferences. Ensuring data privacy and security is crucial to protect individuals' rights.

2. **Autonomy and Informed Consent**: Ethical concerns arise when robots are used in healthcare decision-making. Patients must retain their autonomy, and informed consent should be obtained when robots are involved in medical procedures or care planning.

3. **Depersonalization**: Overreliance on robots for caregiving may lead to depersonalization of the caregiving experience, potentially reducing the quality of human-human interactions in care settings.

4. **Dehumanization**: There is a risk that the use of robots in care roles may dehumanize vulnerable populations, such as the elderly or pediatric patients, if robots are seen as substitutes for human companionship.

5. **Algorithmic Bias**: Robots equipped with AI may inadvertently perpetuate biases present in their training data, potentially leading to unfair treatment, especially if decision-making algorithms are involved in care.

Roboethics in Care and Companionship Roles:

1. **Human Oversight**: It is essential to maintain human oversight in care and companionship roles where robots are involved. Human caregivers should remain responsible for decision-making and ensure that patients' well-being and rights are protected.

2. **Ethical Design**: Robot designers and manufacturers must adhere to ethical design principles that prioritize the well-being and autonomy of patients. Ethical considerations should guide the development of robots for care roles.

3. **Transparency**: The use of robots in care should be transparent to patients, their families, and caregivers. Patients should be informed when interacting with a robot and should have the choice to opt-out if they prefer human care.

4. **Data Privacy and Security**: Stringent data privacy and security measures should be in place to protect patients' personal and medical information collected by robots.

5. **Bias Mitigation**: Developers should implement bias mitigation strategies to ensure that robots do not perpetuate biases and provide equitable care.

The Future of Robots in Care and Companionship:

The integration of robots into care and companionship roles is likely to expand as technology advances. Ethical considerations will continue to play a central role in shaping the use of robots in these contexts. Striking a balance between the benefits of enhanced caregiving and the ethical protection of vulnerable individuals will remain a critical challenge for the future of robotics in care and companionship.

1. **Rise of Robotic Caregivers**: As the global population ages and the demand for caregiving services increases, robots are expected to play a more significant role in assisting with healthcare and daily living tasks. These robotic caregivers have the potential to alleviate the shortage of human caregivers and provide support to the elderly and individuals with disabilities.

2. **Assisting with Activities of Daily Living**: Robotic caregivers are designed to help individuals with activities of daily living (ADLs) such as bathing, dressing, meal preparation, and medication management. They can also assist with instrumental activities of daily living (IADLs) like housekeeping, grocery shopping, and transportation.

3. **Enhancing Independence**: One of the primary goals of robotic caregivers is to enhance the independence and quality of life for those in need of care. By automating routine tasks and providing assistance as needed, these robots can empower individuals to live more autonomously in their homes.

4. **Companionship and Social Interaction**: Beyond practical assistance, robots are being developed to provide companionship and engage in social interactions with users. They can engage in conversations, play games, provide entertainment, and offer emotional support, particularly for individuals who may be isolated or lonely.

5. **Health Monitoring and Telemedicine**: Robotic caregivers can also serve as platforms for health monitoring and telemedicine. They can collect vital signs, remind users to take medications, and connect users with healthcare professionals for remote consultations.

Benefits of Robots in Care and Companionship:

1. **24/7 Availability**: Robots do not require rest or sleep, ensuring 24/7 availability for caregiving and companionship. This can be especially crucial for individuals who need constant monitoring or assistance.

2. **Consistency**: Robots can provide consistent care and assistance, reducing the variability that can occur with human caregivers. They follow programmed routines and guidelines meticulously.

3. **Reduction of Caregiver Burden**: By automating some caregiving tasks, robots can reduce the burden on human caregivers, allowing

them to focus on more complex and emotionally demanding aspects of care.

4. **Safety**: Robots can be equipped with safety features to prevent accidents and respond quickly to emergencies. This can provide peace of mind to both users and their families.

Challenges and Ethical Considerations:

1. **Privacy Concerns**: Robots equipped with cameras and sensors for monitoring and assistance raise privacy concerns. Users may worry about their data being collected and shared without their consent.

2. **Loss of Human Connection**: While robots can provide companionship, they cannot fully replace the depth of human-to-human interaction. There is a risk of individuals becoming socially isolated or emotionally detached if robots replace human companionship entirely.

3. **Ethical Decision-Making**: Robots may face ethical dilemmas in caregiving scenarios, such as balancing a user's autonomy with their safety. Decisions about when to intervene or seek human assistance can be complex.

4. **Quality of Care**: Ensuring that robotic caregivers provide high-quality care and can adapt to the changing needs of users is a significant challenge. The reliability and accuracy of these robots must be rigorously tested and improved.

5. **Affordability and Accessibility**: The cost of robotic caregiving technology may limit its accessibility to certain populations. Ensuring affordability and equitable access to these innovations is essential.

6. **Job Displacement**: The widespread adoption of robotic caregivers may lead to concerns about job displacement in the caregiving industry. It is crucial to consider the impact on human caregivers and the potential need for reskilling and job transition programs.

Ethical Guidelines and Regulations: To address these challenges, ethical guidelines and regulations for the development and use of robotic caregivers are essential. These guidelines should address issues like privacy, transparency, accountability, and the rights and dignity of users. Regulatory bodies may need to establish standards for safety, data security, and the ethical behavior of robotic caregivers.

In conclusion, the future of robots in care and companionship holds great promise for improving the lives of individuals in need of assistance. These robots have the potential to enhance independence, provide consistent care, and offer companionship. However, ethical considerations, privacy concerns, and challenges related to job displacement and affordability must be carefully addressed as this technology continues to evolve. Striking a balance between the benefits of robotic caregiving and the preservation of human connection and values is crucial in shaping the future of care and companionship robotics

Chapter 6: The Human Touch in an Automated World

1. Emotional Intelligence and Empathy:

- Emotional intelligence, the ability to recognize, understand, and manage emotions, is a distinctly human trait. It plays a crucial role in interpersonal relationships, empathy, and effective communication.

- Humans possess the capacity for empathy, allowing them to connect with others on an emotional level, provide comfort, and offer support during challenging times.

2. Complex Problem-Solving and Creativity:

- Humans excel at complex problem-solving and creative thinking. They can navigate ambiguous situations, devise innovative solutions, and adapt to changing circumstances.

- Creativity, a product of human imagination and innovation, drives advancements in art, science, technology, and many other domains.

3. Ethics, Morality, and Value-Based Decisions:

- Humans are responsible for setting ethical and moral standards in society. They engage in value-based decision-making, reflecting cultural, societal, and individual values.

- Ethical considerations, such as fairness, justice, and equity, are deeply rooted in human consciousness and guide decision-making in complex situations.

4. Communication and Empathetic Connections:

- Effective communication is a hallmark of human interaction. Humans can convey thoughts, feelings, and ideas through language, gestures, and expressions.

- Empathetic connections formed through face-to-face communication foster trust, understanding, and meaningful relationships.

5. Ethical and Social Responsibility:

- Humans bear ethical and social responsibility for the consequences of technology and automation. They must ensure that the deployment of AI and automation aligns with societal values and minimizes harm.

- The human role in decision-making related to the ethical use of AI is central to ensuring that technology benefits humanity rather than harms it.

6. Adaptability and Learning:

- Humans possess the capacity to adapt, learn, and acquire new skills throughout their lives. This adaptability allows them to stay relevant in evolving work environments and embrace lifelong learning.

7. A Sense of Purpose and Meaning:

- Humans seek purpose and meaning in their lives, often derived from relationships, personal growth, and contributions to society. These aspects of the human experience go beyond the scope of automation and AI.

Challenges in an Automated World:

1. Technology-Driven Isolation:

- As automation and AI continue to advance, there is a concern that individuals may become isolated or disconnected from genuine human interactions. Overreliance on technology for communication can erode the depth of relationships.

2. Skill Gaps and Job Displacement:

- Automation may lead to job displacement and skill gaps. It is essential to address these challenges through education, reskilling, and workforce development to ensure individuals can thrive in the changing job landscape.

3. Ethical and Accountability Challenges:

- The rapid integration of AI and automation can pose ethical and accountability challenges. Human oversight is critical to ensure that technology aligns with ethical standards and legal frameworks.

4. Privacy and Security Concerns:

- Automation and AI can raise privacy and security concerns as they collect and analyze vast amounts of personal data. Protecting individuals' privacy rights and data security requires vigilant oversight and regulation.

5. Bridging the Digital Divide:

- Access to and proficiency in technology are not equitable worldwide. Bridging the digital divide and ensuring that all individuals have equal access to the benefits of automation is a pressing challenge.

The Human-Machine Partnership:

The future lies in a harmonious partnership between humans and machines. While automation and AI can enhance efficiency and productivity, they cannot replicate the depth of human emotions, creativity, and ethical judgment. The human touch brings warmth, empathy, and values to a world that may otherwise be dominated by cold efficiency.

The challenge is to strike a balance between the advantages of automation and the preservation of what makes us uniquely human. This includes valuing emotional intelligence, creativity, ethical decision-making, and the ability to form deep and meaningful connections with others. The human touch is an essential component of a world where technology serves humanity rather than replaces it. It is through this partnership that we can navigate the complexities of an automated world while preserving the qualities that make us human.

Losing The Personal Connection: Risks and Realities:

As automation and artificial intelligence (AI) continue to advance, there are several significant risks and realities associated with the potential loss of personal connection:

1. Erosion of Authentic Relationships:

- The rise of digital communication and automation can lead to an erosion of authentic human relationships. Online interactions and automated responses lack the depth, nuance, and emotional connection that characterize face-to-face interactions.

- Personal relationships built on empathy, trust, and shared experiences are essential for human well-being. Over-reliance on technology may weaken these bonds.

2. Diminished Empathy and Understanding:

- Automation often involves interactions with algorithms and AI-driven systems that lack the capacity for empathy and understanding of human emotions. This can result in a reduction of empathy in society.

- Genuine understanding often requires emotional intelligence, which is a uniquely human trait. Losing personal connections with fellow humans may contribute to a decline in emotional intelligence.

3. Loneliness and Social Isolation:

- Increased reliance on digital communication and automation may lead to social isolation and loneliness, particularly among vulnerable populations like the elderly. Loneliness is associated with various physical and mental health issues.

- While technology can facilitate connections, it cannot fully replace the benefits of face-to-face human interactions.

4. Dehumanization in Customer Service:

- Automated customer service systems, chatbots, and AI-driven interactions in business can lead to a sense of dehumanization for customers. Customers may feel unheard or frustrated when they cannot access human support.

- The loss of personal connection in customer service can negatively impact brand loyalty and customer satisfaction.

5. Ethical and Privacy Concerns:

- The collection and analysis of vast amounts of personal data by automated systems raise ethical and privacy concerns. Individuals may feel that their personal information is being exploited or manipulated.

- The risks of data breaches and misuse of personal data by automated systems can erode trust and personal connections.

6. Job Displacement and Economic Disparities:

- Automation and AI can lead to job displacement in various industries. As workers lose their jobs to machines, economic disparities may widen, leading to social and economic challenges.

- The loss of employment opportunities can have a significant impact on personal well-being and social cohesion.

7. Education and Skill Gaps:

- The rapid advancement of technology requires individuals to acquire new skills continually. Those who cannot keep up with these skill demands may face challenges in the job market.

- Bridging the skill gaps and ensuring equitable access to education and training is crucial for maintaining personal connections to economic opportunities.

8. Psychological Impact:

- The constant use of technology, including social media and automated communication, can have a psychological impact, leading to addiction, anxiety, and depression.

- Screen time and digital distractions may reduce the time people spend engaging in meaningful, face-to-face interactions.

Addressing the Risks:

While the risks and realities of losing personal connections in an automated world are significant, there are strategies and approaches to mitigate these challenges:

I. Balance Technology Use: Encourage a balanced approach to technology use, emphasizing the importance of in-person interactions while acknowledging the benefits of digital communication.

Balancing technology use is crucial in mitigating the risks and realities of losing personal connections in an increasingly automated world. Here's a detailed exploration of this aspect:

1. Recognizing the Importance of Balance:

- The first step in addressing the risks is recognizing the importance of striking a balance between technology use and personal connections. Technology, when used mindfully, can enhance our lives, but over-reliance on it can lead to negative consequences.

2. Setting Boundaries:

- Encouraging individuals to set boundaries around their technology use is essential. This includes defining specific times for digital interactions and disconnecting from screens during quality face-to-face interactions.

3. Digital Detox:

- Promoting the concept of digital detox, where individuals periodically disconnect from technology, can help them recharge and refocus on personal connections. Suggesting occasional breaks from social media and screens can be beneficial.

4. Family and Social Agreements:

- Families and social groups can establish agreements or guidelines for technology use during gatherings and events. For example, designating "device-free dinners" can encourage more meaningful conversations.

5. Mindful Tech Consumption:

- Encourage mindful consumption of technology by asking individuals to reflect on the purpose of their digital interactions. Are they using technology for information, entertainment, or genuine communication? Being mindful can help prioritize meaningful connections.

6. Promote Offline Activities:

- Encourage participation in offline activities and hobbies that foster face-to-face interactions. These activities can include sports, group classes, volunteering, or attending community events.

7. Digital Sabbaticals:

- Advocating for digital sabbaticals, where individuals take extended breaks from technology, can help reset their relationship with screens and prioritize personal connections.

8. Technology-Free Spaces:

- Designate specific areas or times as technology-free zones or hours. For instance, bedrooms can be technology-free to promote better sleep and intimacy in relationships.

9. Educating about Screen Time Effects:

- Raising awareness about the potential negative effects of excessive screen time on mental health and relationships is essential. Educating individuals, especially young people, about the importance of moderation can be impactful.

10. Role Modeling:

- Adults and role models can set an example by practicing healthy technology use themselves. Children and young adults often mimic the behavior of those they look up to.

11. Utilize Technology Mindfully:

- Emphasize using technology as a tool to enhance personal connections rather than replace them. Encourage individuals to use video calls for face-to-face conversations with distant loved ones and to facilitate group activities online.

12. Prioritize Quality Over Quantity:

- Emphasize the quality of interactions over the quantity of digital connections. Encourage deeper, more meaningful conversations and relationships, even if they occur less frequently.

13. Digital Well-being Apps and Tools:

- Leverage digital well-being apps and tools that can help individuals track and manage their screen time. These tools can provide insights and reminders to maintain a healthy balance.

14. Promote Offline Social Activities:

- Encourage participation in social activities, clubs, or organizations that align with individuals' interests. These in-person gatherings can help people meet others who share their passions.

15. Self-Awareness and Self-Reflection:

- Encourage self-awareness and self-reflection about the impact of technology on personal connections. This introspection can lead to more conscious choices in technology use.

16. Support Systems:

- Establish support systems within families, schools, and workplaces to address technology-related challenges. This can include counseling services, peer support groups, and resources for digital well-being.

Balancing technology use is not about rejecting technology but about using it mindfully to enhance our lives while preserving the depth and authenticity of personal connections. By promoting these strategies and fostering a culture of balance, we can address the risks associated with losing the personal connection in an automated world and ensure that technology serves as a tool for enriching, rather than replacing, our human relationships.

II. Promote Digital Literacy: Teach individuals digital literacy skills to help them navigate the digital landscape effectively and make informed decisions about their online interactions.

Promoting digital literacy is a fundamental approach to empowering individuals to navigate the digital landscape effectively, make informed decisions about their online interactions, and maintain meaningful personal connections. Here's a detailed examination of this aspect:

1. Digital Literacy Defined:

- Digital literacy encompasses a range of skills and competencies, including the ability to access, understand, evaluate, and apply information and communication technologies (ICT) effectively. It involves critical thinking and ethical considerations in the digital realm.

2. Education and Awareness:

- Comprehensive digital literacy education should be integrated into formal education systems. Schools and educational institutions play a crucial role in teaching students how to use digital tools responsibly.

- Awareness campaigns and workshops can target both students and adults, emphasizing the importance of digital literacy in preserving personal connections and privacy.

3. Critical Thinking and Evaluation:

- Digital literacy encourages critical thinking and the ability to evaluate information sources critically. Individuals should be equipped with the skills to discern reliable information from misinformation and disinformation.

- This critical evaluation extends to online interactions, where individuals need to assess the authenticity and trustworthiness of the content they encounter.

4. Privacy and Security:

- Understanding the principles of online privacy and security is a core component of digital literacy. Individuals should be educated on how to protect their personal data, recognize online threats, and take appropriate security measures.

- Recognizing phishing attempts, using strong passwords, and understanding data encryption are essential skills in this context.

5. Responsible Online Behavior:

- Promoting responsible online behavior is a key aspect of digital literacy. This includes respectful communication, empathy, and ethical conduct in online interactions.

- Individuals should be aware of the consequences of their online actions, including cyberbullying and the spread of harmful content.

6. Identifying Digital Manipulation:

- Digital literacy education should cover the identification of digital manipulation techniques, such as deepfakes and image manipulation. Being able to recognize manipulated content is critical for informed decision-making.

7. Protecting Personal Information:

- Individuals should learn how to protect their personal information, including how to adjust privacy settings on social media platforms and other online services. They should be aware of the potential risks of oversharing personal information.

8. Encouraging Ethical Use of Technology:

- Digital literacy promotes ethical considerations when using technology. This involves understanding issues related to copyright, plagiarism, and the responsible use of information.

- Encouraging ethical behavior online contributes to a positive digital environment.

9. Staying Informed About Technology Trends:

- Digital literacy involves staying informed about the latest technology trends and advancements. Individuals should understand the implications of emerging technologies, including AI, IoT, and social media platforms.

10. Parental and Adult Education: Promoting digital literacy should extend to parents and adults who may not have grown up in a digital-native environment. They need to understand the digital landscape to guide and protect the younger generation effectively.

11. Access to Reliable Resources: Providing access to reliable digital literacy resources and online courses can empower individuals to enhance their skills continuously. Governments, educational institutions, and organizations can offer these resources.

12. Encourage Critical Digital Citizenship: Digital literacy goes hand in hand with the concept of digital citizenship, which emphasizes responsible and ethical engagement in the digital world. Individuals should be encouraged to be responsible digital citizens who contribute positively to online communities.

13. Evaluate and Adapt Curricula: Educational institutions should regularly evaluate and adapt their digital literacy curricula to keep pace with technological advancements and emerging digital challenges.

Promoting digital literacy is a proactive approach to addressing the risks associated with losing personal connections in an automated world. It empowers individuals to use technology as a tool for enhancing their lives and relationships while safeguarding their privacy and security. By fostering digital literacy from an early age and throughout one's lifetime, societies can create a more informed, responsible, and connected digital community.

III. Fostering Emotional Intelligence: Promote emotional intelligence education and development to ensure individuals can maintain empathy and understanding in their relationships.

Fostering emotional intelligence is an essential approach to counterbalance the potential erosion of personal connections in an automated world. Emotional intelligence, often referred to as EQ (Emotional Quotient), is the ability to recognize, understand, manage, and express emotions, both in oneself and in others. It plays a crucial role in nurturing meaningful relationships and maintaining the human touch in an increasingly automated society. Here's a detailed examination of this aspect:

1. Emotional Awareness:

- The foundation of emotional intelligence is self-awareness. Individuals need to be in touch with their own emotions, understanding what they feel and why they feel that way. Self-reflection and introspection are key to developing emotional awareness.

2. Empathy Development:

- Empathy, the ability to understand and share the feelings of others, is a core component of emotional intelligence. Empathetic individuals can connect with others on a deeper level, validating their emotions and experiences.

- Education and training programs can teach individuals how to empathize with others, encouraging perspective-taking and active listening.

3. Effective Communication:

- Emotional intelligence enhances effective communication by helping individuals express themselves clearly and empathetically. It enables them to convey their feelings, thoughts, and needs while also understanding the emotions and perspectives of others.

- Teaching communication skills, including nonverbal cues and active listening, can improve interpersonal connections.

4. Emotion Regulation:

- Emotional intelligence involves the ability to regulate one's own emotions. This skill is vital in maintaining composure, managing stress, and responding to situations with emotional balance.

- Techniques such as mindfulness, meditation, and stress management practices can help individuals develop emotion regulation skills.

5. Conflict Resolution:

- Emotional intelligence supports effective conflict resolution by promoting understanding and empathy. It helps individuals navigate conflicts with empathy, respect, and a focus on finding mutually beneficial solutions.

- Conflict resolution training can teach techniques for addressing disagreements constructively.

6. Recognizing Emotions in Others:

- Fostering emotional intelligence includes the ability to recognize emotions in others. This skill allows individuals to offer support and empathy when needed and build stronger connections.

- Training can help individuals become more attuned to nonverbal cues and emotional expressions.

7. Building Positive Relationships:

- Emotional intelligence contributes to building and maintaining positive relationships. It helps individuals establish trust, communicate effectively, and navigate the complexities of interpersonal dynamics.

- Relationship-building skills can be taught and practiced in both personal and professional settings.

8. Resilience and Well-being:

- Emotional intelligence promotes resilience by helping individuals cope with adversity and setbacks. Resilient individuals are better equipped to bounce back from challenges and maintain their overall well-being.

- Programs that focus on resilience and emotional well-being can enhance emotional intelligence.

9. Empathy in Technology Design:

- Incorporating empathy into the design of automated systems and AI interfaces can enhance user experiences. By considering users' emotional needs and reactions, technology can be more human-centered.

- Tech companies should prioritize empathy-driven design principles.

10. Parenting and Education: Parents and educators play a critical role in nurturing emotional intelligence from a young age. Schools can incorporate emotional intelligence education into their curricula, teaching students how to recognize and manage emotions.

11. Workplace Training: Employers can provide training and resources to foster emotional intelligence among employees. This can lead to improved workplace relationships, better teamwork, and increased job satisfaction.

12. Continuous Learning: Fostering emotional intelligence is an ongoing process. Individuals should be encouraged to engage in continuous learning and self-improvement to enhance their emotional intelligence skills throughout their lives.

Fostering emotional intelligence is an integral part of addressing the risks associated with losing personal connections in an automated world. It enables individuals to maintain authentic and meaningful relationships, even in the face of technological advancements. By emphasizing emotional awareness, empathy, effective communication, and conflict resolution skills, societies can ensure that the human touch remains a central aspect of human interaction, both online and offline.

IV. Protect Privacy and Data: Strengthen privacy regulations and data protection measures to safeguard individuals' personal information and restore trust in digital interactions.

In an increasingly automated world, protecting privacy and data is paramount to safeguarding personal connections and preserving the human touch. The proliferation of technology and digital interactions has generated vast amounts of personal information, making it vital to establish robust privacy measures. Here's a detailed examination of this aspect:

1. Data Privacy as a Fundamental Right:

- Recognize data privacy as a fundamental human right. Individuals should have control over their personal data and how it is collected, used, and shared by organizations and technology platforms.

2. Data Protection Regulations:

- Implement comprehensive data protection regulations and legislation, such as the General Data Protection Regulation (GDPR) in the

European Union, to ensure that organizations adhere to strict data privacy standards and practices.

- Enforce penalties for organizations that fail to comply with these regulations, emphasizing the importance of data privacy.

3. Informed Consent:

- Require organizations and digital platforms to obtain informed consent from individuals before collecting their personal data. Consent should be clear, specific, and given freely, without coercion.

4. Transparent Data Practices:

- Promote transparent data practices, where organizations clearly communicate how they collect, store, and use personal data. Individuals should have access to understandable privacy policies and terms of service.

5. Data Minimization:

- Encourage the principle of data minimization, wherein organizations collect only the data necessary for a specific purpose and retain it for as long as needed. Unnecessary data collection should be avoided.

6. Security Measures:

- Strengthen data security measures to protect personal information from data breaches and cyberattacks. Encryption, multi-factor authentication, and regular security audits are essential components of data protection.

7. User Control and Transparency:

- Empower individuals with control over their own data. They should be able to access, rectify, and delete their personal information held by organizations. Transparency in data practices allows individuals to exercise these rights effectively.

8. Ethical Data Handling:

- Encourage ethical data handling practices, emphasizing the responsible and ethical use of personal data. Organizations should consider the potential impact of their data practices on individuals' privacy and well-being.

9. Data Protection Officers:

- Appoint data protection officers within organizations to oversee data privacy compliance and serve as points of contact for privacy-related inquiries from individuals and regulatory authorities.

10. Privacy by Design: Adopt a "privacy by design" approach in the development of technology and automated systems. Privacy considerations should be integrated into the design process from the outset.

11. User Education: Educate individuals about the importance of data privacy and provide them with guidance on how to protect their personal information online. This includes raising awareness about common privacy risks and how to mitigate them.

12. Privacy Tools and Services: Encourage the use of privacy-enhancing tools and services, such as virtual private networks (VPNs), secure messaging apps, and browser extensions that block trackers and protect user privacy.

13. Regular Auditing and Compliance Checks: Conduct regular audits and compliance checks to ensure that organizations are adhering to data privacy regulations. Regulatory authorities should enforce compliance and investigate violations.

14. International Data Protection Cooperation: Foster international cooperation on data protection to address cross-border data flows and global privacy challenges. Harmonizing data protection standards can enhance the effectiveness of privacy regulations.

15. Empowerment Through Privacy Rights: Empower individuals to exercise their privacy rights, including the right to be forgotten (erasure of personal data) and the right to opt out of data collection and profiling.

By focusing on protecting privacy and data in an automated world, individuals can maintain a sense of control over their personal information and trust in digital interactions. This, in turn, contributes to the preservation of personal connections and the human touch in a technologically driven society. Privacy measures not only safeguard individuals but also create an environment where meaningful and authentic relationships can flourish without concerns of data misuse or breaches.

V. Invest in Mental Health: Address mental health concerns related to technology use by providing access to mental health resources and support.

1. Recognize the Impact of Technology on Mental Health:

- Acknowledge that the constant connectivity, information overload, and digital distractions can have a significant impact on mental health. Recognizing this impact is the first step toward addressing it.

2. Promote Digital Detox and Mindfulness:

- Encourage individuals to take regular breaks from technology and engage in mindfulness practices. Mindfulness can help individuals regain focus, reduce stress, and manage anxiety related to technology use.

3. Digital Addiction Awareness:

- Raise awareness about digital addiction and its effects on mental health. Individuals should be educated about the signs of addiction, such as excessive screen time, compulsive social media use, and neglect of offline relationships.

4. Mental Health Education:

- Incorporate mental health education into school curricula and workplace training programs. Teach individuals about the importance of mental health, stress management, and seeking help when needed.

5. Accessible Mental Health Services:

- Ensure that mental health services are readily accessible and affordable. Invest in the expansion of mental health resources, including counseling, therapy, and crisis helplines.

6. Telehealth and Digital Support:

- Leverage technology for the benefit of mental health by offering telehealth services and digital mental health support platforms. These services can provide convenient access to counseling and therapy.

7. Employee Well-being Programs:

- Employers should prioritize employee well-being by offering wellness programs that address the mental health challenges of the digital age.

These programs can include stress reduction workshops, mindfulness sessions, and employee assistance programs.

8. Balanced Screen Time:

- Encourage individuals, especially children and adolescents, to maintain a balanced screen time regimen. Promote outdoor activities, physical exercise, and face-to-face interactions to counteract excessive screen time.

9. Online Mental Health Communities:

- Facilitate the creation of supportive online communities focused on mental health. These platforms can offer peer support, resources, and a sense of belonging for individuals experiencing digital-related mental health challenges.

10. Combating Cyberbullying: Take active measures to combat cyberbullying, which can have severe mental health consequences, particularly among young people. Promote digital etiquette and provide resources for addressing cyberbullying incidents.

11. Self-Care and Resilience Building: Teach individuals self-care practices and resilience-building techniques. This includes strategies for managing stress, setting boundaries with technology, and prioritizing mental well-being.

12. Encourage Face-to-Face Interactions: Promote face-to-face interactions as a means of nurturing personal connections and supporting mental health. Encourage social gatherings, community events, and activities that foster in-person relationships.

13. Digital Well-being Apps: - Advocate the use of digital well-being apps that help individuals track their screen time, set usage limits, and receive notifications when it's time to take a break.

14. Destigmatize Mental Health: Work to destigmatize discussions about mental health. Encourage open conversations about mental well-being, allowing individuals to share their challenges and seek help without fear of judgment.

15. Research and Data Collection: - Invest in research to better understand the impact of technology on mental health and develop evidence-based interventions. Collect data on digital-related mental health issues to inform policies and programs.

16. Public Awareness Campaigns: Launch public awareness campaigns highlighting the importance of mental health in the digital age. These campaigns can emphasize the need for balance, mindfulness, and seeking help when mental health is affected.

Investing in mental health in an automated world is essential to ensure that individuals are equipped to navigate the challenges posed by technology while maintaining meaningful personal connections. By fostering a culture of mental well-being, societies can help individuals thrive in a digitally driven environment, preserving the human touch and nurturing authentic relationships even in the face of technological advancements.

VI. Lifelong Learning: Encourage lifelong learning and skill development to ensure that individuals can adapt to changing job markets and remain connected to economic opportunities.

In an automated world where technology continually evolves, lifelong learning becomes essential. To navigate the digital landscape effectively, individuals must continually acquire new knowledge and skills. Here's a detailed examination of this aspect:

1. Rapid Technological Advancements:

- Acknowledge that technology evolves rapidly, leading to changes in how we communicate, work, and interact. Lifelong learning is necessary to stay updated and relevant in this dynamic environment.

2. Digital Literacy for All Ages:

- Promote digital literacy from an early age and emphasize its importance throughout one's lifetime. This includes educating children, adults, and seniors about digital tools, online safety, and responsible technology use.

3. Continuous Skill Development:

- Encourage individuals to engage in continuous skill development. This could involve acquiring new digital skills, adapting to changing job market demands, and exploring emerging technologies.

4. Technology for Personal Growth:

- Highlight the potential for technology to facilitate personal growth and self-improvement. Online courses, educational apps, and digital platforms can provide access to a wealth of knowledge and skills.

5. Adaptability and Resilience:

- Lifelong learning fosters adaptability and resilience. Individuals who continually acquire new skills are better prepared to navigate career transitions and embrace technological changes.

6. Online Education Resources:

- Promote the availability of online education resources. Encourage the use of platforms like online courses, webinars, and virtual libraries to access a wide range of learning materials.

7. Soft Skills Development:

- Emphasize the importance of soft skills such as emotional intelligence, communication, and empathy. These skills are essential for building and maintaining personal connections in a digital world.

8. Encourage Critical Thinking:

- Teach critical thinking skills to help individuals assess the credibility of digital information, make informed decisions, and engage in meaningful discussions.

9. Addressing the Digital Divide:

- Ensure that lifelong learning opportunities are accessible to all, bridging the digital divide. Efforts should be made to provide technology and internet access to underserved communities.

10. Upskilling and Reskilling: Support initiatives that focus on upskilling and reskilling individuals in response to changing job market demands. This can include programs that teach digital skills, coding, and data literacy.

11. Collaborative Learning: Promote collaborative learning environments where individuals can share knowledge and experiences. Collaborative platforms and online communities can facilitate peer-to-peer learning.

12. Mentorship and Coaching: Encourage mentorship and coaching relationships, where experienced individuals guide and support those who are learning new skills or transitioning into new roles.

13. Lifelong Learning in the Workplace: Employers should recognize the value of lifelong learning and offer opportunities for professional development within the workplace. This can include training, workshops, and access to online courses.

14. Digital Well-being Education: Incorporate digital well-being education into lifelong learning initiatives. Teach individuals how to balance technology use, manage screen time, and maintain healthy online habits.

15. Embrace Emerging Technologies: Encourage individuals to embrace emerging technologies, such as artificial intelligence and automation, by understanding how they work and how they can be applied in various fields.

16. Cultivate a Growth Mindset: Foster a growth mindset that encourages individuals to embrace challenges and view failures as opportunities for learning and improvement.

17. Stay Curious: - Encourage individuals to stay curious and explore new subjects and technologies that pique their interest. Lifelong learning is not just about necessity but also about intellectual curiosity and personal growth.

By promoting lifelong learning, individuals can proactively adapt to the changing technological landscape while preserving the human touch in their personal connections. Lifelong learners are better equipped to understand, navigate, and utilize technology for the enhancement of their lives and relationships. It's a powerful strategy for ensuring that people continue to thrive in an increasingly automated world

VII. Promote Face-to-Face Interaction: Encourage social initiatives that promote face-to-face interaction, community building, and the cultivation of genuine personal connections.

In an increasingly automated world driven by technology and digital interactions, promoting face-to-face interaction is essential to counteract the potential erosion of personal connections. These in-person interactions are crucial for maintaining the human touch and nurturing authentic relationships. Here's a detailed examination of this aspect:

1. Importance of Physical Presence:

- Recognize that face-to-face interactions allow for physical presence, enabling individuals to connect on a deeper and more meaningful level. Body language, facial expressions, and tone of voice all contribute to richer communication.

2. Nurturing Empathy and Emotional Connections:

- Face-to-face interactions foster empathy and emotional connections. Being physically present with someone allows individuals to better understand each other's feelings and experiences, leading to stronger bonds.

3. Overcoming Digital Isolation:

- Combat the feelings of digital isolation and loneliness that can result from excessive screen time and online interactions. Face-to-face connections provide a sense of belonging and reduce feelings of isolation.

4. Building Trust:

- Trust is often built more effectively through face-to-face interactions. In-person meetings allow individuals to gauge sincerity and authenticity, contributing to trustworthiness in relationships.

5. Effective Communication:

- Face-to-face communication is more effective for addressing complex or sensitive topics. It reduces the risk of miscommunication and misunderstandings that can arise in digital interactions.

6. Strengthening Relationships:

- Encourage individuals to prioritize face-to-face time with loved ones, friends, and colleagues. Spending quality time together strengthens relationships and creates lasting memories.

7. Fostering Collaboration:

- In professional settings, face-to-face meetings and collaboration can lead to more innovative ideas and effective problem-solving. The exchange of ideas is often richer in person.

8. Skill Development:

- Face-to-face interactions help individuals develop social skills, including active listening, conflict resolution, and effective communication, which are essential for personal and professional success.

9. Balancing Online and Offline Life:

- Emphasize the importance of balancing online and offline life. Encourage individuals to allocate time for face-to-face interactions, leisure activities, and hobbies that facilitate in-person connections.

10. Family Bonding: Promote family bonding through regular face-to-face activities and gatherings. These moments are essential for maintaining strong family ties and providing emotional support.

11. Community Engagement: Encourage community engagement through local events, volunteer opportunities, and group activities. These in-person interactions contribute to a sense of belonging and community cohesion.

12. Networking and Professional Relationships: In professional contexts, face-to-face networking events, conferences, and meetings are crucial for building and nurturing professional relationships. They provide opportunities for collaboration and career advancement.

13. Reducing Screen Dependency: Educate individuals, especially young people, about the potential negative effects of screen dependency. Promote alternatives to screen-based entertainment and encourage outdoor activities and sports.

14. Public Spaces and Gathering Areas: Create public spaces and gathering areas that facilitate face-to-face interactions. Parks, community centers, and public events can serve as venues for people to connect in person.

15. Encourage Digital Balance: Encourage individuals to set boundaries on screen time and digital interactions to create space for face-to-face encounters. Digital balance is essential for overall well-being.

16. Celebrate Face-to-Face Moments: Celebrate and cherish face-to-face moments. Encourage individuals to capture these experiences through photos and shared memories to reinforce their significance.

By promoting face-to-face interaction, individuals and societies can ensure that personal connections remain authentic and meaningful in an increasingly automated world. These in-person encounters help mitigate the potential drawbacks of technology by fostering empathy, trust, effective communication, and the development of essential social skills. Embracing the value of physical presence contributes to a richer, more fulfilling human experience.

In conclusion, the risks and realities of losing the personal connection in an automated world underscore the importance of balancing technological advancements with the preservation of meaningful human interactions. By addressing the associated challenges and promoting strategies that prioritize authentic relationships, empathy, and emotional intelligence, society can strive for a harmonious coexistence of technology and human connection in an increasingly automated era.

The Ethical Dimensions of Human-AI Collaboration:

In an increasingly automated world, where humans and artificial intelligence (AI) systems work together, a range of ethical considerations emerges. These considerations are crucial to ensure that human-AI collaboration is not only effective but also respectful of human values and rights. Here's a detailed exploration of the ethical dimensions involved:

1. Transparency and Accountability:

- Ethical human-AI collaboration necessitates transparency in how AI systems operate and make decisions. Users should understand the algorithms' functioning and the role of AI in any given task.

- Accountability is essential when errors or biases occur. Determining who is responsible for AI-related decisions or consequences becomes a crucial ethical concern.

2. Bias and Fairness:

- AI systems can inherit biases from their training data, which can lead to unfair or discriminatory outcomes. Ethical considerations require addressing and mitigating these biases to ensure fairness and equal treatment for all individuals.

3. Privacy and Data Protection:

- Collaborative AI systems often process vast amounts of personal data. Protecting user privacy and data security is an ethical imperative. Consent, data anonymization, and robust security measures are vital components.

4. Consent and Autonomy:

- Ethical collaboration with AI should involve informed consent from users. Individuals must retain autonomy over decisions and have the option to opt out or control the level of AI involvement in their tasks.

5. Job Displacement and Reskilling:

- The ethical implications of AI replacing human jobs and tasks should be addressed. Ensuring that individuals have opportunities for reskilling and transitioning to new roles becomes essential to avoid socioeconomic disparities.

6. Dehumanization and Overreliance:

- Overreliance on AI can lead to dehumanization in interactions. Ethical considerations involve finding a balance between AI's efficiency and the preservation of the human touch in various fields, such as customer service or healthcare.

7. Accountability for AI Mistakes:

- When AI makes mistakes or causes harm, ethical frameworks must determine accountability. Legal and ethical responsibility should be clearly defined to protect individuals and ensure justice.

8. Ensuring Ethical AI Development:

- Ethical considerations extend to the development of AI systems. Developers should prioritize ethical principles during the design phase to prevent harmful outcomes.

9. AI in Critical Decision-Making:

- In situations where AI systems influence critical decisions, such as medical diagnoses or legal judgments, ethical safeguards must be in place. Transparency, accountability, and human oversight become crucial.

10. Equity and Accessibility: Ethical collaboration involves ensuring that AI benefits are accessible to all, regardless of socioeconomic status, disability, or geographical location. Narrowing the digital divide is an ethical imperative.

11. Human-AI Interaction Design: Ethical interaction design should prioritize a user-centric approach, making AI systems intuitive and user-friendly. Ensuring that humans can understand and control AI's actions is paramount.

12. Ethical AI Education: Ethical considerations extend to education and training. Providing individuals with knowledge about AI's capabilities, limitations, and ethical implications empowers them to make informed choices.

13. Psychological Well-being: Ethical concerns related to AI and mental health include the potential for AI to exacerbate feelings of loneliness or dependency. Ensuring that AI tools prioritize users' psychological well-being is essential.

14. Cultural Sensitivity: Ethical AI should be culturally sensitive, respecting diverse perspectives and values. Avoiding cultural bias and ensuring inclusivity are ethical imperatives.

15. Ethical AI Regulation: Governments and regulatory bodies play a vital role in setting ethical standards and guidelines for AI development and deployment. Ethical regulation helps create a level playing field and fosters responsible innovation.

16. Ethical Decision-Making Frameworks: Organizations should adopt ethical decision-making frameworks that guide AI use in alignment with moral principles and societal values.

Addressing these ethical dimensions of human-AI collaboration is essential to ensure that technological advancements serve humanity's best interests. Ethical considerations provide a foundation for responsible AI development, deployment, and usage, safeguarding the human touch and ethical values in an automated world. By addressing these dimensions, we can harness AI's potential while upholding the principles of fairness, transparency, accountability, and respect for human rights.

The Irreplaceability of Human Intuition and Emotion:

In an automated world, where AI and technology play increasingly significant roles, it's essential to recognize that certain aspects of human experience, such as intuition and emotion, remain irreplaceable. These uniquely human qualities bring depth, nuance, and ethical considerations to various facets of life and decision-making. Here's a detailed exploration of why human intuition and emotion are irreplaceable:

1. Intuition as a Complex Cognitive Process:

183

- Intuition is a complex cognitive process that involves subconsciously assessing vast amounts of information, patterns, and experiences. It often leads to quick, insightful decision-making, guided by a deep understanding of a situation.

- While AI systems can process large datasets and perform complex calculations, they lack the intuitive capacity to understand context, emotions, and subtle cues that humans naturally pick up on.

2. Emotional Intelligence and Empathy:

- Humans possess emotional intelligence, allowing them to perceive, understand, and manage emotions in themselves and others. This emotional depth enables empathy, which is crucial for connecting with and supporting one another.

- AI lacks genuine emotions and empathy. It may simulate empathy through pre-programmed responses, but it cannot authentically understand or experience human emotions.

3. Ethical Decision-Making:

- Ethical decision-making often requires a blend of intuition and emotion. It involves weighing moral considerations, empathizing with those affected by decisions, and assessing the broader societal impact.

- Human judgment, influenced by moral values and emotions, is critical for navigating complex ethical dilemmas, while AI relies on algorithms that may not fully grasp the ethical nuances.

4. Creativity and Innovation:

- Intuition and emotion play vital roles in creativity and innovation. They inspire new ideas, artistic expressions, and groundbreaking discoveries. Human intuition can connect seemingly unrelated concepts, fostering innovation.

- While AI can assist in data analysis and generating suggestions, it lacks the imaginative and emotional elements that underpin creativity.

5. Complex Problem Solving:

- Humans excel at solving complex, non-linear problems that require holistic thinking and intuition. These problems often involve ambiguity and uncertainty, which humans can navigate through intuition and emotion.

- AI, while proficient at specific tasks, struggles with the unpredictability and ambiguity inherent in many real-world problems.

6. Human Connection and Communication:

- Human intuition and emotion are central to effective communication and building meaningful relationships. They enable individuals to connect on a personal and emotional level, fostering trust and understanding.

- While AI can facilitate communication, it cannot replicate the depth of human connection that arises from shared emotional experiences.

7. Contextual Understanding:

- Human intuition allows individuals to grasp the broader context of a situation, considering not only data but also the emotional and social elements. This contextual understanding is invaluable in decision-making.

- AI tends to rely on data-driven analysis and lacks the ability to comprehend the subtleties of human context fully.

8. Adaptability and Flexibility:

- Humans possess the capacity to adapt and learn from new experiences rapidly. Intuition and emotional responses enable quick adjustments in unfamiliar or dynamic situations.

- AI systems typically require reprogramming or extensive training to adapt to new contexts, making them less agile in rapidly changing environments.

9. Human Values and Morality:

- Human intuition and emotion are closely linked to moral reasoning and the development of ethical values. These qualities inform decisions based on a deep sense of right and wrong.

- AI, on the other hand, relies on programmed algorithms and lacks an inherent moral compass, making it reliant on human guidance for ethical considerations.

While AI and automation offer significant benefits in terms of efficiency, data analysis, and task automation, they cannot replicate the nuanced, emotionally informed, and morally guided decision-making that humans bring to various aspects of life. Recognizing the irreplaceability of human intuition and emotion ensures that technology complements rather than supplants these vital human qualities, preserving the depth and richness of human experience in an increasingly automated world.

Chapter 7: Accountability in the AI Landscape

In the ever-evolving landscape of artificial intelligence (AI), accountability stands as a critical pillar upon which the responsible development, deployment, and use of AI systems depend. Chapter 7 of the book "AI Ethics and Governance: A Comprehensive Guide" delves deeply into the multifaceted concept of accountability, shedding light on its importance and implications within the AI domain.

1. **Defining Accountability:** At its core, accountability refers to the obligation and responsibility of individuals, organizations, and systems for their actions and decisions. In the context of AI, accountability extends to various stakeholders, including developers, policymakers, users, and even the AI systems themselves. It encompasses the notion that those who create, deploy, or use AI should be answerable for the consequences that arise from their actions or the AI systems they interact with.

2. **Developer Accountability:** One of the central themes of this chapter revolves around the accountability of AI developers and organizations. It explores the ethical and legal obligations that developers bear when creating AI systems. This includes ensuring transparency in AI algorithms, guarding against bias and discrimination, and minimizing potential harm to individuals or society at large.

3. **Algorithmic Accountability:** A significant portion of the chapter is dedicated to the concept of algorithmic accountability. It delves into the need for AI systems to be transparent, interpretable, and auditable. The discussion touches upon techniques such as explainable AI (XAI) and the importance of providing clear and understandable reasons for AI-generated decisions, particularly in critical domains like healthcare, finance, and criminal justice.

4. **Regulatory Frameworks:** Chapter 7 also explores the emerging regulatory landscape for AI. It discusses various initiatives and laws that aim to hold organizations accountable for their AI systems, such as the European Union's AI Act, which outlines strict requirements for high-risk AI applications. Additionally, it examines the role of government agencies and their responsibility in enforcing AI regulations.

5. **Ethical Considerations:** The chapter emphasizes the ethical dimensions of accountability in AI. It underscores the need for developers to make ethical

decisions when designing AI algorithms and to take responsibility for the societal impact of their creations. Ethical considerations encompass not only technical aspects but also broader questions of fairness, justice, and the well-being of communities affected by AI systems.

6. **User Accountability:** Accountability is not a one-sided responsibility. Users of AI systems also play a role in ensuring accountability. The chapter explores the importance of user education and awareness, as well as their ability to demand transparency and accountability from AI providers. Users must understand the capabilities and limitations of AI and make informed decisions about their interactions with AI systems.

7. **Future Directions:** The chapter concludes by looking at the evolving nature of accountability in the AI landscape. It discusses emerging challenges, such as the increasing use of AI in autonomous systems like self-driving cars and drones, and the need for new frameworks to address these challenges. It also highlights the importance of ongoing research and collaboration in shaping the future of AI accountability.

In summary, Chapter 7: Accountability in the AI Landscape offers a comprehensive exploration of the multifaceted concept of accountability in the context of artificial intelligence. It underscores the shared responsibility of developers, users, and policymakers in ensuring that AI technologies are developed and used in ways that are ethical, transparent, and accountable to society at large. As AI continues to permeate various aspects of our lives, understanding and addressing accountability will remain paramount for shaping a responsible and ethical AI future.

Who is responsible when AI goes wrong?

The question of responsibility in the realm of artificial intelligence (AI) is one of paramount importance and complexity, and it forms the focal point of Chapter 7 in "AI Ethics and Governance: A Comprehensive Guide." This chapter investigates the intricate web of accountability that arises when AI systems fail or produce unintended consequences, and it scrutinizes the key stakeholders who may bear responsibility in such scenarios.

I. **Primary Stakeholders:** When AI systems malfunction or cause harm, pinpointing responsibility is often a multifaceted endeavor. At the forefront are the primary stakeholders:

➤ **Developers and Organizations:** The chapter underscores the responsibility of AI developers and the organizations behind AI projects. They are responsible for the design, development, and quality assurance of AI systems. Any errors, biases, or ethical lapses in AI algorithms can be attributed to their actions or negligence. Developers must ensure that AI systems are thoroughly tested and audited to minimize risks.

1. **Design and Development Responsibility:** Developers and the organizations they represent are the architects behind AI systems. Their responsibilities extend from the initial design phase to the deployment of AI technologies. Key aspects of their accountability include:

- **Algorithmic Design:** Developers must make deliberate choices in designing AI algorithms. Decisions regarding data selection, model architecture, and training methodologies significantly impact the behavior of AI systems. Responsibility lies with developers when algorithmic design choices lead to unintended consequences.

- **Data Quality and Bias Mitigation:** Ensuring the quality and fairness of training data is vital. Developers must identify and rectify biases within datasets to prevent AI systems from perpetuating discrimination or unfairness. Failure to address data biases can result in ethical and legal accountability.

- **Robustness and Quality Assurance:** Rigorous testing and quality assurance are essential components of AI development. Developers are responsible for conducting thorough testing, validation, and auditing of AI models to identify and address potential issues. Failing to do so can lead to accountability for system failures.

2. **Ethical Considerations:** Beyond the technical aspects of AI development, developers and organizations have ethical responsibilities to consider:

- **Ethical Frameworks:** They should adopt ethical frameworks that guide AI development toward socially responsible outcomes. Ethical considerations should encompass fairness, transparency, accountability, and the overall societal impact of AI systems.

- **Avoiding Harm:** Developers have a moral obligation to prevent harm to individuals or communities. This includes avoiding the creation of AI systems that may endanger public safety, privacy, or well-being.

- **Beneficial Use:** Developers should ensure that AI technology is used for the benefit of society. Responsible AI development means actively seeking ways to enhance the quality of life, solve societal problems, and respect individual rights.

3. **Transparency and Explainability:** To facilitate accountability, developers must prioritize transparency and explainability in AI systems:

- **Transparency:** Developers should make the decision-making processes of AI algorithms transparent. This includes providing information about how AI systems make decisions, what data they use, and the rationale behind their actions.

- **Explainability:** The ability to explain AI decisions in a clear and understandable manner is crucial. Techniques like explainable AI (XAI) are essential tools for achieving this, as they allow developers to provide insights into complex AI models.

4. **Mitigation and Continuous Improvement:** Accountability also entails proactive measures to mitigate risks and ongoing improvement:

- **Risk Mitigation:** Developers and organizations must proactively identify and address risks associated with AI technology. This includes understanding potential vulnerabilities, security threats, and unintended consequences and taking steps to mitigate them.

- **Learning from Failures:** When AI systems do go wrong, developers should view these incidents as opportunities for learning and improvement. Accountability involves analyzing failures, understanding their root causes, and implementing corrective actions.

5. **Legal and Regulatory Compliance:** Developers and organizations must adhere to legal and regulatory frameworks:

- **Legal Responsibility:** Legal accountability may come into play if AI systems violate existing laws or regulations. Developers must be aware of and comply with applicable legal requirements in the regions where they operate.

- **Regulatory Compliance:** Regulatory bodies may impose specific requirements on AI development and deployment. Developers and organizations must ensure compliance with these regulations and cooperate with regulatory authorities.

➢ **Policymakers and Regulators:** Governments and regulatory bodies also play a pivotal role in holding AI systems accountable. They are responsible for crafting and enforcing regulations that govern AI usage. In many cases, they bear the responsibility of overseeing the AI industry and ensuring that developers adhere to ethical and legal standards.

1. **Regulatory Frameworks:** Policymakers and regulators are responsible for creating and enforcing the legal and ethical standards that govern AI systems. Their role involves:

   - **Crafting Regulations:** Policymakers are tasked with the development of comprehensive and adaptable regulations that set the ethical and legal boundaries for AI technologies. These regulations address concerns such as data privacy, transparency, bias mitigation, and the safe deployment of AI in various sectors.

   - **Risk Assessment:** Policymakers are responsible for assessing the potential risks associated with AI systems, particularly those used in critical areas like healthcare, finance, and autonomous vehicles. They must determine the level of oversight and control required to mitigate these risks effectively.

   - **High-Risk AI:** Identifying and defining high-risk AI applications is a crucial responsibility. Policymakers need to specify which AI systems require more stringent oversight and regulation due to their potential to cause significant harm if they fail or are misused.

2. **Enforcement and Oversight:** Accountability extends to the enforcement of regulations and ongoing oversight of the AI industry:

   - **Enforcement:** Regulators are accountable for ensuring that organizations and developers comply with AI-related laws and regulations. This may involve conducting audits, investigations, and imposing fines or penalties on those found in violation.

   - **Monitoring Compliance:** Policymakers and regulators must continuously monitor the AI landscape to keep pace with technological advancements. This includes tracking the emergence of new AI applications and assessing their impact on society.

- **Adaptation:** The AI field evolves rapidly, so regulatory frameworks must adapt accordingly. Policymakers should be agile in amending existing regulations or introducing new ones to address emerging challenges and opportunities.

3. **Ethical and Societal Considerations:** Policymakers and regulators are also responsible for addressing broader ethical and societal implications of AI:

- **Ethical Guidelines:** Beyond legal requirements, they must consider ethical principles and guidelines to ensure AI technologies align with societal values. Ethical responsibility encompasses fairness, transparency, accountability, and the promotion of human well-being.

- **Public Input:** Policymakers should engage with the public and experts to gather input and insights when developing AI regulations. Public engagement ensures that AI governance is reflective of diverse perspectives and societal concerns.

4. **International Cooperation:** In the globalized world of AI, international cooperation is crucial:

- **Harmonization:** Policymakers must work toward harmonizing AI regulations across borders to create a consistent and predictable regulatory environment for AI developers and organizations operating globally.

- **Knowledge Sharing:** Sharing knowledge, best practices, and lessons learned with other nations and international organizations fosters a collective effort to address AI-related challenges and ensures accountability on a global scale.

5. **Balancing Innovation and Safety:** Policymakers face the delicate task of balancing the promotion of AI innovation with the need for safety and ethical responsibility:

- **Innovation Promotion:** Encouraging AI innovation is essential for economic growth and technological progress. Policymakers must create an environment that fosters innovation while maintaining safeguards against potential risks.

- **Safety Measures:** At the same time, policymakers are responsible for putting in place measures that ensure AI technologies are safe, reliable, and accountable, even as they advance.

➤ **Users:** Users of AI systems have a degree of responsibility as well. They should be aware of the limitations of AI, use AI systems appropriately, and report issues when they encounter them. Users also have a role in demanding transparency and accountability from AI providers.

1. Users play a crucial role in ensuring accountability by being informed and educated about AI technology:

- **Awareness:** Users should be aware of the presence and capabilities of AI systems in their interactions with technology. This awareness helps users make informed decisions about how they engage with AI.

- **Education:** Promoting AI literacy among users is essential. Users should understand the basics of how AI works, its limitations, and the potential risks associated with its use. This education empowers individuals and organizations to navigate the AI landscape effectively.

2. **Responsible Usage:** Users bear the responsibility of using AI technology responsibly and within its intended scope:

- **Appropriate Usage:** It is incumbent upon users to use AI systems for their intended purposes. Misuse or abuse of AI technology can lead to unintended consequences and accountability.

- **Ethical Considerations:** Users should also consider the ethical implications of their use of AI systems. This includes respecting privacy, avoiding discrimination, and being mindful of the societal impact of their AI-related decisions.

3. **Demanding Accountability:** Users have the power to hold developers and organizations accountable for their AI systems:

- **Transparency and Accountability:** Users should demand transparency from AI providers. They have the right to know how AI systems make decisions, what data is used, and whether the systems are designed to mitigate bias and discrimination.

- **Feedback and Reporting:** If users encounter problems, biases, or unintended consequences in AI systems, they should provide feedback and report issues to developers and relevant authorities. User feedback is essential in identifying and addressing problems promptly.

4. **Data Responsibility:** Users often provide the data that fuels AI systems, and they must take steps to protect their own data:

- **Data Privacy:** Users should be vigilant about protecting their personal data when interacting with AI systems. This includes understanding the data collection practices of AI applications and ensuring their data is used in compliance with privacy regulations.

- **Data Accuracy:** Users can contribute to the accuracy and fairness of AI systems by providing accurate and representative data. Biased or inaccurate data can lead to biased AI outcomes.

5. **Evaluating Trustworthiness:** Users should evaluate the trustworthiness of AI systems they engage with:

- **Reliability:** Assessing the reliability of AI systems is crucial. Users should be cautious of AI applications that consistently produce unreliable or unsafe results.

- **Third-party Certifications:** Users can look for third-party certifications or evaluations of AI systems to gauge their trustworthiness and adherence to ethical and safety standards.

6. **Collaboration with Developers:** Collaboration between users and developers is essential for accountability:

- **User Input:** Developers can benefit from user input and feedback to improve the performance and safety of their AI systems. Users can contribute valuable insights into real-world usage and potential issues.

II. **Algorithmic Accountability:** A significant portion of the chapter is devoted to algorithmic accountability. It delves into the intricate nature of AI algorithms and highlights the challenges in determining responsibility when algorithms produce unintended consequences. Factors like data quality, bias, and the dynamic nature of AI systems make it difficult to attribute blame to a single party.

1. **Understanding Algorithmic Accountability:** Algorithmic accountability refers to the concept that the algorithms driving AI systems should be transparent, interpretable, and subject to scrutiny.

This accountability framework ensures that AI systems can be held responsible for their actions, and that the decisions made by these systems can be explained and justified.

2. **Transparency and Explainability:** Transparency is a cornerstone of algorithmic accountability:

- **Transparency:** AI developers must design algorithms in a way that makes their operations transparent to external observers. This means that stakeholders, including users and regulators, should have access to information about how the algorithm makes decisions, what data it uses, and why it produces particular outcomes.

- **Explainability:** Beyond transparency, algorithms must be designed to be explainable. Explainable AI (XAI) techniques aim to provide clear and understandable explanations for the decisions AI systems make. This enables users and stakeholders to comprehend the rationale behind AI-generated outcomes.

3. **Bias and Fairness Mitigation:** Addressing bias and ensuring fairness are integral components of algorithmic accountability:

- **Bias Identification:** Developers must actively identify and mitigate biases within AI algorithms. This includes biases present in training data, model architecture, or decision-making processes. Algorithms should not discriminate against individuals or groups based on protected characteristics such as race, gender, or ethnicity.

- **Fairness Considerations:** Algorithms should be designed to promote fairness and avoid disparate impacts on different demographic groups. Developers must implement fairness-aware machine learning techniques to ensure that AI systems do not perpetuate or exacerbate existing societal inequalities.

4. **Auditability and Accountability Measures:** Algorithmic accountability entails measures for auditing and ensuring accountability:

- **Auditing Algorithms:** Auditing involves systematically examining the behavior of algorithms, both during development and in real-world use. This process helps identify and rectify issues, biases, and unintended consequences.

- **Accountability Frameworks:** Developers should establish clear accountability frameworks for AI systems. This includes specifying who is responsible for algorithmic decisions, how decisions are made, and what measures are in place to rectify errors or harm caused by the algorithm.

5. **Ethical Considerations:** Algorithmic accountability goes beyond technical aspects and delves into ethical dimensions:

- **Ethical Responsibility:** Developers bear an ethical responsibility to ensure that their algorithms are used for the benefit of society and do not cause harm. Ethical considerations include respecting individual rights, privacy, and the broader societal impact of algorithmic decisions.

6. **Regulatory Requirements:** Regulatory frameworks increasingly emphasize algorithmic accountability:

- **Legal Compliance:** Algorithms must adhere to legal requirements and regulations governing AI technology. Developers must ensure that their algorithms comply with data protection, anti-discrimination, and other relevant laws.

- **Transparency Reporting:** Some regulations require transparency reporting, where organizations disclose information about their AI systems, including how they make decisions and handle sensitive data. This promotes accountability and regulatory compliance.

7. **Ongoing Monitoring and Improvement:** Accountability is an ongoing process:

- **Continuous Assessment:** Developers must continuously assess the performance and behavior of their algorithms, taking into account changing data distributions and user feedback.

- **Iterative Development:** Accountability involves iterating on algorithmic design and model improvement to address identified issues and enhance system performance and fairness.

III. **Legal and Ethical Considerations:** The chapter examines the legal and ethical dimensions of responsibility. It explores how existing legal frameworks can be applied to AI-related harm, including product liability laws. Additionally, it underscores the importance of ethical considerations, emphasizing that ethical responsibility goes beyond legal obligations.

1. **Legal Responsibility:** Legal responsibility refers to the obligation of individuals, organizations, and AI systems to comply with established laws and regulations. Key aspects of legal responsibility in the AI context include:

- **Compliance with Regulations:** Developers and organizations must adhere to legal frameworks governing AI technology. This includes data protection laws, anti-discrimination laws, and sector-specific regulations in domains like healthcare and finance.

- **Product Liability:** Legal liability can extend to AI developers and manufacturers if AI systems are considered products. Product liability laws may hold developers accountable for any harm caused by defective or unsafe AI systems.

- **Contractual Agreements:** Contracts between AI providers and users often contain legal clauses that define responsibilities and liabilities. Violations of contractual agreements can lead to legal action.

2. **Ethical Responsibility:** Ethical responsibility transcends legal obligations and pertains to the moral duty to ensure the ethical and responsible use of AI technology:

- **Ethical Frameworks:** Developers and organizations should adopt ethical frameworks that guide AI development and usage in ways that align with societal values and norms. Ethical considerations encompass fairness, transparency, accountability, and the promotion of human well-being.

- **Avoiding Harm:** Ethical responsibility involves the moral obligation to prevent harm to individuals or communities. Developers should take proactive measures to ensure that AI systems do not cause harm, discriminate, or infringe upon privacy.

- **Beneficial Use:** Ethical AI development means actively seeking ways to enhance the quality of life, solve societal problems, and respect individual rights. Ethical considerations go beyond legal requirements to promote the greater good.

3. **Alignment and Conflict:** Legal and ethical considerations may align in many cases, but they can also come into conflict:

- **Harmonization:** Ideally, legal and ethical principles should align and reinforce each other, fostering a consistent framework for AI development and use.

- **Ethical Dilemmas:** Ethical considerations may lead developers and organizations to go beyond legal requirements to ensure responsible AI usage. Ethical dilemmas may arise when there is a conflict between ethical principles and legal obligations.

4. **User Rights and Privacy:** Legal and ethical considerations often converge in the protection of user rights and privacy:

- **Informed Consent:** Both legal and ethical frameworks emphasize the importance of obtaining informed consent from users when collecting and processing their data. Users should be aware of how their data will be used.

- **Data Protection:** Legal frameworks such as the General Data Protection Regulation (GDPR) in Europe impose strict requirements for data protection. Ethical responsibility extends to ensuring that data is handled responsibly and in a manner that respects privacy.

5. **Ethical AI Development Principles:** Ethical considerations should guide AI development principles:

- **Fairness and Bias Mitigation:** Ethical AI development demands the proactive mitigation of biases and the promotion of fairness to avoid discriminatory outcomes.

- **Transparency and Accountability:** Ethical principles emphasize transparency in AI decision-making and the ability to hold AI systems accountable for their actions.

- **Human-Centered Design:** Ethical AI development prioritizes human well-being, safety, and the enhancement of human capabilities.

6. **Ethical Review Boards:** In some cases, organizations establish ethical review boards or committees to assess the ethical implications of AI projects and provide guidance on ethical considerations.

IV. **Transparency and Explainability:** An essential aspect of accountability is transparency and explainability in AI systems. Developers must design AI algorithms that can be understood and audited, making it easier to identify the source of issues when things go wrong. Techniques like explainable AI (XAI) are discussed as a means to enhance accountability.

1. **Transparency:** Transparency in AI refers to the openness and accessibility of information regarding how AI systems operate, make decisions, and use data. The key components of transparency include:

- **Algorithmic Processes:** Transparency entails making the inner workings of AI algorithms accessible to stakeholders. This means providing insight into how algorithms process data, make predictions, and arrive at decisions.

- **Data Usage:** Transparency involves disclosing the sources and types of data used to train AI models. This allows users and regulators to understand the data landscape and assess potential biases or data-related issues.

- **Decision Logic:** Transparency extends to explaining the logic behind AI system decisions. Users should have access to the rationale and factors considered when AI generates outcomes or recommendations.

- **Model Performance:** Information about the performance and limitations of AI models should be readily available. Transparency helps users gauge the reliability and trustworthiness of AI systems.

2. **Explainability:** Explainability takes transparency a step further by ensuring that AI systems can provide clear, interpretable, and justifiable explanations for their actions and decisions. Key elements of explainability include:

- **Interpretable Models:** Developers should strive to create AI models that produce results that can be easily interpreted and understood by both experts and non-experts. This aids in making AI more transparent.

- **User-Friendly Explanations:** AI systems should generate explanations that are user-friendly and tailored to the audience. This means presenting explanations in a language and format that users can comprehend.

- **Causal Understanding:** Explainability goes beyond surface-level explanations and aims to reveal the causal relationships and factors contributing to AI decisions. This provides a deeper understanding of why AI behaves as it does.

- **Contextual Explanations:** AI should be able to provide explanations that consider the broader context of a given decision, taking into account various factors and nuances.

3. **Importance of Transparency and Explainability:** Transparency and explainability are crucial for several reasons:

- **Accountability:** These principles facilitate accountability by allowing stakeholders to trace the decisions and actions of AI systems. In cases where AI goes wrong, transparency and explainability help identify the source of errors or bias.

- **Trust Building:** Making AI transparent and explainable builds trust among users, regulators, and the general public. When users understand why AI makes certain decisions, they are more likely to trust and accept the technology.

- **Bias Mitigation:** Transparency and explainability are vital tools in identifying and mitigating bias in AI systems. They enable developers to pinpoint biases in training data or algorithmic design and take corrective measures.

- **Ethical Compliance:** Ethical considerations, such as fairness and non-discrimination, are more effectively addressed when AI systems are transparent and explainable. Stakeholders can assess whether AI systems adhere to ethical guidelines.

4. **Challenges and Trade-offs:** Achieving transparency and explainability in AI is not without challenges:

- **Complex Models:** Highly complex AI models, like deep neural networks, can be challenging to explain comprehensively. Striking a balance between model complexity and explainability is an ongoing challenge.

- **Performance Trade-offs:** Some AI systems may sacrifice performance for the sake of transparency and explainability.

Developers must carefully weigh the trade-offs between accuracy and interpretability.

- **User Comprehension:** Ensuring that explanations are understandable to a wide range of users can be challenging, as technical details may not always align with user knowledge and expertise.

V.   **Emerging Challenges:** As AI technologies advance, new challenges emerge in determining responsibility. For instance, when AI systems operate autonomously in fields like healthcare or autonomous vehicles, the lines of responsibility become blurrier. This chapter discusses these emerging challenges and the need for novel frameworks and standards to address them.

1. **Autonomous Systems:** One of the most significant emerging challenges is the proliferation of autonomous AI systems. These systems, such as self-driving cars and autonomous drones, can make decisions and take actions with minimal human intervention. Determining responsibility becomes complex when AI operates independently:

- **Human Oversight:** Ensuring accountability and transparency in autonomous AI systems is challenging. There is a need to establish mechanisms for human oversight and intervention when AI systems make critical decisions.

- **Liability:** Questions surrounding liability arise. Should responsibility for accidents involving autonomous vehicles, for example, fall on the manufacturer, the developer of the AI system, or the human "operator" (if there is one)?

2. **AI in Healthcare:** The use of AI in healthcare is on the rise, presenting unique challenges in terms of accountability:

- **Diagnostic Errors:** When AI systems are used for medical diagnosis, who is responsible for errors or misdiagnoses? Is it the healthcare provider, the AI developer, or the data used to train the system?

- **Informed Consent:** Obtaining informed consent from patients is crucial. Ensuring that patients understand the role of AI in their diagnosis and treatment and can make informed decisions poses ethical and legal challenges.

201

3. **AI in Criminal Justice:** The deployment of AI in criminal justice systems, such as risk assessment tools and predictive policing, raises concerns:

- **Bias and Discrimination:** AI algorithms in this domain may perpetuate biases present in historical data, leading to unfair outcomes. Determining responsibility for biased AI decisions is challenging.

- **Transparency in Sentencing:** AI systems used in sentencing decisions should be transparent and explainable. However, complex models may make it difficult to provide understandable explanations for sentencing recommendations.

4. **Privacy and Data Protection:** The growing use of AI for data analysis and processing presents challenges in maintaining privacy and data protection:

- **Data Privacy:** Ensuring the privacy of individuals' data used to train AI models is a challenge. Data breaches or misuse can lead to significant harm, but determining responsibility can be complex.

- **Data Ownership:** Who owns the data used in AI systems, and who bears responsibility if that data is mishandled or misused? Clear data ownership and governance frameworks are needed.

5. **Cross-Border AI:** AI systems often operate globally, transcending national borders. This creates challenges for regulatory harmonization and determining responsibility:

- **Global Regulations:** Harmonizing AI regulations across jurisdictions is difficult but necessary to establish consistent standards for accountability.

- **Jurisdictional Challenges:** When an AI system operates across multiple countries, it can be challenging to determine which legal and ethical standards apply and who is responsible for compliance.

6. **AI Malfunction and Security:** As AI becomes more integrated into critical systems (e.g., infrastructure, energy, finance), the potential for AI malfunction or security breaches grows:

- **Cybersecurity:** Ensuring the security of AI systems is crucial to prevent malicious attacks and data breaches. Determining responsibility for security failures is complex.

- **Systemic Failures:** If an AI system that controls critical infrastructure fails, such as a power grid or transportation system, the consequences can be severe. Establishing responsibility for systemic failures is a major challenge.

7. **Public Perception and Trust:** As AI becomes more prevalent, public perception and trust become central concerns:

- **Trust Deficits:** High-profile AI failures can erode public trust in the technology. Rebuilding trust and determining responsibility in such cases is challenging.

- **User Expectations:** Managing user expectations regarding what AI can and cannot do is vital. Ensuring that users understand the limitations of AI technology is an ongoing challenge.

VI. **Mitigation and Prevention:** Accountability is not merely about assigning blame but also about mitigating and preventing AI-related harms. The chapter explores strategies for mitigating risks, such as robust testing, ongoing monitoring, and proactive efforts to address bias and discrimination in AI systems.

1. **Risk Assessment and Management:** Mitigation begins with identifying and assessing potential risks associated with AI systems. Developers and organizations must conduct thorough risk assessments to understand the vulnerabilities and potential consequences of AI failures:

- **Risk Identification:** Identify potential risks, including technical vulnerabilities, data quality issues, and unintended consequences of AI decisions.

- **Risk Quantification:** Assign probabilities and severity levels to identified risks to prioritize mitigation efforts effectively.

- **Risk Mitigation Plans:** Develop plans to address and mitigate identified risks, including technical solutions, process improvements, and contingency plans.

2. **Testing and Quality Assurance:** Rigorous testing and quality assurance are essential in mitigating AI failures:

- **Testing Protocols:** Develop comprehensive testing protocols to evaluate AI systems under various conditions and scenarios. This includes both simulated and real-world testing.

- **Validation:** Ensure that AI models are thoroughly validated to confirm their reliability and performance. This may involve benchmarking against existing solutions or industry standards.

- **Auditing:** Implement regular audits of AI systems to identify issues, vulnerabilities, and areas for improvement. Auditing should be an ongoing process throughout the AI system's lifecycle.

3. **Bias Mitigation and Fairness:** Addressing bias and ensuring fairness in AI systems is a proactive measure to prevent unintended consequences:

- **Bias Detection:** Implement mechanisms to detect and quantify biases within AI algorithms and datasets. This includes using fairness metrics and continuous monitoring.

- **Bias Mitigation Techniques:** Utilize bias mitigation techniques, such as re-sampling, re-weighting, or algorithmic adjustments, to reduce the impact of biases on AI decisions.

- **Fairness-Aware AI:** Develop AI models with fairness-awareness, ensuring that they do not discriminate against specific demographic groups and that they promote equitable outcomes.

4. **Explainability and Transparency:** Proactive measures in enhancing explainability and transparency contribute to mitigation:

- **Explainable AI (XAI):** Adopt XAI techniques that make AI decisions interpretable and transparent. This helps users and stakeholders understand why AI systems make specific decisions.

- **Transparency Reporting:** Publish transparency reports that provide insights into AI system operations, data usage, and decision-making processes. Transparency builds trust and allows for external scrutiny.

5. **Security Measures:** Cybersecurity is vital in preventing AI failures resulting from malicious attacks or data breaches:

- **Cybersecurity Protocols:** Implement robust cybersecurity protocols to protect AI systems from unauthorized access, data breaches, and other security threats.

- **Secure Data Handling:** Ensure that sensitive data used in AI training and operation is securely stored, transmitted, and processed to prevent data leaks or compromises.

6. **User Education and Training:** Educating users and stakeholders about AI technology and its limitations is a proactive measure to prevent misunderstandings:

- **User Training:** Provide training and guidance to users on how to interact with AI systems effectively and responsibly.

- **Transparency Efforts:** Educate users about the transparency and accountability measures in place within AI systems, so they can make informed decisions.

7. **Continuous Improvement:** Mitigation and prevention are ongoing processes that involve continuous improvement:

- **Learning from Failures:** When AI systems do fail or produce unintended consequences, view these incidents as opportunities for learning and improvement. Analyze the root causes and implement corrective actions.

- **Iterative Development:** Iterate on AI model design and system architecture to address identified issues and enhance performance and safety continually.

VII. **Collaborative Efforts:** Ultimately, the chapter advocates for collaborative efforts among all stakeholders. Developers, regulators, users, and ethicists must work together to establish a culture of accountability in the AI landscape. This includes sharing best practices, learning from past failures, and continuously improving AI systems.

1. **Stakeholder Collaboration:** Collaborative efforts should involve all relevant stakeholders in the AI ecosystem. This includes developers, organizations, policymakers, regulators, users, ethicists, and the public. Each group plays a distinct role in fostering accountability:

- **Developers and Organizations:** Developers have a primary responsibility for the technical aspects of AI accountability, such as model design, testing, and bias mitigation. Collaborating with organizations ensures that AI systems align with organizational values and goals.

- **Policymakers and Regulators:** Policymakers and regulators create the legal and ethical framework for AI. Collaboration with developers and organizations helps policymakers understand the practical challenges and nuances of AI implementation.

- **Users:** Users provide valuable feedback on AI systems' usability, effectiveness, and potential issues. Developers and organizations should actively seek user input to improve AI technology.

- **Ethicists and Experts:** Ethicists and AI experts contribute to the ethical discourse surrounding AI and help ensure that AI systems align with societal values and ethical principles.

- **Public Engagement:** Engaging with the broader public fosters transparency and accountability. Public input can shape AI regulations and standards to reflect diverse perspectives and concerns.

2. **Industry Collaboration:** Collaboration within the AI industry is essential to establish best practices, share knowledge, and address common challenges:

- **Industry Standards:** AI industry organizations and consortiums can develop industry-wide standards for ethical AI development, transparency, and accountability.

- **Information Sharing:** Sharing insights, lessons learned, and best practices among AI developers and organizations can accelerate responsible AI adoption.

- **Peer Review:** Encouraging peer review of AI models and systems within the industry can help identify and address issues before they lead to unintended consequences.

3. **Government and Industry Cooperation:** Collaboration between governments and industry is crucial in setting regulatory frameworks while ensuring technological advancement:

- **Regulatory Input:** Governments can seek input from industry experts and organizations when formulating AI regulations. This collaboration ensures that regulations are practical and effective.

- **Compliance and Reporting:** Developers and organizations should collaborate with regulators to ensure compliance with AI-related laws and regulations. Reporting mechanisms can facilitate transparency and accountability.

4. **Research and Development Collaboration:** Collaboration among research institutions, academia, and industry drives innovation while addressing emerging challenges:

- **Research Funding:** Government agencies, private organizations, and academic institutions can collaborate on funding research into AI safety, ethics, and accountability.

- **Academic Expertise:** Collaboration between academia and industry brings academic expertise into real-world AI development, helping to ensure responsible practices.

5. **Cross-Border Collaboration:** AI operates on a global scale, making international collaboration necessary:

- **Harmonization:** Collaborative efforts among countries can harmonize AI regulations and standards, reducing complexity and inconsistencies for organizations operating globally.

- **Knowledge Sharing:** Sharing knowledge and experiences across borders fosters a collective approach to addressing AI-related challenges and ensuring global accountability.

6. **Multi-Disciplinary Teams:** Collaborative AI development teams should be multi-disciplinary, consisting of professionals with diverse backgrounds and expertise:

- **Ethical Considerations:** Ethicists and social scientists contribute to ethical considerations, ensuring that AI aligns with societal values.

- **Legal Expertise:** Legal experts provide guidance on compliance with existing laws and help navigate regulatory frameworks.

- **Technical Prowess:** Technical experts drive the development of AI systems, ensuring they meet technical standards and operate effectively.

7. **Sharing Incident and Failure Data:** Collaboration involves sharing data on AI incidents, failures, and near-misses to learn from mistakes:

- **Incident Reporting:** Organizations should report AI-related incidents and failures to relevant authorities and industry bodies to facilitate shared learning and prevention.

- **Post-Incident Analysis:** Collaborative post-incident analysis helps uncover root causes and develop strategies to prevent similar incidents in the future.

The Challenges of Tracing Decision-Making Processes

1. **Complexity of AI Algorithms:** AI algorithms, particularly deep learning models, are often highly complex and composed of millions or even billions of parameters. Tracing decision-making within these intricate models is challenging because:

- **Opacity:** Deep learning models are often considered "black boxes" because their inner workings are not easily interpretable. The decision-making process occurs across multiple layers, making it difficult to discern how inputs are transformed into outputs.

- **Non-linearity:** AI algorithms frequently use non-linear activation functions, making it challenging to track how individual inputs contribute to final decisions. This non-linearity can obscure the relationship between inputs and outputs.

2. **Data-Driven Decision-Making:** Many AI systems rely on extensive datasets for training, and these datasets may contain inherent biases or anomalies. Tracing decision-making is complicated by:

- **Data Complexity:** Understanding how specific data points influence AI decisions can be challenging, especially when dealing with large and diverse datasets.

- **Bias Amplification:** Biases present in training data can be amplified by AI algorithms, leading to unfair or discriminatory outcomes. Tracing the origin of such biases within the decision-making process is a non-trivial task.

3. **Interconnected Features:** In some AI applications, numerous features or factors interact to make a decision. Tracing the contribution of each feature to the final decision is difficult because:

- **Feature Interactions:** Features may interact in complex ways, and their relative importance can vary depending on the context. Tracing these interactions can be computationally intensive.

- **Feature Engineering:** The process of feature engineering, where relevant features are selected or engineered for input, can further obscure the decision-making process.

4. **Real-Time and Dynamic Environments:** AI systems often operate in real-time and dynamic environments. Tracing decision-making in such contexts is challenging due to:

- **Temporal Factors:** Decisions may depend on the temporal order of inputs or events, making it difficult to trace the decision process over time.

- **Changing Data Distributions:** In dynamic environments, data distributions can shift, impacting the decision-making process. Tracing these changes is essential for accountability.

5. **Third-Party Components:** AI systems may incorporate third-party components, such as pre-trained models or external data sources. Tracing decisions becomes more complex because:

- **Dependency on External Inputs:** Decisions may rely on external data or models, making it necessary to trace decision processes beyond the immediate AI system.

- **Lack of Control:** Developers may have limited control over third-party components, making it challenging to ensure transparency and traceability.

6. **Privacy and Confidentiality:** Tracing decision-making processes must balance transparency with privacy and confidentiality concerns:

- **Data Privacy:** Revealing the entire decision-making process may involve exposing sensitive data. Striking a balance between transparency and data privacy is a challenging ethical consideration.

- **Confidential Algorithms:** In some cases, organizations may consider their AI algorithms proprietary and may be hesitant to fully disclose their inner workings.

7. **Regulatory Compliance:** Meeting regulatory requirements for transparency and traceability can be demanding:

- **Regulatory Expectations:** Regulations may mandate transparency and accountability in AI decision-making processes. Ensuring compliance while safeguarding proprietary information can be a complex task.

8. **Scalability:** Tracing decision-making processes becomes more challenging as AI systems scale:

- **Large-Scale Deployment:** In large-scale AI deployments, tracking individual decisions across vast datasets and complex models can strain computational resources.

- **Real-Time Monitoring:** Monitoring decisions in real-time across a wide user base requires efficient and scalable systems.

Addressing the challenges of tracing decision-making processes in AI involves a multi-faceted approach that combines technical advancements, ethical considerations, regulatory frameworks, and collaboration among stakeholders. Despite these challenges, the pursuit of greater transparency and traceability in AI decision-making is essential for accountability, fairness, and responsible AI deployment.

Legal Frameworks and Proposals for AI Accountability:

1. **Existing Legal Frameworks:** Various legal frameworks and regulations form the foundation for AI accountability. These include:

- **Data Protection Laws:** Laws like the General Data Protection Regulation (GDPR) in Europe require organizations to ensure that AI systems handling personal data are transparent, secure, and accountable. Non-compliance can result in significant fines.

- **Anti-Discrimination Laws:** Existing anti-discrimination laws, such as the Civil Rights Act in the United States, may apply to AI systems that result in discriminatory outcomes. Organizations can be held accountable for AI systems that perpetuate biases.

- **Product Liability Laws:** In cases where AI systems are considered products, product liability laws can be applied if AI systems cause harm due to defects or unsafe design.

2. **Proposed AI Accountability Regulations:** Recognizing the unique challenges posed by AI, policymakers and regulators around the world are actively developing and proposing new regulations. Some notable examples include:

- **EU AI Act:** The European Union's proposed AI Act aims to establish a comprehensive regulatory framework for AI. It introduces a risk-based approach, categorizing AI systems as low, medium, or high risk. High-risk systems face stricter requirements, including conformity assessments, documentation, and human oversight.

- **AI Transparency Act (US):** In the United States, the AI Transparency Act has been introduced to require AI system developers to provide detailed information about the functioning, training data, and potential biases of their systems. This legislation seeks to enhance transparency and accountability in AI.

- **AI Governance Frameworks (Canada):** Canada is developing AI governance frameworks that emphasize responsible AI development and deployment. These frameworks include guidelines for transparency, fairness, accountability, and privacy.

- **AI Ethics Guidelines (UNESCO):** UNESCO has proposed global AI ethics guidelines aimed at ensuring that AI respects human rights, promotes transparency, and is accountable to individuals and society at large.

3. **Accountability Mechanisms in Proposed Regulations:** Proposed AI accountability regulations include specific mechanisms to ensure responsible AI development and deployment:

- **Transparency Requirements:** Many regulations emphasize the need for transparency in AI systems. Developers may be required to disclose information about how AI systems make decisions, the data they use, and their potential biases.

- **Documentation and Record-Keeping:** Regulations often mandate that developers maintain detailed records of the development process, including data collection, model training, and testing. This documentation helps trace decision-making processes.

- **Conformity Assessments:** High-risk AI systems may be subject to conformity assessments to ensure that they meet regulatory requirements. These assessments involve third-party evaluations of system performance and compliance.

- **Human Oversight:** Some regulations require human oversight of AI systems, especially in high-risk domains. Human experts or operators may be responsible for making or reviewing critical decisions.

- **Bias Mitigation:** Regulations may stipulate that AI developers implement bias mitigation techniques and regularly audit their systems for bias. Organizations can be held accountable for discriminatory AI outcomes.

4. **Global Harmonization:** Achieving global harmonization of AI accountability regulations is a challenge due to differing legal systems and cultural norms. However, efforts are being made to align international standards to facilitate cross-border AI deployment while ensuring accountability.

5. **Challenges and Controversies:** The development and implementation of AI accountability regulations are not without challenges and controversies:

- **Balancing Innovation:** Striking a balance between promoting innovation and safeguarding accountability is a delicate task. Regulations must avoid stifling AI advancements while addressing risks.

- **Enforcement:** Effective enforcement of AI regulations can be challenging, especially when AI systems operate across borders or when there is a lack of resources for oversight.

- **Overreliance on Regulation:** Critics argue that overreliance on regulation may not be sufficient for addressing complex ethical and societal issues associated with AI. Ethical considerations may extend beyond legal compliance.

Legal frameworks and regulations are critical tools for holding developers and organizations accountable when AI systems go wrong, while also fostering transparency and ethical AI practices. However, the dynamic nature of AI technology and the need for international cooperation present ongoing challenges in this evolving accountability landscape.

Chapter 8: Steering the AI Future

This chapter examines the strategies, principles, and considerations necessary to ensure that AI technologies align with societal values and ethical standards as they continue to evolve.

1. **Ethical Principles and Values:** Steering the AI future begins with a foundation of ethical principles and values that guide AI development and use. Some key principles include:

- **Transparency:** Promoting transparency in AI systems ensures that their decision-making processes are understandable and can be scrutinized for fairness and accountability.

- **Fairness:** The principle of fairness emphasizes the need to prevent discrimination and bias in AI algorithms, ensuring that they provide equitable outcomes for all individuals and groups.

- **Accountability:** Developers and organizations should be held accountable for the consequences of AI systems. Accountability mechanisms help address harm caused by AI failures or misuse.

- **Privacy:** Protecting individuals' privacy in AI systems is essential. AI developers must handle personal data responsibly and in accordance with data protection laws.

- **Beneficence:** AI technologies should be designed to benefit humanity, enhance well-being, and address societal challenges, rather than causing harm or exacerbating existing problems.

- **Non-Maleficence:** AI systems should strive to avoid harm and minimize potential negative impacts. This includes mitigating biases and risks associated with AI deployment.

2. **Governance Models:** Effective governance models are critical for steering the AI future. These models establish the structures and processes for oversight, regulation, and decision-making. Key aspects include:

- **Multi-Stakeholder Approach:** Encouraging input and collaboration among multiple stakeholders, including developers, regulators, users, ethicists, and the public, ensures a balanced and inclusive governance framework.

- **Regulatory Oversight:** Governments play a vital role in setting and enforcing regulations that guide AI development and use. Effective regulatory bodies are essential for oversight.

- **Industry Self-Regulation:** AI industries and organizations can develop self-regulatory standards and best practices to complement government regulations and ensure responsible AI development.

- **Ethics Committees:** Establishing ethics committees or review boards within organizations can help assess the ethical implications of AI projects and provide guidance on responsible practices.

- **Global Cooperation:** Given the global nature of AI, international cooperation is necessary to harmonize regulations and standards, ensuring consistency in AI governance across borders.

3. **Research and Innovation:** Steering the AI future involves promoting research and innovation that align with ethical principles. Key considerations include:

- **Ethics in Research:** Researchers should adhere to ethical guidelines, including informed consent and responsible data handling, when conducting AI-related research.

- **Responsible Innovation:** AI development should follow principles of responsible innovation, considering societal impacts, potential risks, and ethical implications from the outset.

- **Human-Centered Design:** AI technologies should prioritize the well-being, safety, and empowerment of individuals and communities, promoting human-centered design principles.

4. **Education and Awareness:** Raising awareness and educating stakeholders about AI's capabilities, limitations, and ethical considerations is essential for steering the AI future:

- **User Education:** Educating users about how to interact with AI systems responsibly and ethically helps ensure informed use.

- **Ethical Training:** Developers, data scientists, and AI professionals should receive training on ethical AI practices to embed responsible considerations into their work.

- **Public Engagement:** Involving the public in discussions about AI's societal impacts and ethical use fosters a sense of shared responsibility.

5. **Continuous Assessment and Adaptation:** Steering the AI future requires ongoing assessment and adaptation to evolving technologies and ethical standards:

- **Ethics Audits:** Conducting ethics audits of AI systems and projects helps identify and rectify ethical concerns and biases.

- **Feedback Loops:** Establishing feedback mechanisms allows stakeholders to provide input on AI systems' performance and ethical considerations.

- **Ethics by Design:** Implementing an "ethics by design" approach ensures that ethical considerations are integral to AI system development from the start.

6. **Ethical AI Leadership:** Ethical leadership in AI development and deployment is crucial for steering the AI future:

- **Organizational Culture:** Organizations should foster a culture of ethical AI development, with leadership setting an example and promoting ethical behavior at all levels.

- **Ethical Considerations in Decision-Making:** Ethical considerations should be central to decision-making processes, including choices related to AI system design, deployment, and risk assessment.

In conclusion, Chapter 8 underscores the importance of steering the AI future in a direction that aligns with ethical principles, societal values, and responsible practices. By emphasizing transparency, fairness, accountability, and continuous assessment, stakeholders can work together to shape the development and deployment of AI technologies in ways that benefit individuals and society as a whole while minimizing harm and ethical pitfalls.

Global Initiatives in AI Ethics:

Global initiatives in AI ethics play a pivotal role in shaping the responsible development and deployment of artificial intelligence (AI) technologies on a worldwide scale. In this chapter, we delve into the significance of these initiatives and the various efforts aimed at establishing international standards and ethical guidelines for AI.

1. **AI Ethics on the Global Stage:** As AI technologies transcend national borders, the need for global collaboration in defining ethical standards becomes evident. Several key initiatives and organizations have emerged to address this imperative:

- **United Nations (UN):** The UN has recognized the importance of AI ethics through initiatives like the United Nations Educational, Scientific and Cultural Organization (UNESCO) Guidelines on AI Ethics. These guidelines emphasize the need for AI to align with human rights and ethical principles.

- **OECD AI Principles:** The Organisation for Economic Co-operation and Development (OECD) has developed a set of AI Principles that emphasize responsible AI innovation. These principles focus on AI that respects human rights, is transparent and accountable, and provides a fair distribution of benefits.

- **Partnership on AI (PAI):** The Partnership on AI is a collaboration between major tech companies, civil society organizations, and academic institutions. PAI aims to address global challenges related to AI ethics, including fairness, transparency, and accountability.

- **Global AI Ethics Consortium:** This consortium comprises leading AI ethics organizations, think tanks, and institutions from around the world. It seeks to harmonize AI ethics guidelines and promote global collaboration on ethical AI development.

2. **AI Ethics Guidelines and Principles:** Global initiatives often result in the creation of AI ethics guidelines and principles that serve as reference points for responsible AI development:

- **Human Rights Emphasis:** Many global guidelines stress the importance of AI respecting and upholding human rights, including principles related to privacy, non-discrimination, and freedom of expression.

217

- **Transparency and Accountability:** Ethical principles emphasize transparency in AI systems' decision-making processes and accountability mechanisms to address AI failures.

- **Beneficence and Non-Maleficence:** Principles related to AI's beneficial impact on society and the avoidance of harm are recurring themes in global AI ethics.

- **Fairness and Equity:** Guidelines often highlight the need for AI systems to be designed and deployed in a manner that promotes fairness and equity, avoiding discriminatory outcomes.

3. **International Collaboration and Harmonization:** Global initiatives in AI ethics encourage international collaboration and the harmonization of ethical standards:

- **Standardization Efforts:** Organizations like the International Organization for Standardization (ISO) are working on AI standardization to create a common framework for ethical AI development.

- **Cross-Border Partnerships:** Collaborations between countries, industries, and institutions facilitate the sharing of best practices and ethical insights, leading to a more unified approach to AI ethics.

- **Data Sharing:** International cooperation also extends to sharing data and research related to AI ethics, enabling a broader understanding of AI's ethical challenges.

4. **Ethical Considerations in AI Research:** Global initiatives often stress the importance of ethics in AI research:

- **Ethical Review Boards:** Researchers are encouraged to establish ethical review boards to assess and address the ethical implications of their AI research projects.

- **Ethics Training:** Researchers are encouraged to undergo ethics training to ensure that ethical considerations are integrated into AI research practices.

5. **AI Governance and Accountability:** Global initiatives emphasize the need for governance structures that ensure accountability in AI development and use:

- **Oversight Bodies:** Establishing oversight bodies at the national and international levels is crucial for enforcing ethical guidelines and holding AI developers accountable.

- **Compliance Mechanisms:** Global initiatives often recommend the implementation of compliance mechanisms to ensure that AI systems adhere to ethical principles and standards.

6. **Public Engagement and Inclusivity:** Ethical AI development requires active involvement from a diverse range of stakeholders:

- **Public Input:** Engaging the public in AI ethics discussions and policy-making processes ensures that a variety of perspectives are considered.

- **Inclusivity:** Global initiatives aim to be inclusive, welcoming input from individuals, organizations, and countries with diverse backgrounds and interests.

In conclusion, Chapter 8 underscores the critical role of global initiatives in AI ethics in steering the AI future responsibly. These initiatives help establish a common ethical framework, promote international collaboration, and ensure that AI technologies align with human values and global ethical standards. As AI continues to shape the world, these global efforts are essential for safeguarding ethical AI development and use on a global scale.

Collaborations Between Tech Companies, Governments, and Academia:

I. **Tech Companies and Ethical AI:** Tech giants and AI industry leaders have a substantial influence on the development and deployment of AI technologies. Collaborative efforts between tech companies and other stakeholders are crucial for ensuring that AI aligns with ethical principles:

➤ **Research and Development:** Tech companies are at the forefront of AI research and development. They have the expertise and resources to pioneer ethical AI practices and innovations.

1. **Research and Development Pioneers:**

- **Cutting-Edge Innovation:** Tech companies are at the forefront of AI research and development, driving innovation in the field. They possess the resources, talent, and infrastructure to pioneer advancements in AI technologies.

- **Ethical Prototyping:** Tech companies can lead by example by integrating ethical considerations into the earliest stages of AI development. This includes embedding ethical principles in prototypes and proof-of-concept projects.

2. **Responsible AI Development:**

- **Ethical Commitment:** Collaboration encourages tech companies to commit to ethical AI development practices. They emphasize transparency, fairness, accountability, and the avoidance of harm in their AI projects.

- **Internal Guidelines:** Tech companies often establish internal ethical guidelines and policies that guide their AI R&D teams. These guidelines reflect their commitment to responsible AI practices.

3. **Ethics Boards and Oversight:**

- **External Ethics Advisors:** Some tech companies establish ethics boards or advisory committees composed of external experts in ethics, law, and social sciences. These experts provide impartial oversight and guidance on the ethical dimensions of AI projects.

- **Review and Accountability:** Ethics boards ensure that AI projects align with ethical principles and help identify and address ethical concerns. This external review mechanism enhances transparency and accountability.

4. **Bias Mitigation and Fairness:**

- **Biased Algorithm Mitigation:** Tech companies actively invest in research and development to mitigate biases in AI algorithms. They aim to reduce disparities and ensure fair and equitable outcomes.

- **Diverse Data:** Tech companies focus on sourcing diverse and representative data to train AI models, minimizing the risk of perpetuating biases.

5. **Algorithmic Transparency and Explainability:**

- **User-Friendly AI:** Tech companies prioritize making AI algorithms transparent and explainable. Users should be able to understand how AI systems make decisions, enhancing trust and accountability.

- **Interpretable AI Models:** They develop interpretable AI models and provide tools for users to inspect and interpret AI-generated recommendations or decisions.

6. **User-Centered Design:**

- **Feedback Mechanisms:** Tech companies actively seek feedback from users during AI product development. This user-centered approach ensures that AI systems align with users' needs and expectations.

- **Accessibility:** They design AI systems to be accessible to individuals with disabilities, promoting inclusivity and ethical considerations in AI development.

7. **Data Privacy and Security:**

- **Data Protection:** Tech companies adhere to robust data privacy and security practices, ensuring that personal and sensitive data are handled responsibly and ethically.

- **Compliance with Regulations:** They ensure compliance with data protection regulations such as the General Data Protection Regulation (GDPR) and implement measures to protect user privacy.

8. **Ethical Considerations in Product Design:**

- **Ethical by Design:** Tech companies embrace an "ethics by design" approach, where ethical considerations are integral to the design and development of AI products from the outset.

- **Ethical Impact Assessment:** They conduct ethical impact assessments to evaluate the potential ethical consequences of AI products and make necessary adjustments.

9. **Public Engagement and Transparency:**

- **Transparency Initiatives:** Tech companies engage with the public by providing information about their AI systems, including how they work, what data they use, and the ethical principles guiding their development.

- **User Control:** They empower users with control over their data and interactions with AI systems, fostering a sense of agency and transparency.

10. **Cross-Industry Collaboration:**

- **Sharing Best Practices:** Tech companies collaborate across industries to share best practices and ethical insights, contributing to the development of responsible AI standards and guidelines.

- **Addressing Global Challenges:** Collaboration ensures that tech companies are involved in addressing global AI challenges, including those related to ethics, fairness, and societal impact.

Tech companies are pivotal in fostering an ethical AI research and development culture through their commitment to responsible practices, innovation, and collaboration. Their role extends beyond innovation to encompass transparency, fairness, accountability, and the promotion of ethical considerations at every stage of AI development. Through active collaboration with governments, academia, and other stakeholders, tech companies contribute significantly to the responsible steering of the AI future.

➢ **Responsible AI Development:** Collaborations promote responsible AI development, where companies commit to ethical considerations, transparency, fairness, and accountability in their AI projects.

1. **Ethical Commitment and Culture:**

- **Embedding Ethical Principles:** Tech companies demonstrate a commitment to ethical AI by integrating ethical principles into their corporate culture. This includes valuing transparency, fairness, accountability, and the societal impact of their AI projects.

- **Leadership Influence:** Ethical leadership within tech companies sets the tone for responsible AI development. Company executives and leaders emphasize the importance of ethical considerations in all AI initiatives.

2. **Ethical Guidelines and Frameworks:**

- **Internal Guidelines:** Tech companies often establish internal ethical guidelines and frameworks that serve as a compass for their AI R&D

teams. These guidelines outline best practices and principles for ethical AI development.

- **Adherence to International Standards:** Companies align their ethical guidelines with internationally recognized standards and principles such as those outlined by the European Commission's "Principles for Trustworthy AI" or the OECD's AI Principles.

3. **External Ethics Oversight:**

- **Ethics Boards and Advisory Committees:** Some tech companies set up ethics boards or advisory committees comprising external experts in ethics, law, and social sciences. These experts provide an external perspective and offer guidance on ethical considerations in AI projects.

- **Ethical Audits:** Ethics boards conduct ethical audits of AI systems and projects to assess their alignment with ethical principles. They help identify potential biases, ethical concerns, and areas for improvement.

4. **Bias Mitigation and Fairness:**

- **Bias Awareness:** Tech companies actively work to raise awareness of potential biases in AI systems. They educate their teams about the risks associated with biased data and algorithms.

- **Bias Mitigation Techniques:** Companies invest in research and development to develop and implement bias mitigation techniques. These techniques aim to reduce and rectify biases within AI systems, ensuring fair and equitable outcomes.

5. **Algorithmic Transparency and Explainability:**

- **Transparency Initiatives:** Tech companies prioritize making AI algorithms transparent. They provide users with insights into how AI systems make decisions, which enhances user trust and accountability.

- **Explainable AI:** Companies develop explainable AI models and tools that enable users and developers to interpret AI-generated decisions. This focus on explainability fosters understanding and ethical scrutiny of AI systems.

6. **User-Centered Design:**

- **User Feedback:** Tech companies actively seek user feedback throughout the AI product development lifecycle. This iterative process ensures that AI systems align with users' needs, values, and expectations.

- **Accessibility:** They design AI systems with accessibility in mind, making them usable and inclusive for individuals with disabilities. Ethical considerations extend to ensuring that technology benefits everyone.

7. **Data Privacy and Security:**

- **Data Protection Measures:** Tech companies adhere to stringent data privacy and security measures. They implement robust data protection protocols to safeguard personal and sensitive data, adhering to global data protection regulations.

- **User Data Control:** Companies provide users with control over their data, allowing them to make informed choices about how their data is collected, used, and shared.

8. **Ethical Considerations in Product Design:**

- **Ethics by Design:** Tech companies embrace an "ethics by design" approach, integrating ethical considerations into the design and development of AI products from the initial concept stage. This ensures that ethics are a fundamental part of the product's DNA.

- **Ethical Impact Assessment:** Prior to launch, companies conduct ethical impact assessments to evaluate potential ethical consequences. Adjustments are made to address any identified risks.

9. **Public Engagement and Transparency:**

- **Transparency Initiatives:** Tech companies engage in transparent communication with the public. They provide clear and accessible information about their AI systems, including how they work, what data is used, and the ethical principles guiding their development.

- **User Empowerment:** Companies empower users by providing options for data control, allowing them to exercise agency over their interactions with AI systems.

10. **Cross-Industry Collaboration:**

- **Sharing Best Practices:** Tech companies actively collaborate with other industries to share best practices and ethical insights. These collaborations contribute to the development of responsible AI standards and guidelines that benefit society as a whole.

- **Addressing Global Challenges:** By participating in cross-industry collaborations, tech companies ensure that they are part of the global conversation addressing challenges related to ethics, fairness, and societal impact in AI development.

➢ **Ethics Boards:** Some tech companies establish ethics boards or advisory committees composed of external experts to provide guidance and ethical oversight of their AI initiatives.

Ethics boards play a critical role in guiding and overseeing the ethical dimensions of artificial intelligence (AI) research and development within tech companies. These boards are composed of external experts in ethics, law, social sciences, and related fields. Their purpose is to provide impartial guidance, ethical scrutiny, and accountability in AI projects. Here, we delve into the importance and functions of ethics boards in tech companies:

1. **Impartial Oversight:**

- **External Expertise:** Ethics boards consist of independent experts who bring fresh perspectives and impartial judgments to the ethical considerations of AI projects. Their external status ensures objectivity and reduces conflicts of interest.

- **Ethical Scrutiny:** Ethics boards evaluate AI projects from an ethical standpoint, assessing potential ethical risks, biases, and societal implications. They provide recommendations and raise ethical concerns that internal teams may overlook.

2. **Alignment with Ethical Principles:**

- **Ensuring Compliance:** Ethics boards ensure that AI projects adhere to established ethical guidelines and principles. They verify that projects prioritize transparency, fairness, accountability, and societal benefit.

- **Ethical Frameworks:** These boards assess projects against ethical frameworks, such as those outlined by international bodies like the

European Commission or the OECD, to guarantee alignment with global ethical standards.

3. **Ethical Audits and Impact Assessments:**

- **Regular Audits:** Ethics boards conduct ethical audits of AI systems and projects at various stages of development. These audits help identify ethical concerns and potential biases, promoting transparency and accountability.

- **Impact Assessment:** Prior to project initiation, ethics boards may require ethical impact assessments. These assessments evaluate the potential societal consequences and ethical risks associated with the AI technology, guiding responsible development.

4. **Mitigating Ethical Concerns:**

- **Risk Mitigation:** When ethics boards identify ethical concerns, they work collaboratively with AI teams to develop strategies for mitigating risks. This may involve adjusting algorithms, data collection methods, or decision-making processes to reduce biases and ethical issues.

- **Ethical Roadmaps:** Ethics boards assist in creating ethical roadmaps for AI projects, outlining steps to address and rectify identified ethical challenges. These roadmaps promote responsible development and compliance with ethical guidelines.

5. **Transparency and Accountability:**

- **Enhancing Transparency:** Ethics boards advocate for transparency in AI development. They ensure that companies disclose their ethical considerations, methodologies, and data sources to the public, users, and regulatory bodies.

- **Accountability Mechanisms:** In cases of ethical breaches or concerns, ethics boards help establish accountability mechanisms, ensuring that individuals and organizations take responsibility for any ethical lapses and implement corrective actions.

6. **User-Centered Ethical Development:**

- **User Feedback Integration:** Ethics boards encourage tech companies to incorporate user feedback into their AI projects. This user-centered approach ensures that AI systems align with users' values, expectations, and ethical concerns.

- **Ethical by Design:** Ethics boards advocate for an "ethics by design" approach, where ethical considerations are embedded into the design and development of AI products from the very beginning.

7. **Cross-Industry Collaboration:**

- **Sharing Ethical Insights:** Ethics boards often comprise experts from diverse fields, allowing them to share ethical insights and best practices with other industries. This cross-industry collaboration fosters a more comprehensive and informed approach to AI ethics.

- **Global Ethical Standards:** Collaboration with other sectors contributes to the development of global ethical standards for AI, ensuring that ethical considerations are consistent and applicable across industries and regions.

8. **Ethical Public Relations:**

- **Public Trust:** Ethics boards contribute to building public trust by verifying and validating the ethical claims made by tech companies. Their involvement assures the public that ethical principles are taken seriously and that external experts oversee AI projects.

- **Transparency Initiatives:** Ethics boards support transparency initiatives by advocating for clear communication about the ethical aspects of AI projects to the public and stakeholders.

In conclusion, ethics boards in tech companies are instrumental in ensuring that AI projects are developed and deployed responsibly and ethically. Their impartiality, expertise, and commitment to ethical principles serve as a critical safeguard against potential ethical lapses and biases in AI technologies. By actively engaging with ethics boards, tech companies demonstrate their dedication to responsible AI development and contribute to building a trustworthy and ethically sound AI landscape.

II. **Government Regulation and Oversight:** Governments play a vital role in setting legal frameworks and regulations that guide AI development and use. Collaborations between tech companies and governments are essential for achieving a balance between innovation and responsible AI:

➢ **Regulatory Input:** Tech companies can provide valuable input to governments in the formulation of AI-related policies and regulations. This ensures that regulations are practical and consider the nuances of AI technology.

Collaboration between tech companies, governments, and academia is essential to strike a balance between innovation and regulatory control. Here, we explore the concept of "regulatory input" in more detail:

1. **Stakeholder Engagement:**

- **Collaborative Approach:** Government regulation benefits from input and insights from various stakeholders, including tech companies, academic experts, and civil society organizations. Collaboration ensures that regulations are well-informed, comprehensive, and practical.

- **Dialogue with Tech Companies:** Governments engage in a dialogue with tech companies to understand the nuances and complexities of AI technology. This exchange of information helps regulators make informed decisions and design regulations that are effective and adaptable.

2. **Regulatory Design:**

- **Regulatory Frameworks:** Government regulators work on crafting regulatory frameworks that govern AI development and use. These frameworks may encompass areas such as data privacy, algorithmic transparency, bias mitigation, and safety standards.

- **Input from Tech Companies:** Tech companies provide valuable input on the feasibility and practicality of proposed regulations. They share their expertise in AI technology to help regulators design rules that foster responsible AI while allowing for innovation.

3. **Policy Formulation:**

- **Consultation Periods:** Governments often hold consultation periods during which tech companies and other stakeholders can provide feedback on draft regulations. This collaborative process allows for refinement and improvement of regulatory proposals.

- **Balancing Interests:** Tech companies and government regulators work together to balance the interests of innovation and public welfare. They aim to create regulations that protect individual rights, promote fairness, and mitigate risks while still fostering technological advancement.

4. **Ethical Standards:**

- **Defining Ethical Standards:** Collaboratively, tech companies and governments establish ethical standards and principles that underpin AI development and use. These standards guide the creation of regulations that promote responsible AI.

- **Alignment with International Norms:** Tech companies and governments ensure that their regulations align with international norms and standards, contributing to a global framework for AI governance.

5. **Monitoring and Compliance:**

- **Compliance Mechanisms:** Governments establish mechanisms for monitoring AI systems and enforcing compliance with regulations. These mechanisms may include audits, reporting requirements, and penalties for non-compliance.

- **Tech Company Responsibility:** Tech companies play a crucial role in ensuring that their AI systems adhere to regulatory standards. They are responsible for implementing measures to comply with ethical guidelines and regulatory mandates.

6. **Evolving Regulations:**

- **Adaptive Governance:** Tech companies and governments collaborate on the concept of adaptive governance. This approach allows for the flexible adjustment of AI regulations as technology evolves and new challenges emerge.

- **Ongoing Collaboration:** Tech companies maintain ongoing collaboration with governments to assess the impact of existing regulations and adapt them as needed to address emerging ethical and technological issues.

7. **Global Harmonization:**

- **International Collaboration:** Tech companies and governments engage in international collaborations and partnerships to harmonize AI regulations across borders. This global effort aims to create a consistent and predictable regulatory environment for AI development and deployment.

- **Avoiding Fragmentation:** Collaboration helps prevent regulatory fragmentation, where different regions have conflicting or incompatible AI regulations. A harmonized approach reduces compliance burdens and ensures a level playing field for tech companies operating globally.

8. **Public Input and Transparency:**

- **Incorporating Public Perspective:** Tech companies and governments encourage public input in the regulatory process. Public consultations and transparency initiatives ensure that the regulatory framework reflects the values and concerns of society at large.

- **Building Trust:** Collaboration between tech companies and governments in engaging the public and maintaining transparency helps build trust in AI technologies and the regulatory process.

Regulatory input in the context of collaborations between tech companies, governments, and academia is essential for developing responsible and effective AI regulations. This input ensures that regulations strike a balance between fostering innovation and protecting the interests of individuals and society. By working together, tech companies and governments can create a regulatory framework that promotes ethical AI while advancing the responsible development and use of this transformative technology.

➤ **Compliance and Reporting:** Collaborations help companies understand and comply with AI-related laws and regulations. Governments can establish reporting mechanisms to ensure transparency and accountability.

Compliance and reporting mechanisms are essential components of these regulations, ensuring that AI development and deployment align with ethical standards, safety requirements, and legal mandates. Here, we delve into the concepts of compliance and reporting in the context of government regulation and oversight:

1. **Compliance Frameworks:**

- **Regulatory Requirements:** Government regulators establish compliance frameworks that outline the specific rules, standards, and guidelines that AI developers and users must adhere to. These requirements may cover a wide range of areas, including data privacy, bias mitigation, safety, and transparency.

- **Alignment with Ethical Principles:** Compliance frameworks are designed to align with ethical principles and international norms, promoting the responsible and ethical use of AI technologies.

2. **Oversight and Monitoring:**

- **Regulatory Authorities:** Government agencies are tasked with overseeing AI compliance. They monitor AI systems, practices, and applications to ensure that they meet regulatory standards.

- **Audit and Assessment:** Regulatory authorities conduct audits and assessments to evaluate AI systems for compliance with established regulations. These assessments may include technical evaluations, algorithmic audits, and ethical impact assessments.

3. **Reporting Requirements:**

- **Mandatory Reporting:** Government regulations often impose mandatory reporting requirements on tech companies and organizations that develop or use AI systems. These requirements necessitate the submission of relevant information to regulatory authorities.

- **Transparency Initiatives:** Reporting requirements promote transparency by compelling organizations to disclose details about their AI systems, including their functionalities, data sources, decision-making processes, and potential risks.

4. **Ethical and Safety Audits:**

- **Ethical Audits:** Tech companies and organizations may be required to undergo ethical audits, where external or internal auditors assess the ethical considerations of AI systems. These audits help identify and rectify ethical concerns.

- **Safety Audits:** Safety audits focus on evaluating the safety and reliability of AI systems, particularly in critical applications such as autonomous vehicles or medical diagnostics. Auditors assess the systems' ability to handle unforeseen scenarios and mitigate risks.

5. **Accountability Mechanisms:**

- **Corrective Actions:** In cases of non-compliance or ethical violations, government regulators and oversight bodies establish accountability mechanisms. These mechanisms may require tech companies to take corrective actions, modify their AI systems, or rectify ethical issues promptly.

- **Penalties and Fines:** Regulatory authorities have the power to impose penalties and fines on organizations that fail to comply with AI regulations. These penalties serve as a deterrent against unethical or unsafe AI practices.

6. **User Rights and Protections:**

- **Data Privacy:** Government regulations often include provisions for safeguarding user data privacy. Users have the right to know how their data is used by AI systems and the option to control its collection and sharing.

- **Transparency and Explanations:** Regulations may require AI systems to provide transparent explanations of their decisions to users. This empowers users to understand and challenge AI-generated outcomes.

7. **Public Trust and Accountability:**

- **Public Oversight:** Compliance and reporting mechanisms contribute to building public trust in AI technologies. They reassure the public that tech companies and organizations are held accountable for the ethical and legal implications of their AI systems.

- **Ethical Commitment:** Demonstrating compliance with regulations and reporting requirements signals a tech company's commitment to ethical AI development. It fosters a culture of responsibility and accountability within the industry.

8. **International Collaboration:**

- **Global Harmonization:** Government regulation and oversight are increasingly harmonized at the international level. Collaboration between governments from different regions helps avoid regulatory fragmentation and ensures consistent AI standards on a global scale.

- **Data Sharing:** International collaboration also facilitates the sharing of information and best practices related to AI compliance and reporting, allowing governments to learn from one another's experiences and approaches.

Compliance and reporting mechanisms within government regulation and oversight are essential for ensuring that AI technologies are developed and used responsibly and ethically. These mechanisms promote transparency, user rights, and public trust in AI systems while holding tech companies and organizations accountable for their ethical and legal obligations. Collaboration between governments, tech companies, and academia is instrumental in crafting effective and adaptive compliance frameworks that enable the responsible steering of the AI future.

➢ **Ethical Standards:** Governments may work with tech companies to set ethical standards and guidelines for AI development, promoting responsible practices across the industry.

Government regulation and oversight in the realm of artificial intelligence (AI) extend to the establishment and enforcement of ethical standards. These standards are critical for ensuring that AI technologies are developed, deployed, and used in a manner that aligns with societal values, human rights, and responsible innovation. In this context, let's explore the importance and details of ethical standards in government regulation and oversight:

1. **Defining Ethical Standards:**

- **Ethical Principles:** Government regulators, often in collaboration with experts from academia and industry, define a set of ethical principles that serve as the foundation for AI development and use. These principles typically include transparency, fairness, accountability, privacy, safety, and the promotion of human well-being.

- **Alignment with International Norms:** Ethical standards in AI regulation are typically designed to align with internationally recognized ethical norms and principles. This alignment promotes consistency and facilitates international cooperation on AI ethics.

2. **Translating Ethics into Regulations:**

-   **Regulatory Frameworks:** Ethical standards are translated into concrete regulatory frameworks. These frameworks specify the requirements, guidelines, and legal obligations that AI developers, users, and organizations must adhere to.

-   **Cross-Sectoral Approach:** Ethical standards are applied across various sectors and industries where AI is used, ensuring that they are not confined to a specific domain but are comprehensive and widely applicable.

3. **Data Privacy and Security:**

-   **Data Protection:** Ethical standards emphasize the importance of data privacy and security. They require organizations to handle personal and sensitive data responsibly, adhering to data protection regulations like GDPR (General Data Protection Regulation).

-   **User Consent:** Ethical standards often mandate that organizations obtain informed consent from users before collecting and processing their data for AI applications.

4. **Transparency and Explainability:**

-   **Algorithmic Transparency:** Ethical standards demand that AI algorithms are transparent and explainable. Users and stakeholders should be able to understand how AI systems arrive at their decisions or recommendations.

-   **User Rights:** Ethical standards prioritize the rights of users to access information about how AI systems work and the basis for their outputs.

5. **Bias Mitigation and Fairness:**

-   **Bias Awareness:** Ethical standards recognize the importance of mitigating bias in AI systems. They require organizations to actively identify and rectify biases in data and algorithms to ensure fair and equitable outcomes.

-   **Algorithmic Fairness:** Organizations are obligated to design and deploy AI systems that do not discriminate against individuals based on factors like race, gender, or socioeconomic status.

6. **Safety and Accountability:**

- **Safety Protocols:** Ethical standards in AI regulation mandate the development and implementation of safety protocols. AI systems must be designed to minimize risks and ensure they operate reliably.

- **Accountability Mechanisms:** Ethical standards require organizations to establish accountability mechanisms. This includes taking responsibility for AI-related outcomes, implementing corrective actions, and reporting incidents or ethical violations.

7. **Human-Centric Development:**

- **Human Rights Perspective:** Ethical standards adopt a human rights perspective, ensuring that AI technologies respect and uphold fundamental human rights such as privacy, freedom of expression, and non-discrimination.

- **Human Well-Being:** Ethical standards prioritize the well-being of individuals and society as a whole. AI systems should contribute positively to societal progress and not harm human interests.

8. **Public Consultation and Transparency:**

- **Public Engagement:** Governments often seek public input and consultation when formulating and revising ethical standards for AI. This ensures that diverse perspectives and concerns are considered in the regulatory process.

- **Transparency Initiatives:** Ethical standards require transparency in the regulatory process itself. Governments are expected to provide clear information about AI regulations, their objectives, and the rationale behind specific standards.

9. **Enforcement and Accountability:**

- **Regulatory Compliance:** Ethical standards are enforceable through legal and regulatory mechanisms. Organizations found in violation of these standards may face penalties, fines, or other regulatory actions.

- **Stakeholder Responsibility:** Ethical standards also place a responsibility on AI developers, organizations, and users to actively comply with and uphold ethical principles in AI development and deployment.

10. **Global Cooperation:**

- **International Collaboration:** Ethical standards are often designed with international cooperation in mind. Governments collaborate on developing shared ethical norms to ensure a consistent and harmonized approach to AI regulation on a global scale.

- **Ethical Diplomacy:** Countries engage in ethical diplomacy to promote common values and standards for AI ethics and governance, reducing the potential for regulatory fragmentation.

    In conclusion, ethical standards in government regulation and oversight of AI are essential for promoting responsible and ethical development and use of AI technologies. They provide a clear framework for ensuring that AI aligns with societal values, protects individual rights, and contributes positively to human well-being. Ethical standards, when enforced and followed, play a pivotal role in building trust in AI systems and fostering a responsible AI ecosystem. Collaboration among governments, tech companies, and academia is crucial in crafting, implementing, and evolving these standards to address the ever-evolving landscape of AI ethics and technology.

III. **Academic Expertise and Ethical Guidance:** Academia brings a wealth of expertise in ethics, research, and critical thinking to the table. Collaborations with academia enrich AI development and governance:

➤ **Ethical Research:** Academics can conduct research on the ethical implications of AI, offering insights into potential risks, biases, and societal impacts.

Academic expertise and ethical research are fundamental components of collaborations between tech companies, governments, and academia in steering the future of artificial intelligence (AI) responsibly. Ethical research in AI involves conducting studies, investigations, and analyses to address ethical dilemmas, challenges, and implications associated with AI technologies. Here, we delve into the importance and details of ethical research in this context:

1. **Ethical Analysis and Assessment:**

- **Ethical Dilemmas:** Ethical research explores complex ethical dilemmas arising from AI technologies, such as bias in algorithms, privacy concerns, and decision-making accountability. It seeks to identify and understand the underlying ethical issues.

- **Impact Assessment:** Ethical research assesses the potential impact of AI on society, individuals, and vulnerable populations. It aims to foresee ethical challenges and prevent harm.

2. **Algorithmic Bias and Fairness:**

- **Bias Detection:** Ethical researchers investigate and develop methods to detect and mitigate bias in AI algorithms. They analyze data sources, algorithmic decision-making processes, and outcomes to ensure fairness and reduce discriminatory impacts.

- **Fairness Metrics:** Research in this area involves the development of fairness metrics and methodologies for evaluating AI systems. It strives to provide tools for quantifying and addressing bias.

3. **Transparency and Explainability:**

- **Explainable AI (XAI):** Ethical research focuses on making AI systems more transparent and explainable. It explores techniques for generating human-understandable explanations for AI-generated decisions.

- **User Understanding:** Researchers work on methods to help users understand AI outputs and the reasoning behind them. This empowers users to make informed decisions and challenge AI outcomes when necessary.

4. **Data Privacy and Security:**

- **Privacy-Preserving AI:** Ethical research explores techniques and technologies for preserving data privacy while leveraging data for AI applications. This includes methods like differential privacy and federated learning.

- **Secure AI:** Researchers develop strategies to enhance the security of AI systems, protecting them from adversarial attacks and data breaches that could compromise user privacy.

5. **Ethical Guidelines and Principles:**

- **Principled Development:** Ethical research contributes to the formulation of ethical guidelines and principles for AI development and use. These guidelines often prioritize fairness, transparency, accountability, and human well-being.

- **Cross-Cultural Considerations:** Research takes into account cultural and societal variations in ethical values, ensuring that AI principles are applicable and adaptable to diverse global contexts.

6. **Human-AI Interaction:**

- **User-Centered Design:** Ethical research promotes user-centered design in AI systems. It investigates how AI interacts with humans and aims to enhance the user experience while respecting ethical boundaries.

- **User Feedback Integration:** Researchers explore methods for effectively integrating user feedback into AI systems to improve their ethical performance.

7. **Societal and Ethical Impact:**

- **Stakeholder Engagement:** Ethical research encourages stakeholder engagement, including discussions with the public, policymakers, and civil society. This inclusive approach seeks to incorporate diverse perspectives into AI ethics considerations.

- **Ethical Scenarios:** Researchers create ethical scenarios and thought experiments to evaluate how AI systems would respond to various ethical challenges. This helps identify potential shortcomings and areas for improvement.

8. **Regulatory Input:**

- **Policy Recommendations:** Ethical research provides valuable input for the formulation of AI regulations and policies. Researchers offer evidence-based recommendations to policymakers, ensuring that regulations are grounded in ethical considerations.

- **Impact Assessments:** Researchers conduct ethical impact assessments of proposed regulations, helping governments understand the potential consequences and ethical implications of regulatory decisions.

9. **Cross-Disciplinary Collaboration:**

- **Interdisciplinary Research:** Ethical research often involves collaboration between experts from diverse fields, including philosophy, computer science, law, sociology, and psychology. This interdisciplinary approach enriches ethical discussions and solutions.

- **Cross-Sectoral Cooperation:** Researchers engage with tech companies, governments, and civil society to create a holistic understanding of AI ethics. Collaborations ensure that ethical research addresses real-world challenges effectively.

10. **Educational Initiatives:**

- **Ethics Education:** Ethical research contributes to educational initiatives that promote AI ethics awareness and literacy. It prepares future AI professionals and decision-makers to navigate ethical complexities.

- **Public Awareness:** Research findings are often translated into educational materials and public awareness campaigns to inform the general population about AI ethics, fostering a more informed and engaged society.

Ethical research in AI is a cornerstone of responsible AI development and governance. It addresses the ethical implications, challenges, and potential benefits of AI technologies. Through collaboration between academia, tech companies, and governments, ethical research contributes to the establishment of ethical standards, regulatory frameworks, and best practices that guide the responsible development and deployment of AI systems. It empowers stakeholders to make informed decisions, mitigate ethical risks, and ensure that AI technologies align with societal values and human well-being.

➢ **Ethical Education:** Collaborations support ethical education and training for AI professionals, ensuring that ethical considerations are an integral part of AI development.

Ethical education is a crucial component of collaborations between tech companies, governments, and academia in steering the future of artificial intelligence (AI) responsibly. This form of education focuses on raising awareness, imparting ethical principles, and fostering a deep understanding of the ethical considerations surrounding AI technologies.

Here, we explore the importance and details of ethical education in this context:

1. **Awareness and Ethics Literacy:**

- **Raising Awareness:** Ethical education programs aim to raise awareness about the ethical dimensions of AI among various stakeholders, including AI developers, policymakers, users, and the general public.

- **Ethics Literacy:** These programs provide foundational knowledge about AI ethics, ensuring that individuals can identify, understand, and navigate ethical challenges associated with AI technologies.

2. **Ethical Principles and Frameworks:**

- **Teaching Ethical Principles:** Ethical education introduces learners to key ethical principles such as fairness, transparency, accountability, privacy, and human well-being. It emphasizes the importance of integrating these principles into AI development and use.

- **Ethical Frameworks:** Learners are introduced to ethical frameworks that guide responsible AI development. This includes frameworks proposed by international organizations, regulatory bodies, and academic institutions.

3. **AI Bias and Fairness:**

- **Understanding Bias:** Ethical education delves into the concept of bias in AI and its potential consequences. It equips learners with the knowledge and tools to recognize and address bias in AI algorithms and data.

- **Promoting Fairness:** Programs emphasize the importance of fairness in AI systems, teaching methods to evaluate and improve fairness in algorithmic decision-making.

4. **Transparency and Explainability:**

- **Transparency Education:** Ethical education highlights the significance of transparency in AI. It explains why transparent AI systems are essential for accountability and user trust.

- **Explainability Training:** Learners are taught about the importance of explainable AI (XAI) and methods for making AI algorithms more interpretable. This empowers them to demand and design transparent AI systems.

5. **Privacy and Data Protection:**

- **Data Privacy Education:** Ethical education addresses data privacy concerns in AI. It teaches learners about data protection regulations, user consent, and responsible data handling practices.

- **Security Awareness:** Learners are educated about the importance of AI system security to safeguard against data breaches and unauthorized access.

6. **Ethical Decision-Making:**

- **Ethical Frameworks:** Ethical education equips individuals with ethical decision-making frameworks. It encourages thoughtful consideration of ethical dilemmas and the application of ethical principles in decision-making.

- **Case Studies:** Real-world case studies are used to illustrate ethical decision-making processes and the consequences of different choices in AI development and deployment.

7. **User-Centered Design:**

- **User Empowerment:** Ethical education promotes a user-centered design approach. It teaches AI developers to actively seek user input, incorporate user feedback, and design systems that align with user values and expectations.

- **Inclusivity:** Programs emphasize inclusivity in AI design, ensuring that AI systems are accessible and beneficial to all individuals, including those with disabilities.

8. **Ethical Impact Assessment:**

- **Ethical Scenarios:** Ethical education includes the study of ethical scenarios and thought experiments related to AI. Learners analyze these scenarios to evaluate the ethical implications and consider possible solutions.

- **Ethical Impact Assessment:** Learners are trained in conducting ethical impact assessments of AI systems. This involves assessing potential consequences, risks, and societal impacts of AI technologies.

9. **Regulatory Understanding:**

- **Regulatory Compliance:** Ethical education provides an understanding of AI regulations and the legal obligations associated with AI development and use. It ensures that individuals and organizations are aware of their responsibilities.

- **Contributing to Compliance:** Ethical education empowers individuals to contribute to regulatory compliance within their organizations, promoting a culture of ethics and responsibility.

10. **Public Engagement and Advocacy:**

- **Advocacy Skills:** Ethical education fosters skills for public engagement and advocacy in AI ethics. It encourages individuals to participate in discussions, provide input on AI regulations, and advocate for ethical AI practices.

- **Building Trust:** Educated individuals are more likely to advocate for ethical AI, contributing to building public trust in AI technologies and the responsible governance of AI.

11. **Interdisciplinary Approach:**

- **Collaboration Across Disciplines:** Ethical education often adopts an interdisciplinary approach, bringing together experts from philosophy, computer science, law, psychology, sociology, and other fields. This interdisciplinary collaboration enriches ethical discussions and solutions.

- **Cross-Sectoral Cooperation:** Ethical education encourages collaboration between academia, tech companies, governments, and civil society to ensure that ethical considerations in AI are addressed comprehensively.

Ethical education is a cornerstone of responsible AI development and governance. It equips individuals with the knowledge, skills, and ethical awareness necessary to navigate the complex landscape of AI ethics. By raising awareness, promoting ethical principles, and fostering ethical decision-making, ethical education contributes to the development of a responsible and ethical AI ecosystem. Collaboration between tech companies, governments, and academia in delivering ethical education ensures that all stakeholders are well-prepared to address the ethical challenges posed by AI technologies.

> **Ethical Audits:** Academics may participate in ethical audits of AI systems and projects, helping identify and address ethical concerns and biases.

Ethical audits involve comprehensive assessments of AI systems, algorithms, and practices to ensure they align with ethical principles, regulations, and societal values. Here, we delve into the importance and details of ethical audits in this context:

1. **Assessing Ethical Compliance:**

- **Alignment with Ethical Principles:** Ethical audits evaluate the extent to which AI systems adhere to ethical principles such as fairness, transparency, accountability, and privacy. They ensure that AI technologies align with established ethical norms.

- **Legal and Regulatory Compliance:** Audits also assess whether AI systems comply with relevant laws and regulations, including data protection and anti-discrimination laws. This ensures that AI deployment meets legal standards.

2. **Bias Mitigation and Fairness:**

- **Bias Identification:** Ethical audits involve identifying and assessing potential biases in AI algorithms and data sources. They aim to uncover any disparities in how AI systems treat different groups or individuals.

- **Fairness Evaluation:** Auditors use fairness metrics and evaluation techniques to assess the fairness of AI decisions and outcomes, particularly concerning sensitive attributes like race or gender.

3. **Transparency and Explainability:**

- **Transparency Assessment:** Ethical audits examine the level of transparency in AI systems. They assess whether AI processes are clear and understandable to stakeholders, including users and decision-makers.

- **Explainability Evaluation:** Auditors assess the explainability of AI algorithms, focusing on their ability to provide coherent and interpretable explanations for their decisions.

4. **Privacy and Data Handling:**

- **Data Privacy Analysis:** Ethical audits scrutinize data privacy practices in AI systems. They ensure that data collection, storage, and processing align with privacy regulations and user consent.

- **Security Check:** Auditors evaluate the security measures implemented in AI systems to safeguard against data breaches, unauthorized access, and other security risks that may compromise user privacy.

5. **Accountability Mechanisms:**

- **Responsibility Assessment:** Ethical audits investigate the presence of accountability mechanisms within AI systems. They examine whether there are processes in place for identifying and rectifying errors, biases, or ethical violations.

- **User Redress:** Auditors ensure that AI systems provide avenues for users to seek redress in cases of adverse outcomes or ethical concerns.

6. **Ethical Impact Assessment:**

- **Ethical Scenarios:** Ethical audits may use hypothetical scenarios and thought experiments to assess how AI systems would respond to various ethical challenges. This helps identify potential shortcomings and areas for improvement.

- **Impact Evaluation:** Auditors consider the broader societal and ethical impact of AI technologies, assessing their consequences on individuals, communities, and vulnerable populations.

7. **User-Centered Design:**

- **User Empowerment:** Ethical audits check whether AI systems adopt a user-centered design approach. They evaluate whether user input and feedback are actively sought and integrated into system development.

- **Inclusivity Examination:** Auditors assess whether AI systems are designed inclusively to serve diverse user needs and accommodate individuals with disabilities.

8. **Regulatory Compliance:**

- **Legal Adherence:** Ethical audits ensure that AI systems comply with applicable regulations and standards. They verify that AI technologies meet the legal requirements of different jurisdictions.

- **Contribution to Compliance:** Ethical audits may assist organizations in ensuring that their AI systems and practices align with ethical and legal standards, helping them meet regulatory obligations.

9. **Continuous Improvement:**

- **Feedback Loop:** Ethical audits establish a feedback loop for ongoing improvement. Auditors provide recommendations and action items for addressing identified ethical issues and enhancing AI system performance.

- **Adaptive Governance:** Audits contribute to adaptive governance by identifying emerging ethical challenges and opportunities for refinement in AI technologies and practices.

10. **Public Trust and Accountability:**

- **Building Trust:** Ethical audits contribute to building and maintaining public trust in AI technologies. They signal to the public that organizations are committed to ethical and responsible AI deployment.

- **Accountability Reporting:** Organizations may use the findings of ethical audits to report on their commitment to ethical AI and their efforts to address ethical concerns.

11. **Interdisciplinary Collaboration:**

- **Expert Collaboration:** Ethical audits often involve collaboration between experts from various disciplines, including ethics, computer science, law, and social sciences. This interdisciplinary approach enriches the audit process and findings.

- **Stakeholder Involvement:** Auditors may engage with stakeholders, including tech companies, governments, civil society organizations, and users, to gather diverse perspectives on AI ethics.

  Ethical audits are essential for ensuring that AI systems and practices align with ethical principles, legal requirements, and societal values. They provide a systematic and rigorous evaluation of AI technologies to identify and rectify ethical issues and shortcomings. Collaboration between tech companies, governments, and academia in conducting ethical audits contributes to the responsible development and deployment of AI, fosters accountability, and builds public trust in AI technologies.

IV. **Shared Research and Innovation:** Collaborations often result in shared research and innovation projects that promote ethical AI:

➢ **Joint Research Initiatives:** Tech companies, governments, and academia can collaborate on research projects focused on AI ethics, transparency, fairness, and accountability.

Joint research initiatives are a cornerstone of collaborations between tech companies, governments, and academia when steering the future of artificial intelligence (AI) responsibly. These initiatives involve cooperative efforts to conduct research, innovation, and development activities related to AI technologies. Here, we explore the importance and details of joint research initiatives in this context:

1. **Combining Expertise:**

- **Interdisciplinary Collaboration:** Joint research initiatives bring together experts from various fields, including computer science, ethics, law, psychology, and more. This interdisciplinary collaboration enriches research outcomes and ensures a holistic approach to AI development.

- **Tech Industry Involvement:** Collaboration with tech companies allows academia and governments to tap into industry expertise, access proprietary data and resources, and gain insights into cutting-edge AI technologies and practices.

2. **Ethical Considerations:**

- **Ethical Research:** Joint research initiatives often include ethical research components. Researchers work together to address ethical dilemmas, assess the ethical implications of AI technologies, and propose solutions for responsible AI development.

- **Policy Recommendations:** Research findings from joint initiatives can inform the development of AI ethics policies and regulatory frameworks. Collaboration with governments ensures that ethical considerations are integrated into policy recommendations.

3. **Data Sharing and Access:**

- **Data Collaboration:** Tech companies participating in joint initiatives may provide access to their data resources. This enables researchers to conduct data-driven studies and experiments, fostering innovation in AI algorithms and applications.

- **Data Privacy and Security:** Collaborative efforts emphasize the importance of data privacy and security, ensuring that data sharing complies with legal and ethical standards and that sensitive information is protected.

4. **Transparency and Explainability:**

- **Development of Explainable AI (XAI):** Joint research often focuses on making AI algorithms more transparent and explainable. Researchers work together to develop and refine XAI techniques, enhancing user understanding of AI decisions.

- **User-Centered Design:** Collaboration with academia helps tech companies adopt user-centered design principles, ensuring that AI systems are designed with transparency and user needs in mind.

5. **Bias Mitigation and Fairness:**

- **Bias Research:** Joint initiatives address bias in AI algorithms and data. Researchers collaborate to develop bias-detection tools, fairness metrics, and strategies for mitigating bias and ensuring equitable outcomes.

- **Cross-Sectoral Perspectives:** Collaboration between academia, governments, and tech companies ensures that bias research considers a wide range of perspectives and societal contexts.

6. **Safety and Accountability:**

- **Safety Protocols:** Joint initiatives focus on safety in AI, particularly in applications like autonomous vehicles and healthcare. Researchers work on safety protocols and standards to minimize risks and ensure reliable AI performance.

- **Accountability Measures:** Collaboration supports the development of accountability mechanisms within AI systems. Researchers address issues related to algorithmic accountability and user redress.

7. **Ethical Impact Assessments:**

- **Scenario Planning:** Joint research initiatives often include the creation of ethical scenarios and thought experiments. These scenarios are used to assess the ethical implications and potential consequences of AI technologies.

- **Impact Evaluation:** Researchers evaluate the broader societal impact of AI systems, including their effects on individuals, communities, and vulnerable populations.

8. **Policy Input and Advocacy:**

- **Policy Expertise:** Academia provides policy expertise in joint initiatives, helping to shape AI regulations and governance structures. Researchers offer evidence-based recommendations to policymakers.

- **Ethical Advocacy:** Collaboration enables academia to advocate for ethical AI practices and principles within the tech industry and government, contributing to responsible AI development and deployment.

9. **Education and Public Awareness:**

- **Educational Initiatives:** Joint research initiatives often extend to educational programs. Collaboration between academia, tech companies, and governments fosters the development of AI ethics education and awareness campaigns for the public.

- **Informed Society:** Educated individuals are better equipped to understand AI ethics and advocate for responsible AI practices, contributing to a more informed and ethically aware society.

10. **Cross-Sectoral Cooperation:**

- **Diverse Perspectives:** Collaboration between academia, tech companies, and governments ensures that a wide range of perspectives are considered in AI research and development. This inclusivity promotes comprehensive and equitable AI solutions.

- **Regulatory Alignment:** Joint initiatives contribute to aligning AI research, innovation, and development with regulatory standards and ethical principles, reducing the potential for regulatory fragmentation.

In summary, joint research initiatives are instrumental in advancing responsible AI development and governance. They combine the strengths of academia, tech companies, and governments to address ethical challenges, enhance transparency, and promote user-centric AI. By working together, these stakeholders foster innovation, contribute to ethical AI practices, and help steer the future of AI in a manner that aligns with societal values and human well-being.

➢ **Innovation Challenges:** Competitions and innovation challenges can encourage the development of AI solutions that align with ethical principles.

Innovation challenges are an integral part of collaborations between tech companies, governments, and academia when it comes to steering the future of artificial intelligence (AI) responsibly. These challenges serve as structured competitions or initiatives designed to stimulate creative thinking, problem-solving, and the development of novel AI solutions. Here, we explore the importance and details of innovation challenges in this context:

1. **Problem Identification:**

- **Defining Ethical and Societal Problems:** Innovation challenges start by identifying specific ethical, societal, or technological problems related to AI. These problems can include bias in algorithms, privacy concerns, safety in autonomous systems, or AI's impact on employment.

- **Public Input:** Some challenges involve gathering input from the public, users, and stakeholders to ensure that the identified problems are relevant and resonate with the broader community.

2. **Cross-Sectoral Collaboration:**

- **Multi-Stakeholder Participation:** Innovation challenges encourage participation from diverse stakeholders, including tech experts, researchers, policymakers, and representatives from civil society. This diversity of perspectives enriches problem-solving and solution development.

- **Tech-Industry Involvement:** Collaboration with tech companies ensures that real-world expertise and resources are brought to the table. Companies may sponsor challenges, provide datasets, or offer technical mentorship to participants.

3. **Innovation and Solution Development:**

- **Encouraging Creativity:** Innovation challenges provide a platform for creative thinking and out-of-the-box solutions. Participants are encouraged to propose innovative approaches to address the identified problems.

- **Prototyping and Development:** Many challenges require participants to develop prototypes or working models of their proposed solutions. This practical aspect fosters hands-on experience and encourages tangible results.

4. **Ethical Considerations:**

- **Ethical Guidelines:** Innovation challenges often include ethical guidelines to ensure that proposed solutions align with ethical principles. This can involve guidelines for fairness, transparency, accountability, and user privacy.

- **Ethics Review:** In some cases, challenges may require participants to undergo ethics reviews or assessments to ensure that their solutions do not pose ethical risks or harm.

5. **Data Access and Privacy:**

- **Data Availability:** Challenges may provide participants with access to datasets relevant to the problem at hand. Data access can be crucial for training and testing AI models.

- **Data Privacy:** Safeguarding data privacy is a priority. Challenges ensure that data used by participants is anonymized, consent-based, and compliant with data protection regulations.

6. **Transparency and Accountability:**

- **Explainability Requirements:** Challenges may require participants to make their AI models transparent and explainable. This promotes the development of AI systems that can justify their decisions.

- **Accountability Measures:** Challenges often include mechanisms to hold participants accountable for their solutions. This can involve evaluation criteria related to system performance, fairness, or bias mitigation.

7. **Fair Competition:**

- **Impartial Judging:** Challenges appoint impartial panels of judges who evaluate solutions based on predetermined criteria. This ensures a fair competition and reduces the potential for biases.

- **Validation and Verification:** Rigorous validation and verification processes may be in place to confirm the accuracy and reliability of submitted solutions.

8. **Impact Assessment:**

- **Assessing Societal Impact:** Innovation challenges consider the potential impact of solutions on society, individuals, and vulnerable populations. They evaluate whether proposed solutions contribute positively to societal well-being.

- **Ethical Scenarios:** Challenges may include scenarios or case studies that participants must address to assess the real-world ethical implications of their solutions.

9. **Regulatory Alignment:**

- **Adherence to Regulations:** Challenges often require participants to ensure that their solutions comply with existing AI regulations and standards. This promotes regulatory alignment and responsible innovation.

- **Policy Input:** Solutions proposed in challenges may inform policymakers and regulatory bodies, contributing to the development of ethical AI policies.

10. **Public Awareness and Education:**

- **Communication and Outreach:** Innovation challenges often involve communication and outreach efforts to raise public awareness about AI ethics and responsible innovation. This fosters a more informed and engaged society.

- **Educational Initiatives:** Challenges may include educational components to teach participants and the public about the ethical considerations associated with AI.

11. **Iterative Improvement:**

- **Feedback Loop:** Challenges provide feedback to participants, enabling iterative improvement of solutions. This encourages continuous learning and refinement.

- **Adaptive Governance:** The insights gained from challenges can contribute to adaptive governance and the development of AI technologies that evolve responsibly over time.

In summary, innovation challenges are a dynamic and collaborative way to address ethical, societal, and technological issues in AI. They foster creative problem-solving, encourage ethical considerations, and promote responsible innovation. By engaging participants from academia, tech companies, and governments, these challenges contribute to the development of innovative AI solutions that align with societal values, human well-being, and ethical principles.

➤ **Public-Private Partnerships:** Public-private partnerships facilitate shared resources and knowledge, fostering responsible AI innovation.

Public-private partnerships are pivotal in collaborations between tech companies, governments, and academia when steering the future of artificial intelligence (AI) responsibly. These partnerships involve joint efforts between governmental or public entities and private-sector organizations, such as tech companies, to address ethical, societal, and technological challenges posed by AI. Here, we explore the importance and details of public-private partnerships in this context:

1. **Resource Sharing:**

- **Data and Expertise:** Public-private partnerships facilitate the sharing of critical resources. Tech companies often have access to large datasets and technical expertise, while governments can provide regulatory guidance and public interest perspectives.

- **Financial Support:** Governmental entities may provide funding for research projects and initiatives, enabling academia and tech companies to conduct research and innovation in AI ethics.

2. **Collaborative Research:**

- **Interdisciplinary Teams:** Partnerships bring together interdisciplinary teams comprising experts from academia, tech companies, and government agencies. This diversity of knowledge and skills enhances research outcomes.

- **Joint Projects:** Collaborators work on joint research projects focused on ethical AI development, transparency, fairness, privacy, and other relevant topics. These projects aim to develop practical solutions and guidelines.

3. **Ethical Frameworks and Standards:**

- **Policy and Regulation Development:** Public-private partnerships contribute to the development of ethical frameworks, guidelines, and regulatory standards for AI. Governments and tech companies work together to create rules that ensure responsible AI development and deployment.

- **Industry Adoption:** Collaboration between tech companies and governments helps to promote the adoption of ethical guidelines and standards within the tech industry, aligning industry practices with societal values.

4. **Ethical Impact Assessments:**

- **Societal Consequences:** Public-private partnerships assess the societal and ethical impact of AI technologies. Researchers analyze how AI affects individuals, communities, and vulnerable populations, informing ethical considerations.

- **Mitigation Strategies:** Insights from impact assessments lead to the development of strategies to mitigate potential harms and maximize the benefits of AI.

5. **Transparency and Accountability:**

- **Explainable AI (XAI):** Partnerships often focus on XAI research to make AI systems more transparent and accountable. This involves developing methods for generating human-understandable explanations for AI decisions.

- **Accountability Mechanisms:** Collaborators work to establish accountability mechanisms within AI systems, ensuring that errors, biases, and ethical violations are identified and rectified.

6. **Bias Mitigation and Fairness:**

- **Bias Detection:** Public-private partnerships address bias in AI algorithms. Researchers develop tools and techniques to detect and mitigate bias, promoting fairness in AI decision-making.

- **Fairness Metrics:** Partnerships work on the development of fairness metrics and methodologies for evaluating AI systems, helping to quantify and address bias.

7. **Data Privacy and Security:**

- **Privacy-Preserving AI:** Public-private partnerships explore privacy-preserving AI techniques, allowing AI systems to operate on sensitive data without compromising user privacy.

- **Secure AI:** Researchers develop strategies to enhance the security of AI systems, safeguarding them from adversarial attacks and data breaches.

8. **User-Centered Design:**

- **Enhancing User Experience:** Partnerships promote user-centered design in AI systems. They investigate how AI interacts with humans and aim to enhance the user experience while respecting ethical boundaries.

- **User Feedback Integration:** Research informs methods for effectively integrating user feedback into AI systems to improve their ethical performance.

9. **Regulatory Input:**

- **Policy Recommendations:** Public-private partnerships provide valuable input for the formulation of AI regulations and policies. Researchers offer evidence-based recommendations to policymakers, ensuring that regulations are grounded in ethical considerations.

- **Impact Assessments:** Researchers conduct ethical impact assessments of proposed regulations, helping governments understand the potential consequences and ethical implications of regulatory decisions.

10. **Educational Initiatives:**

- **Ethics Education:** Partnerships contribute to educational initiatives that promote AI ethics awareness and literacy. They prepare future AI professionals and decision-makers to navigate ethical complexities.

- **Public Awareness:** Research findings are often translated into educational materials and public awareness campaigns to inform the general population about AI ethics, fostering a more informed and engaged society.

11. **Cross-Sectoral Cooperation:**

- **Interdisciplinary Research:** Public-private partnerships involve collaboration between experts from diverse fields, including philosophy, computer science, law, sociology, and psychology. This interdisciplinary approach enriches ethical discussions and solutions.

- **Cross-Sectoral Engagement:** Researchers engage with tech companies, governments, and civil society to create a holistic understanding of AI ethics. Collaborations ensure that ethical considerations address real-world challenges effectively.

Public-private partnerships are essential for advancing responsible AI development and governance. They leverage the resources, expertise, and perspectives of governments, tech companies, and academia to address ethical challenges, develop ethical guidelines, and promote the responsible deployment of AI technologies. By working together, these stakeholders contribute to the establishment of ethical standards, regulatory frameworks, and best practices that guide the development of AI systems in alignment with societal values and human well-being.

V.   **Ethical Considerations in AI Education:** Collaborations between these sectors also extend to AI education and training:

➤ **Curriculum Development:** Tech companies and academia collaborate to develop AI curricula that emphasize ethics, responsible AI, and societal implications.

Curriculum development is a critical aspect of collaborations between tech companies, governments, and academia when steering the future of artificial intelligence (AI) responsibly. Developing comprehensive AI ethics curricula ensures that students, professionals, policymakers, and the broader community are equipped with the knowledge and skills to navigate the ethical complexities of AI. Here, we explore the importance and details of curriculum development in AI ethics education:

1. **Defining Ethical Foundations:**

- **Core Ethical Principles:** Curriculum development begins with defining the core ethical principles that underpin AI ethics, including fairness, transparency, accountability, privacy, and human well-being.

- **Ethical Frameworks:** Curricula introduce learners to established ethical frameworks that guide responsible AI development, such as those proposed by international organizations and regulatory bodies.

2. **Interdisciplinary Approach:**

- **Multidisciplinary Expertise:** Curriculum development involves collaboration between experts from various fields, including philosophy, computer science, law, social sciences, and psychology. This multidisciplinary approach ensures a holistic understanding of AI ethics.

- **Tech Industry Input:** Collaboration with tech companies allows curricula to incorporate real-world industry perspectives, ensuring that educational content is relevant and up-to-date.

3. **Curriculum Components:**

- **Foundational Knowledge:** Curricula provide foundational knowledge about AI technologies, their capabilities, and their societal implications. This ensures that learners understand the context in which AI ethics operates.

- **Ethical Principles:** Educational materials emphasize ethical principles and values that should guide AI development and use. These principles serve as the ethical compass for decision-making.

4. **Case Studies and Ethical Scenarios:**

- **Real-World Application:** Curricula include case studies and ethical scenarios to illustrate ethical dilemmas and challenges faced in AI development and deployment. Learners analyze these cases to understand the practical implications of ethical decisions.

- **Critical Thinking:** Ethical scenarios encourage critical thinking and help learners develop the skills to identify, assess, and resolve ethical issues.

5. **Regulatory and Legal Awareness:**

- **Understanding Regulations:** Curricula provide an overview of AI regulations and legal frameworks. Learners gain an understanding of the legal obligations and responsibilities associated with AI development and use.

- **Compliance Education:** Education on compliance with regulations ensures that individuals and organizations adhere to legal standards in AI applications.

6. **Bias and Fairness:**

- **Bias Awareness:** Curriculum development addresses bias in AI algorithms and data. Learners are educated about the sources and consequences of bias and the importance of bias mitigation.

- **Fairness Metrics:** Curricula introduce fairness metrics and evaluation techniques that learners can use to assess and improve the fairness of AI systems.

7. **Transparency and Explainability:**

- **Transparency Education:** Educational materials highlight the significance of transparency in AI. They explain why transparent AI systems are essential for accountability and user trust.

- **Explainability Training:** Curricula equip learners with knowledge about the importance of explainable AI (XAI) and methods for making AI algorithms more interpretable.

8. **Privacy and Data Protection:**

- **Data Privacy Education:** Curriculum development addresses data privacy concerns in AI. Learners are educated about data protection regulations, user consent, and responsible data handling practices.

- **Security Awareness:** Learners are informed about the importance of AI system security to safeguard against data breaches and unauthorized access.

9. **Ethical Decision-Making:**

- **Ethical Frameworks:** Curricula provide learners with ethical decision-making frameworks. They encourage thoughtful consideration of ethical dilemmas and the application of ethical principles in decision-making.

- **Case-Based Learning:** Case-based learning exercises challenge learners to apply ethical frameworks to real-world scenarios, enhancing their ethical reasoning skills.

10. **User-Centered Design:**

- **User Empowerment:** Curriculum development promotes a user-centered design approach. It teaches AI developers to actively seek user input, incorporate user feedback, and design systems that align with user values and expectations.

- **Inclusivity:** Educational materials emphasize inclusivity in AI design, ensuring that AI systems are accessible and beneficial to all individuals, including those with disabilities.

11. **Ethical Impact Assessment:**

- **Ethical Scenarios:** Curricula include ethical scenarios and thought experiments related to AI. Learners analyze these scenarios to evaluate the ethical implications and consider possible solutions.

- **Impact Assessment Training:** Curriculum development involves training learners to conduct ethical impact assessments of AI systems, ensuring that they can assess potential consequences, risks, and societal impacts.

12. **Public Engagement and Advocacy:**

- **Advocacy Skills:** Curricula foster advocacy skills in AI ethics. They teach individuals to participate in discussions, provide input on AI regulations, and advocate for ethical AI practices.

- **Building Trust:** Educated individuals are more likely to advocate for ethical AI, contributing to building public trust in AI technologies and responsible AI governance.

13. **Continuous Learning and Adaptation:**

- **Adaptive Curriculum:** Curriculum development recognizes the evolving nature of AI ethics. Materials are designed to be adaptable and regularly updated to address emerging ethical challenges and technological advancements.

- **Professional Development:** Ongoing education and training opportunities are provided to professionals, ensuring that they stay updated on the latest developments in AI ethics.

14. **Assessment and Certification:**

- **Ethical Competency Assessment:** Curricula include assessments to evaluate learners' ethical competency in AI. This ensures that learners have absorbed the ethical principles and can apply them effectively.

- **Certification Programs:** Certification programs may be offered to individuals who demonstrate proficiency in AI ethics, enhancing their credibility in the field.

Curriculum development in AI ethics education is essential for preparing individuals and organizations to navigate the ethical complexities of AI responsibly. It provides the knowledge, skills, and ethical awareness necessary to develop, use, and regulate AI technologies in a manner that aligns with societal values and human well-being. Collaborations between tech companies, governments, and academia in curriculum development ensure that AI ethics education is comprehensive, up-to-date, and responsive to emerging challenges.

➢ **Ethical AI Courses:** Universities offer courses and programs dedicated to ethical AI, ensuring that future AI professionals have a strong ethical foundation.

Ethical AI courses play a central role in collaborations between tech companies, governments, and academia when steering the future of artificial intelligence (AI) responsibly. These courses are designed to provide comprehensive instruction and training on the ethical dimensions of AI development, deployment, and regulation. Here, we delve into the importance and details of ethical AI courses:

1. **Foundational Knowledge:**

- **Introduction to AI Ethics:** Ethical AI courses begin with an introduction to the fundamental concepts and principles of AI ethics. Learners gain an understanding of why ethical considerations are critical in AI development.

- **Interdisciplinary Approach:** These courses often adopt an interdisciplinary approach, drawing from philosophy, computer science, law, psychology, and social sciences to provide a well-rounded perspective.

2. **Core Ethical Principles:**

- **Principle-Centered Learning:** Courses focus on core ethical principles, including fairness, transparency, accountability, privacy, and human well-being. Learners delve into these principles to understand their significance in AI ethics.

- **Real-World Application:** Ethical AI courses emphasize the practical application of ethical principles in AI decision-making and system development.

3. **Regulatory and Legal Awareness:**

- **Understanding Legal Frameworks:** Courses educate participants about AI regulations, legal frameworks, and standards. Learners gain insights into the legal obligations and responsibilities associated with AI.

- **Compliance Training:** Ethical AI courses teach compliance with regulations to ensure that individuals and organizations adhere to legal standards in AI applications.

4. **Bias Mitigation and Fairness:**

- **Bias Identification:** Courses address bias in AI algorithms and data sources. Participants learn techniques to identify and mitigate bias, ensuring fair AI outcomes.

- **Fairness Metrics:** These courses introduce fairness metrics and evaluation methods, allowing learners to assess and improve the fairness of AI systems.

5. **Transparency and Explainability:**

- **Importance of Transparency:** Ethical AI courses stress the importance of transparency in AI systems. Learners understand why transparent AI is essential for accountability and user trust.

- **Explainable AI (XAI):** Courses delve into XAI techniques, helping participants make AI algorithms more interpretable and accountable.

6. **Privacy and Data Protection:**

- **Data Privacy Education:** Courses address data privacy concerns in AI, covering topics such as user consent, responsible data handling, and compliance with data protection regulations.

- **Security Awareness:** Participants are educated about AI system security to safeguard against data breaches, cyberattacks, and unauthorized access.

7. **User-Centered Design:**

- **Enhancing User Experience:** Ethical AI courses promote a user-centered design approach. They teach participants how to actively involve users in AI development and design systems that align with user values and expectations.

- **Inclusivity:** Courses emphasize the importance of inclusive AI design to ensure that AI systems are accessible and beneficial to all individuals, including those with disabilities.

8. **Ethical Decision-Making:**

- **Ethical Frameworks:** These courses provide learners with ethical decision-making frameworks. Participants practice applying these frameworks to real-world ethical dilemmas in AI.

- **Case-Based Learning:** Case studies challenge learners to analyze and make ethical decisions in practical scenarios, enhancing their ethical reasoning skills.

9. **Regulatory Input:**

- **Policy Recommendations:** Ethical AI courses involve discussions on policy and regulation development. Learners contribute to the formation of evidence-based policy recommendations in AI ethics.

- **Impact Assessments:** Participants conduct ethical impact assessments of proposed regulations, helping governments understand potential consequences and ethical implications.

10. **Public Engagement and Advocacy:**

- **Advocacy Skills:** Courses foster advocacy skills in AI ethics. Participants learn how to engage in discussions, provide input on AI regulations, and advocate for ethical AI practices.

- **Building Public Trust:** Educated individuals are more likely to advocate for ethical AI, contributing to building public trust in AI technologies and responsible AI governance.

11. **Continuous Learning and Adaptation:**

- **Adaptive Curriculum:** Ethical AI courses recognize the evolving nature of AI ethics. They are designed to be adaptable and regularly updated to address emerging ethical challenges and technological advancements.

- **Professional Development:** Ongoing education and training opportunities are provided to professionals, ensuring that they stay updated on the latest developments in AI ethics.

12. **Assessment and Certification:**

- **Ethical Competency Assessment:** Courses include assessments to evaluate learners' ethical competency in AI. This ensures that learners have absorbed the ethical principles and can apply them effectively.

- **Certification Programs:** Some courses offer certification programs to individuals who demonstrate proficiency in AI ethics, enhancing their credibility in the field.

13. **Public Awareness and Education:**

- **Communication and Outreach:** Ethical AI courses often include communication and outreach efforts to raise public awareness about AI ethics and responsible AI practices.

- **Educational Initiatives:** Course materials are used to develop educational resources and public awareness campaigns, fostering a more informed and engaged society.

Ethical AI courses are essential for equipping individuals with the knowledge and skills to navigate the ethical complexities of AI responsibly. Through collaboration between tech companies, governments, and academia, these courses provide a robust foundation in AI ethics, promoting responsible AI development, deployment, and governance. They empower individuals to make ethical decisions, advocate for responsible AI practices, and contribute to the creation of a more ethical and trustworthy AI landscape.

VI. **Public Engagement and Trust Building:** Collaboration enhances public engagement and trust building in AI:

➤ **Public Awareness:** Joint efforts between tech companies, governments, and academia can raise public awareness about AI ethics, promoting responsible AI use.

Public awareness initiatives are a crucial component of collaborations between tech companies, governments, and academia when steering the future of artificial intelligence (AI) responsibly. These initiatives aim to inform and engage the public in discussions about AI ethics, governance, and the societal impact of AI technologies. Here, we explore the importance and details of public awareness efforts in this context:

1. **Raising AI Ethics Awareness:**

- **Educational Campaigns:** Public awareness campaigns are designed to educate the public about the ethical considerations associated with AI. These campaigns use various media channels, such as websites, social media, and educational materials, to disseminate information.

- **Workshops and Webinars:** Organizations collaborate to conduct workshops and webinars on AI ethics, inviting the public to participate and learn about the ethical implications of AI technologies.

2. **Transparency in AI Development:**

- **Highlighting Transparency:** Public awareness initiatives emphasize the importance of transparency in AI development. They explain why transparent AI systems are essential for accountability and user trust.

- **Demonstrating Explainability:** Campaigns may use real-world examples and demonstrations to show how AI systems can be made more explainable and accountable to the public.

3. **Ethical Decision-Making:**

- **Public Involvement:** Initiatives encourage public involvement in ethical decision-making processes related to AI. This can include soliciting public input on AI policy and regulations.

- **Case Studies:** Public awareness materials often include case studies and ethical scenarios that the public can analyze and provide feedback on, fostering critical thinking about AI ethics.

4. **AI Regulations and Policies:**

- **Informing the Public:** Public awareness campaigns inform the public about AI regulations and policies under consideration by governments. This ensures that citizens are aware of proposed regulatory changes that may impact their lives.

- **Soliciting Input:** Some initiatives actively seek public input on AI regulations, providing channels for individuals to voice their concerns and suggestions.

5. **Bias and Fairness:**

- **Addressing Bias Concerns:** Public awareness efforts discuss the issue of bias in AI algorithms and its potential consequences. They raise awareness about ongoing efforts to detect and mitigate bias.

- **Promoting Fairness:** Initiatives emphasize the importance of fairness in AI systems and the role of the public in advocating for fair AI practices.

6. **Data Privacy and Security:**

- **Data Protection Education:** Public awareness campaigns educate individuals about data privacy and protection in the context of AI. They inform the public about their rights and how to safeguard their personal information.

- **Security Awareness:** Initiatives highlight the importance of AI system security to protect against data breaches and cyber threats, promoting security best practices.

7. **Inclusivity and Accessibility:**

- **Accessible AI:** Public awareness initiatives stress the need for AI systems that are accessible to all, including individuals with disabilities. They advocate for AI inclusivity and equal access.

- **Promoting Inclusive Design:** Campaigns encourage the public to demand and support AI systems that consider diverse user needs and abilities.

8. **Building Public Trust:**

- **Trustworthiness of AI:** Public awareness efforts aim to build trust in AI technologies by demonstrating the commitment of tech companies, governments, and academia to responsible AI development.

- **Highlighting Ethical AI Practices:** Campaigns showcase examples of ethical AI practices to reassure the public that AI technologies are being developed and used responsibly.

9. **Advocacy and Engagement:**

- **Public Advocacy:** Public awareness initiatives empower individuals to become advocates for ethical AI. They provide information and resources for the public to engage in discussions and advocate for responsible AI practices.

- **Engaging the Youth:** Some campaigns target educational institutions to engage young learners in AI ethics discussions, preparing the next generation to be informed and active participants in AI governance.

10. **Transparency in Collaboration:**

- **Showcasing Collaborations:** Initiatives highlight collaborative efforts between tech companies, governments, and academia in steering AI responsibly. They showcase the commitment to transparency and shared responsibility.

- **Public-Private Partnerships:** Campaigns explain the role of public-private partnerships in addressing AI ethics challenges and promoting responsible AI innovation.

11. **Feedback Channels:**

- **Soliciting Feedback:** Public awareness initiatives often provide channels for individuals to provide feedback on AI technologies and ethical considerations. This feedback can inform further developments and policies.

- **Responsive Engagement:** Organizations actively respond to public inquiries and concerns, demonstrating a commitment to listening and addressing public feedback.

12. **Educational Initiatives:**

- **AI Ethics Education:** Public awareness campaigns may include educational components, such as online courses and materials, to inform the public about AI ethics and responsible AI practices.

- **AI Ethics Literacy:** Initiatives aim to improve AI ethics literacy among the public, enabling them to make informed decisions about AI technologies.

13. **Continuous Engagement:**

- **Sustainability:** Public awareness efforts are designed for sustainability, ensuring that ongoing engagement and education on AI ethics persist over time.

- **Adaptive Messaging:** Messages and materials are adapted to address emerging ethical challenges and to remain relevant in a rapidly evolving AI landscape.

  Public awareness initiatives are vital for engaging the public in discussions about AI ethics and building trust in AI technologies. By educating individuals about ethical considerations, transparency, and responsible AI practices, these efforts empower the public to advocate for responsible AI development, contribute to policy discussions, and participate in shaping the future of AI in alignment with societal values and human well-being.

➢ **Trust-Building Initiatives:** Initiatives that involve transparency, user education, and external oversight foster trust in AI technologies.

Trust-building initiatives are a critical component of collaborations between tech companies, governments, and academia when steering the future of artificial intelligence (AI) responsibly. These initiatives focus on fostering trust among various stakeholders, including the public, policymakers, and industry players. Here, we explore the importance and details of trust-building efforts in this context:

1. **Transparency and Accountability:**

- **Openness in AI Development:** Trust-building initiatives emphasize transparency in AI development. Tech companies commit to sharing information about their AI systems, their functioning, and data sources used.

- **Accountability Mechanisms:** Initiatives highlight the implementation of accountability mechanisms within AI systems. These mechanisms help identify errors, biases, and ethical violations and ensure that corrective actions are taken.

2. **Ethical AI Practices:**

- **Demonstrating Ethical Commitment:** Trust-building campaigns showcase tech companies' commitment to ethical AI practices. They communicate that ethical considerations are integral to AI development.

- **Promoting Fairness:** Initiatives underscore the importance of fairness in AI systems, demonstrating efforts to detect and mitigate bias and to ensure equitable outcomes.

3. **Data Privacy and Security:**

- **Data Protection Assurance:** Trust-building efforts focus on assuring the public of data privacy protection measures. They communicate adherence to data protection regulations and secure data handling practices.

- **Security Measures:** Initiatives highlight the security measures in place to safeguard AI systems from cyber threats, data breaches, and unauthorized access.

4. **User-Centered Design:**

- **User Empowerment:** Trust-building campaigns promote user-centered design in AI systems. They convey that users' interests and feedback are actively sought and integrated into AI development.

- **Inclusivity:** Initiatives advocate for AI systems that are inclusive and accessible to individuals of all backgrounds and abilities.

5. **Ethical Decision-Making:**

- **Transparent Decision Processes:** Trust-building initiatives elucidate the decision-making processes behind AI systems. They communicate that decisions are made following ethical frameworks and principles.

- **Public Involvement:** Some campaigns involve the public in ethical decision-making, allowing individuals to provide input and perspectives on AI-related ethical dilemmas.

6. **Regulatory Compliance:**

- **Compliance with Regulations:** Trust-building efforts convey a commitment to complying with AI regulations and legal standards. They ensure that AI systems adhere to relevant laws.

- **Supporting Regulation:** Initiatives may actively support regulatory efforts by providing insights and recommendations for effective AI governance.

7. **Bias Mitigation and Fairness:**

- **Bias Awareness:** Trust-building campaigns address bias in AI algorithms and data sources. They raise awareness about ongoing efforts to detect and address bias.

- **Fairness Assurance:** Initiatives communicate the use of fairness metrics and evaluation techniques to assess and improve the fairness of AI systems.

8. **Transparency in Collaboration:**

- **Showcasing Collaborations:** Trust-building initiatives highlight collaborative efforts between tech companies, governments, and academia in steering AI responsibly. They showcase the commitment to transparency and shared responsibility.

- **Public-Private Partnerships:** Campaigns explain the role of public-private partnerships in addressing AI ethics challenges and promoting responsible AI innovation.

9. **Feedback Channels:**

- **Soliciting Feedback:** Trust-building efforts often provide channels for stakeholders, including the public, to provide feedback on AI technologies and ethical considerations. This feedback is used to improve AI systems and practices.

- **Responsive Engagement:** Organizations actively respond to feedback, inquiries, and concerns, demonstrating a commitment to listening and addressing stakeholders' needs and expectations.

10. **Continuous Improvement:**

- **Adaptive Strategies:** Trust-building campaigns are designed for adaptability. They continuously evolve to address emerging ethical challenges and technological advancements.

- **Learning from Mistakes:** Initiatives acknowledge that mistakes may occur in AI development but emphasize a commitment to learning from them and improving AI systems.

11. **Public Awareness and Education:**

- **Communication and Outreach:** Trust-building initiatives include communication and outreach efforts to raise public awareness about AI ethics and responsible AI practices.

- **Educational Initiatives:** They may develop educational materials and public awareness campaigns, translating complex AI ethics concepts into easily understandable information for the public.

12. **Demonstrating Benefits:**

- **Societal Value:** Trust-building campaigns highlight the positive societal impact of AI technologies, showcasing how AI can address critical challenges and improve lives.

- **Responsible Innovation:** Initiatives convey that tech companies, governments, and academia are committed to responsible AI innovation that benefits society at large.

13. **Advocacy and Engagement:**

- **Engaging Stakeholders:** Trust-building efforts engage stakeholders, including the public, policymakers, and civil society, in discussions about AI ethics and governance.

- **Advocacy Empowerment:** They empower individuals and organizations to advocate for ethical AI practices, contributing to a more responsible AI landscape.

14. **Building Public Trust:**

- **Trustworthiness of AI:** Trust-building initiatives aim to build trust in AI technologies by demonstrating the commitment of tech companies, governments, and academia to responsible AI development.

- **Reinforcing Trust:** Through transparent practices, ethical commitment, and open communication, these initiatives work to reinforce and maintain public trust.

Trust-building initiatives are essential for fostering trust among stakeholders and ensuring responsible AI development and governance. By promoting transparency, ethical practices, data privacy, and inclusivity, these efforts empower the public and stakeholders to engage in discussions about AI ethics and advocate for responsible AI practices. Ultimately, they contribute to building a more ethical, trustworthy, and accountable AI landscape that aligns with societal values and human well-being.

VII.   **Adaptive Governance:** Collaborations facilitate adaptive governance in AI:

➢ **Flexible Frameworks:** Adaptive governance models allow for the adjustment of AI regulations and guidelines as the technology evolves, ensuring that ethical standards remain relevant.

Adaptive governance with flexible frameworks is a critical aspect of collaborations between tech companies, governments, and academia when steering the future of artificial intelligence (AI) responsibly. In a rapidly evolving AI landscape, flexibility in governance frameworks is essential to address emerging challenges, adapt to technological advancements, and ensure that AI development remains ethical and aligned with societal values. Here, we explore the importance and details of adaptive governance and flexible frameworks:

1. **Rapid Technological Advancements:**

- **Accelerated Innovation:** The AI field experiences continuous advancements, making it crucial for governance frameworks to adapt swiftly. Collaborative efforts between tech companies, governments, and academia ensure that regulations and policies keep pace with innovation.

- **Emerging Technologies:** Flexible frameworks are designed to accommodate emerging AI technologies like autonomous vehicles, quantum computing, and advanced robotics, ensuring responsible deployment and regulation.

2. **Ethical and Regulatory Alignment:**

- **Alignment with Ethical Standards:** Adaptive governance frameworks prioritize alignment with ethical principles and values. They provide mechanisms to review and update policies to reflect evolving ethical considerations in AI development and use.

- **Compliance and Accountability:** Flexible frameworks emphasize compliance with AI regulations and standards while holding tech companies accountable for ethical lapses or regulatory violations.

3. **Agility in Policy Development:**

271

- **Iterative Policy Formation:** Adaptive governance involves iterative policy development. Policies are continuously refined based on real-world experiences, feedback from stakeholders, and emerging challenges.

- **Pilot Programs:** Frameworks may include provisions for pilot programs, allowing governments and tech companies to test and adapt policies in controlled environments before wider implementation.

4. **Ethical Impact Assessments:**

- **Proactive Assessment:** Adaptive governance encourages the proactive assessment of AI technologies' ethical impact. Tech companies are expected to conduct impact assessments, and governments may set guidelines for these evaluations.

- **Mitigation Strategies:** If assessments reveal potential ethical risks, flexible frameworks provide mechanisms for implementing mitigation strategies and making necessary adjustments.

5. **Public Engagement and Input:**

- **Soliciting Public Input:** Adaptive governance actively solicits public input on AI regulations and policies. Public consultations, open forums, and feedback mechanisms are integrated into the framework.

- **Transparency:** The process of policy development and decision-making is transparent, enabling the public to understand and contribute to governance discussions.

6. **Collaborative Approach:**

- **Multi-Stakeholder Engagement:** Adaptive governance involves collaboration between tech companies, governments, academia, civil society, and industry experts. This diverse input ensures well-informed policies and regulations.

- **International Cooperation:** Flexible frameworks facilitate international cooperation, allowing nations to harmonize AI regulations and standards, reducing fragmentation and promoting global ethical AI development.

7. **Data Governance and Privacy:**

- **Data Ethics:** Adaptive governance frameworks address data governance and privacy concerns, including data collection, storage, and sharing. They evolve to accommodate changing data ethics and privacy requirements.

- **Data Protection:** Regulatory adjustments are made to ensure the protection of personal data and adherence to evolving data protection laws.

8. **Bias and Fairness:**

- **Bias Mitigation Strategies:** Adaptive governance includes strategies to detect and mitigate bias in AI systems. As new bias detection techniques emerge, frameworks incorporate them to enhance fairness.

- **Fairness Metrics:** Frameworks promote the use of fairness metrics and evaluation methods, which can be updated to address emerging fairness challenges.

9. **Transparency and Explainability:**

- **Explainable AI (XAI):** Adaptive governance acknowledges the importance of XAI and incorporates evolving XAI techniques to enhance AI system transparency.

- **Auditability:** Policies require AI developers to ensure that AI systems are auditable, allowing for transparent tracing of decision-making processes.

10. **Continuous Monitoring and Reporting:**

- **Ongoing Assessment:** Adaptive governance involves continuous monitoring of AI systems in operation. Tech companies are required to provide regular reports on system performance, ethical compliance, and impact assessments.

- **Adaptive Enforcement:** If issues arise, governance frameworks can adapt enforcement mechanisms to address challenges and ensure compliance.

11. **Flexibility in Regulatory Models:**

- **Proportional Regulation:** Flexible frameworks allow for proportional regulation, where the level of regulation is adapted based on the potential risks and impacts of specific AI applications.

- **Sandbox Environments:** Regulatory sandboxes may be established to allow tech companies to experiment with new AI technologies within controlled environments while adhering to ethical guidelines.

12. **Adaptive Education and Training:**

- **Continuous Learning:** Adaptive governance promotes continuous education and training on AI ethics and regulations for stakeholders. This ensures that individuals remain updated on evolving standards.

- **Professional Development:** Tech companies are encouraged to invest in the ongoing professional development of their employees to enhance their ethical AI competency.

13. **Stakeholder Feedback Loops:**

- **Feedback Integration:** Governance frameworks incorporate feedback loops that enable stakeholders to provide insights and suggestions for improvements. These loops are integral to continuous refinement.

- **Responsive Governance:** If a significant issue arises, frameworks are designed to respond quickly to address the concern and adjust policies accordingly.

Adaptive governance with flexible frameworks is essential for steering the AI future responsibly. It enables tech companies, governments, and academia to navigate the ever-changing AI landscape while upholding ethical standards, ensuring transparency, and fostering public trust. By embracing flexibility and iterative policy development, adaptive governance promotes the responsible development and deployment of AI technologies that benefit society and align with ethical values.

➢ **Ongoing Collaboration:** Tech companies, governments, and academia work together to assess the impact of AI regulations and adapt them as needed.

Ongoing collaboration is a cornerstone of adaptive governance within collaborations between tech companies, governments, and academia when steering the future of artificial intelligence (AI) responsibly. This collaborative approach ensures that governance frameworks remain effective and responsive to the evolving AI landscape. Here, we explore the importance and details of ongoing collaboration in adaptive governance:

1. **Multi-Stakeholder Engagement:**

- **Inclusivity:** Ongoing collaboration involves a wide range of stakeholders, including tech companies, governments, academia, civil society, and industry experts. This inclusivity ensures that diverse perspectives are considered in policy development.

- **Expert Input:** Collaboration with experts in AI ethics, law, and technology provides valuable insights that inform governance decisions and helps address complex ethical and technical challenges.

2. **Cross-Border Cooperation:**

- **International Engagement:** Adaptive governance encourages cross-border collaboration. Governments and organizations work together to harmonize AI regulations and standards on an international scale, reducing fragmentation and promoting global ethical AI development.

- **Information Sharing:** Collaborative efforts involve the sharing of best practices, lessons learned, and regulatory approaches across nations, facilitating a cohesive global approach to AI governance.

3. **Policy Co-Creation:**

- **Collaborative Policy Development:** Stakeholders collaboratively participate in policy creation. This co-creation ensures that policies are well-informed, practical, and representative of societal values.

- **Iterative Policy Refinement:** Ongoing collaboration allows policies to evolve iteratively. As new information emerges and ethical considerations evolve, policies are continuously refined to align with emerging needs and challenges.

4. **Stakeholder Input:**

- **Public Engagement:** Ongoing collaboration includes mechanisms for public input and engagement in the policymaking process. Public consultations, open forums, and feedback channels provide avenues for citizens to contribute to AI governance.

- **Responsive Governance:** Stakeholder input is taken seriously, and governance frameworks are designed to be responsive. When concerns are raised, mechanisms are in place to address them swiftly and effectively.

5. **Ethical Oversight:**

- **Ethical Review Boards:** Tech companies may establish ethical review boards comprising external experts. Ongoing collaboration with these boards ensures ethical compliance and provides an external perspective on AI development.

- **Audits and Assessments:** Governments collaborate with tech companies to conduct regular audits and ethical impact assessments, fostering transparency and accountability in AI systems.

6. **Continuous Learning:**

- **Professional Development:** Tech companies invest in the ongoing professional development of their employees. Collaborative efforts with academic institutions and training providers ensure that AI professionals remain updated on evolving ethical standards.

- **Ethical Education:** Academia collaborates with industry to develop and deliver ethical AI education and training programs, fostering a culture of responsible AI development.

7. **Data Sharing and Research:**

- **Research Collaboration:** Ongoing collaboration supports joint research initiatives between academia and tech companies. These collaborations generate insights into AI ethics and inform policy decisions.

- **Data Sharing:** Tech companies collaborate with academic institutions to share anonymized and privacy-preserving data for research purposes, enabling advancements in AI while respecting data privacy.

8. **Innovative Solutions:**

- **Sandbox Environments:** Governments and tech companies may establish regulatory sandboxes that encourage innovation within a controlled environment. Ongoing collaboration ensures that these sandboxes adhere to ethical guidelines.

- **Emerging Technologies:** Collaborative efforts address emerging AI technologies, such as autonomous vehicles or AI in healthcare, to develop ethical guidelines and regulations that keep pace with innovation.

9. **Global Ethical Leadership:**

- **Leading by Example:** Governments, tech companies, and academia collaborate to set global ethical standards in AI development and governance. By leading by example, they inspire other nations and organizations to follow suit.

- **Ethical Diplomacy:** Ongoing collaboration may involve diplomatic efforts to encourage nations to adopt responsible AI practices and align with global ethical norms.

10. **Flexible Framework Adaptation:**

- **Iterative Feedback:** Ongoing collaboration involves regular feedback loops from stakeholders. This feedback informs adaptive changes to governance frameworks to address emerging ethical, technical, and societal challenges.

- **Responsive Governance:** Frameworks are designed to be responsive to evolving needs. When significant issues arise, ongoing collaboration ensures swift adaptation and policy adjustments.

11. **Trust Building:**

- **Transparency and Openness:** Ongoing collaboration fosters a culture of transparency and openness among stakeholders. Trust is built by demonstrating a commitment to ethical AI practices and responsible governance.

- **Responsive Communication:** Collaborative efforts include responsive communication channels, ensuring that stakeholders are informed about AI developments and governance decisions.

12. **Public Awareness:**

- **Educational Initiatives:** Collaboration between academia, tech companies, and governments extends to public awareness campaigns. These campaigns educate the public about AI ethics, regulations, and responsible AI practices.

- **Engaging the Youth:** Ongoing collaboration may involve educational initiatives in schools and universities, preparing the next generation to be informed and active participants in AI governance.

Ongoing collaboration is essential for adaptive governance in the AI landscape. By engaging a diverse range of stakeholders, fostering international cooperation, and embracing continuous learning, tech companies, governments, and academia can collectively navigate the complex ethical, technical, and societal challenges posed by AI technologies. This collaborative approach ensures that AI development remains ethical, accountable, and aligned with the values and needs of society.

Collaborations between tech companies, governments, and academia are essential for steering the AI future responsibly and ethically. These partnerships combine the technical expertise of the industry, the regulatory power of governments, and the ethical insights of academia to ensure that AI technologies benefit society while adhering to ethical principles and legal standards. By working together, these sectors can address the challenges and complexities of AI in a holistic and responsible manner.

Fostering An Ethical AI Research and Development Culture:

Fostering an ethical AI research and development (R&D) culture is a pivotal aspect of steering the future of artificial intelligence (AI) in a responsible and beneficial direction. This chapter delves into the significance of cultivating a culture that places ethics, transparency, fairness, and accountability at the core of AI innovation. Here, we explore this topic in greater detail:

1. **Ethical Awareness and Education:**

- **Ethics Training:** Cultivating an ethical AI R&D culture begins with educating AI professionals, data scientists, and developers about the ethical considerations surrounding AI technologies. This training helps individuals understand the potential ethical challenges and biases that can arise during AI development.

- **Ethical Awareness:** Encouraging ethical awareness ensures that AI practitioners are conscious of the societal impact of their work. Ethical considerations should be integrated into every stage of AI development, from data collection to model deployment.

2. **Ethical Guidelines and Frameworks:**

- **Establishing Ethical Guidelines:** Organizations involved in AI R&D should create and implement ethical guidelines that provide clear principles for responsible AI development. These guidelines should align with internationally recognized ethical standards and be regularly updated to reflect evolving ethical concerns.

- **Ethical Frameworks:** Organizations can adopt established ethical frameworks, such as the "Principles for Trustworthy AI" by the European Commission, to guide their AI projects. These frameworks emphasize transparency, fairness, accountability, and societal benefit.

3. **Ethics Committees and Review Boards:**

- **Institutional Oversight:** Organizations should establish ethics committees or review boards responsible for evaluating the ethical implications of AI projects. These bodies ensure that AI R&D aligns with ethical principles and best practices.

- **External Expertise:** Ethics committees often include external experts in ethics, law, and social sciences who provide unbiased assessments of the ethical aspects of AI projects.

4. **Ethical Audits and Impact Assessments:**

- **Ethical Audits:** Regular ethical audits of AI systems and projects help identify and mitigate potential biases, risks, and ethical concerns. These audits provide transparency and accountability in AI R&D.

- **Ethical Impact Assessments:** Before initiating AI projects, organizations should conduct ethical impact assessments to evaluate the potential societal consequences and ethical risks associated with the technology.

5. **Ethical Considerations in AI Research:**

- **Responsible Research:** AI researchers should adopt responsible research practices, including the responsible collection and handling of data, transparency in methodology, and ethical data sharing.

- **Bias Mitigation:** Researchers should actively work on developing and implementing bias mitigation techniques to reduce unfair discrimination in AI systems.

- **Algorithmic Transparency:** AI researchers should focus on making AI algorithms transparent and interpretable to understand how they make decisions.

6. **User-Centered Design:**

- **User Feedback:** Ethical AI R&D culture involves actively seeking feedback from end-users to ensure that AI systems are designed with their needs and concerns in mind.

- **Usability and Accessibility:** AI systems should be designed to be user-friendly and accessible to a diverse range of users, including those with disabilities.

7. **Cross-Disciplinary Collaboration:**

- **Ethical Expertise:** Collaboration with ethicists, sociologists, psychologists, and experts from diverse fields enhances the ethical considerations in AI R&D. These experts can provide valuable insights into the societal impacts of AI technologies.

- **Legal Experts:** Collaboration with legal experts ensures that AI R&D complies with existing laws and regulations related to privacy, data protection, and anti-discrimination.

8. **Ethical Leadership and Accountability:**

- **Organizational Leadership:** Leadership within AI organizations should set the example by promoting an ethical culture. They should communicate the importance of ethics, transparency, and accountability in AI development.

- **Accountability Mechanisms:** Implementing mechanisms for accountability ensures that individuals and organizations take responsibility for the ethical implications of their AI projects. This may involve corrective actions, disclosures, or reporting to regulatory bodies.

9. **Public Engagement and Ethical Discourse:**

- **Transparency with the Public:** Organizations should engage with the public, providing information about their AI projects and their ethical considerations. Transparency fosters trust and allows for public input.

- **Ethical Discourse:** Encouraging discussions about AI ethics in the public sphere and involving diverse stakeholders in ethical decision-making processes is crucial for fostering an ethical AI R&D culture.

10. **Adaptive Ethical Frameworks:**

- **Flexibility and Adaptation:** Ethical AI R&D culture should be flexible and adaptive, allowing for the continuous assessment and adjustment of ethical guidelines and practices in response to evolving technology and societal norms.

In summary, fostering an ethical AI research and development culture is essential for steering the AI future responsibly. It involves comprehensive education, the establishment of ethical guidelines, the creation of oversight mechanisms, and a commitment to ethical principles throughout the AI development lifecycle. Such a culture ensures that AI technologies benefit society while minimizing harm and upholding ethical standards. It also fosters public trust in AI and encourages responsible innovation in this rapidly evolving field.

Conclusion

"Beyond the Code: Ethical Dilemma in the AI Era" concludes with a thoughtful reflection on the ethical challenges and responsibilities that come with the rise of artificial intelligence (AI). The conclusion encapsulates the key takeaways and emphasizes the imperative for a collaborative, ethical, and responsible approach to navigate the AI era. Here, we delve into the conclusion in detail:

1. **Acknowledgment of Ethical Complexity:**

- The conclusion recognizes the profound ethical complexity that AI introduces into society. It underscores that ethical dilemmas are not isolated incidents but rather woven into the fabric of AI development and deployment.

2. **Human-Centered Values:**

- It emphasizes the need to prioritize human-centered values in AI development. The conclusion asserts that AI should augment human capabilities and well-being, rather than compromise them.

3. **Shared Responsibility:**

- Collaborative responsibility is a central theme. The conclusion underscores that addressing AI's ethical challenges requires a collective effort involving tech companies, governments, academia, civil society, and individual users.

4. **Transparency and Accountability:**

- Transparency and accountability are deemed non-negotiable. It highlights the importance of transparent AI development processes, accountable decision-making, and mechanisms to trace the logic behind AI-driven outcomes.

5. **Bias Mitigation and Fairness:**

- Bias mitigation and fairness are recognized as imperative. The conclusion calls for continuous efforts to detect, reduce, and eliminate biases in AI systems to ensure fairness and equity.

6. **Data Privacy and Security:**

- Data privacy and security remain paramount. It emphasizes the necessity of robust data protection measures and safeguards against data breaches and misuse.

7. **Adaptive Governance:**

- Adaptive governance is presented as a vital approach. The conclusion underscores that governance frameworks should be flexible, responsive, and capable of evolving to meet the evolving ethical challenges posed by AI.

8. **Public Engagement:**

- Public engagement is emphasized. It encourages active participation of individuals in AI discussions, public awareness initiatives, and ethical advocacy, highlighting the role of the public in shaping AI's future.

9. **Continuous Learning and Education:**

- Continuous learning and education are regarded as essential. The conclusion stresses the importance of educational initiatives and professional development to equip individuals with AI ethics literacy.

10. **Collaborative Research:**

- Collaborative research is celebrated. It underscores the value of interdisciplinary collaboration between academia and industry to generate ethical insights and guide AI development.

11. **Global Cooperation:**

- Global cooperation is encouraged. The conclusion advocates for international partnerships and agreements to establish common ethical standards and prevent a fragmented AI landscape.

12. **Trust Building:**

- Building trust is a recurring theme. The conclusion asserts that trust is built through transparency, responsible practices, and consistent ethical behavior.

13. **Responsible Innovation:**

- Responsible innovation is championed. It emphasizes that tech companies should prioritize ethical considerations in the design and deployment of AI technologies.

14. **Reflection on Ethical Choices:**

- The conclusion prompts readers to reflect on their own ethical choices in the AI era. It encourages individuals to consider the ethical implications of their AI-related decisions.

15. **Call to Action:**

- Ultimately, the conclusion issues a call to action. It invites stakeholders, from tech leaders to policymakers and citizens, to take an active role in shaping the ethical trajectory of AI.

In summary, the conclusion of "Beyond the Code: Ethical Dilemma in the AI Era" serves as a rallying cry for responsible AI development and governance. It underscores that the ethical challenges of AI are ongoing and evolving, requiring continuous vigilance, collaboration, and ethical introspection to ensure that AI technologies align with human values and societal well-being.

The Ongoing Journey of Ethics in The AI Epoch:

The conclusion of "Beyond the Code: Ethical Dilemma in the AI Era" reflects on the ongoing journey of ethics in the AI epoch. It recognizes that ethical considerations are not a one-time endeavor but a continuous, dynamic process that must evolve alongside the development and deployment of artificial intelligence. Here, we delve into the conclusion's exploration of the ongoing journey of ethics in the AI era in detail:

1. **Ethics as a Dynamic Challenge:**

- The conclusion acknowledges that ethics in the AI era is not a static problem with fixed solutions. Instead, it's a dynamic challenge that evolves with technological advancements, societal changes, and the emergence of new AI applications.

2. **Unforeseen Ethical Dilemmas:**

- It highlights the inevitability of unforeseen ethical dilemmas. As AI technologies continue to expand into various domains, new ethical challenges may emerge, requiring adaptive responses and innovative solutions.

3. **Technological Progress vs. Ethical Progress:**

- The conclusion underscores that while technological progress in AI may move at a rapid pace, ethical progress must keep pace or even lead. This requires a proactive approach to anticipate and address potential ethical issues.

4. **Evolving Ethical Frameworks:**

- It emphasizes the need for evolving ethical frameworks. As AI systems become more complex, ethical guidelines and principles must also evolve to cover a broader spectrum of considerations, from fairness and transparency to bias mitigation.

5. **Interdisciplinary Collaboration:**

- The conclusion highlights the importance of interdisciplinary collaboration. Ethical discussions and solutions should involve experts from diverse fields, including philosophy, law, psychology, and social sciences, to gain a comprehensive understanding of AI's impact.

6. **Public Participation:**

- It encourages active public participation in shaping AI ethics. Public input is vital for ensuring that ethical AI development aligns with societal values and addresses the concerns and expectations of individuals who interact with AI systems.

7. **Continuous Learning and Education:**

- The conclusion stresses the role of continuous learning and education. To navigate the evolving landscape of AI ethics, individuals, organizations, and institutions should invest in ongoing education to stay informed about ethical best practices.

8. **Tech Companies' Ethical Leadership:**

- It calls upon tech companies to take a leadership role in ethical AI development. Companies should prioritize ethical considerations from the inception of AI projects and foster a culture of responsible innovation.

9. **Ethical Audits and Impact Assessments:**

- The conclusion recommends the use of ethical audits and impact assessments. These tools allow organizations to regularly evaluate and measure the ethical implications of their AI systems, identifying areas for improvement.

10. **International Cooperation:**

- It underscores the importance of international cooperation. Ethical standards in AI should not be confined by national borders but should involve collaboration between nations to create a harmonized global framework.

11. **Responsiveness to Ethical Failures:**

- The conclusion acknowledges that ethical failures may occur. What matters is how organizations and societies respond to these failures, learning from them and implementing measures to prevent recurrence.

12. **Building and Rebuilding Trust:**

- Trust is a recurring theme. It acknowledges that trust is not a one-time achievement but an ongoing process. Organizations and governments must continuously work to build and rebuild trust through transparent practices and ethical behavior.

13. **Ethical Leadership in Innovation:**

- It emphasizes the role of ethical leadership in driving innovation. Ethical considerations should be at the forefront of AI research and development to ensure that innovation benefits humanity.

14. **Resilience in Ethical Decision-Making:**

- The conclusion encourages resilience in ethical decision-making. Ethical considerations should withstand external pressures, such as economic incentives or competitive pressures, to maintain a focus on the greater good.

15. **Ethical Awareness and Empowerment:**

- It advocates for raising ethical awareness and empowerment. Individuals and organizations should be empowered with the knowledge and tools to make ethical decisions in the AI era.

16. **Shared Responsibility:**

- The conclusion ultimately emphasizes that ethics in the AI epoch is a shared responsibility. It calls upon all stakeholders, from tech companies and governments to individuals, to actively participate in the ongoing journey of ethical development in AI.

The conclusion of "Beyond the Code: Ethical Dilemma in the AI Era" paints a picture of ethics as a continuous and evolving journey rather than a destination. It emphasizes the importance of proactive, interdisciplinary, and inclusive approaches to address the ever-changing ethical landscape in the AI era. The ongoing journey of ethics in AI requires vigilance, adaptability, and a commitment to aligning AI technologies with human values and societal well-being.

The Collective Responsibility of Society In Guiding AI's Moral Compass:

The conclusion of "Beyond the Code: Ethical Dilemma in the AI Era" underscores the collective responsibility of society in guiding AI's moral compass. It emphasizes that the ethical development and responsible use of artificial intelligence (AI) technologies are not the sole responsibilities of tech companies, governments, or specific stakeholders but a shared duty that extends to all members of society. Here, we delve into the conclusion's exploration of the collective responsibility of society in guiding AI's moral compass in detail:

1. **Democratizing Ethical Discourse:**

- The conclusion advocates for the democratization of ethical discourse around AI. It encourages individuals, communities, and organizations to engage in meaningful discussions about the ethical implications of AI technologies.

2. **Informed Citizenry:**

- It highlights the importance of an informed citizenry. To guide AI's moral compass, individuals must actively seek knowledge about AI ethics, staying informed about the potential benefits and risks associated with AI systems.

3. **Educational Initiatives:**

- The conclusion underscores the role of educational initiatives. Schools, universities, and online courses can play a crucial part in teaching individuals about AI ethics, fostering a generation of responsible AI users and decision-makers.

4. **Media and Journalism:**

- It acknowledges the influence of media and journalism. These platforms should contribute to public awareness by reporting on AI developments, ethical dilemmas, and societal impacts, thereby helping shape public opinion.

5. **Advocacy and Activism:**

- The conclusion encourages advocacy and activism. Individuals and organizations can advocate for ethical AI practices, call for transparency, and demand accountability when ethical violations occur.

6. **Consumer Choices:**

- It highlights the power of consumer choices. By supporting ethical AI products and services and boycotting those that compromise ethical principles, consumers can influence the direction of AI development.

7. **Civil Society and NGOs:**

- The conclusion recognizes the critical role of civil society and non-governmental organizations (NGOs). These groups can provide independent oversight, conduct research, and advocate for ethical AI practices on behalf of the public.

8. **Public Consultations:**

- It calls for active participation in public consultations. Governments and organizations often seek public input on AI policies and regulations, making it crucial for individuals to voice their concerns and recommendations.

9. **Ethical Entrepreneurship:**

- It encourages ethical entrepreneurship. Entrepreneurs and startups can prioritize ethical considerations in their AI solutions, demonstrating that ethical innovation is not only possible but also profitable.

10. **Community Engagement:**

- The conclusion emphasizes community engagement. Local communities can play a role in advocating for responsible AI use, especially in contexts such as urban planning, healthcare, and public services.

11. **Vigilance and Accountability:**

- It underscores the importance of vigilance and accountability. Society must hold tech companies and governments accountable for their AI-related decisions and actions, ensuring that ethical standards are upheld.

12. **Transparency and Access to Information:**

- It advocates for transparency and access to information. Governments and organizations should provide accessible information about AI technologies and their ethical implications, empowering individuals to make informed decisions.

13. **Inclusivity and Diversity:**

- The conclusion highlights the significance of inclusivity and diversity. Ethical discussions about AI should include diverse perspectives, ensuring that the moral compass of AI reflects the values of a global and multicultural society.

14. **Ethical Leadership:**

- It acknowledges the role of ethical leadership. Leaders in various sectors can set an example by prioritizing ethics in AI decisions and policies, inspiring others to follow suit.

15. **Cultural Sensitivity:**

- The conclusion recognizes the importance of cultural sensitivity. AI systems should respect and align with cultural values and norms, requiring input and guidance from diverse cultural backgrounds.

16. **Cross-Generational Responsibility:**

- It calls for cross-generational responsibility. Younger generations must take up the mantle of ethical AI stewardship, carrying forward the commitment to responsible AI use.

17. **Balancing Innovation and Ethics:**

- The conclusion underscores the delicate balance between innovation and ethics. Society must navigate the tension between pushing the boundaries of AI technology and ensuring ethical safeguards are in place.

18. **Collective Vision for AI:**

- It envisions a collective vision for AI. Society should work together to define the ethical parameters and goals for AI development, shaping AI in a way that aligns with human values.

In summary, the conclusion of "Beyond the Code: Ethical Dilemma in the AI Era" asserts that the moral compass of AI is not predetermined but collectively guided by the actions, choices, and values of society as a whole. It underscores that AI ethics is a shared endeavor, where every individual, organization, and community has a role to play in steering AI towards a future that prioritizes human well-being, fairness, transparency, and accountability.

Appendices

"Appendices" in a document typically contain supplementary information that supports or enhances the main content. These sections are often used to provide additional context, data, or references that can be useful for readers who want to delve deeper into the subject matter. Here, we'll explore the purpose and common content found in appendices in detail:

Purpose of Appendices: Appendices serve several purposes in a document:

1. **Provide Additional Information:** Appendices offer a space to include data, charts, graphs, images, or other materials that complement or expand upon the main content. They can include information that might be too detailed or tangential for the main body of the document.

2. **Support Citations and References:** Authors can use appendices to include full citations, references, or bibliographies for sources cited within the main text. This allows readers to find the original sources easily.

3. **Clarify Concepts:** Appendices can clarify complex concepts, equations, or methodologies used in the main content. They provide a space to elaborate on technical details without cluttering the main text.

4. **Compliance with Guidelines:** In academic or professional documents, appendices may be used to comply with specific style guidelines, formatting requirements, or regulatory standards.

Common Content in Appendices:

The content of appendices can vary depending on the nature and purpose of the document, but common elements include:

1. **Supplementary Data:** This may include raw data, survey results, experimental findings, or any additional information that supports the document's arguments or findings.

2. **Visuals:** Appendices can contain visuals like charts, graphs, tables, maps, or images that provide visual representation of the data or concepts discussed in the main text.

3. **Technical Details:** Complex equations, algorithms, or technical specifications that require in-depth explanation or documentation can be placed in the appendices.

4. **Case Studies:** In reports or research papers, appendices might include detailed case studies or examples that illustrate the document's main points or arguments.

5. **Extended Citations:** For scholarly or academic writing, appendices can list full citations for sources referenced in the main text, following a specific citation style.

6. **Questionnaires or Surveys:** When research involves surveys or questionnaires, the full text of these instruments can be placed in an appendix for transparency and reference.

7. **Legislation or Regulations:** In legal documents or policy reports, appendices may include the text of relevant laws, regulations, or policies for reference.

8. **Glossary:** A glossary of specialized terms used in the document can be included in an appendix to aid readers in understanding the terminology.

9. **Additional Resources:** Links to external resources, websites, or documents that provide further information or context related to the document's subject matter.

10. **Author Biographies:** In certain documents, particularly books or academic papers, author biographies or credentials may be included in an appendix.

11. **Permissions and Copyright:** Documents that include copyrighted material may include permissions obtained from copyright holders in an appendix to demonstrate compliance with copyright law.

Formatting and Organization:

Appendices should be clearly labeled, numbered, and referenced within the main text. They often follow the main body of the document but precede the references or bibliography section. Each appendix is typically titled and labeled with a letter or number (e.g., "Appendix A: Survey Results" or "Appendix 1: Data Tables"). Cross-references from the main text to the appendices should be provided to direct readers to relevant supplementary material.

A: Glossary Of Terms in AI And Ethics:

An "Appendix A: Glossary of Terms in AI and Ethics" is an essential reference tool that provides readers with a clear and comprehensive understanding of key terminology and concepts used within a document focused on the intersection of artificial intelligence (AI) and ethics. This glossary serves several critical functions, and here we'll delve into the details of its purpose, content, and significance:

Purpose of the Glossary:

1. **Clarification of Technical Language:** AI and ethics discussions often involve complex and technical terms that may be unfamiliar to a broad readership. The glossary's primary purpose is to clarify these terms and provide concise, accessible definitions.

2. **Accessibility:** It enhances the accessibility of the document by ensuring that even readers without a deep background in AI or ethics can follow and engage with the content.

3. **Consistency:** The glossary promotes consistency in the use of terminology throughout the document, ensuring that each term is used with the same meaning and context.

4. **Quick Reference:** Readers can easily reference the glossary while reading the document, enabling them to grasp the meaning of specific terms without the need for external sources.

5. **Educational Value:** In educational or instructional materials, the glossary serves as a valuable learning aid, helping students or participants grasp the nuances of AI and ethics terminology.

Contents of the Glossary:

The glossary typically includes the following components:

1. **Alphabetical Listing:** Terms are arranged alphabetically for easy navigation.

2. **Term:** Each entry begins with the term itself, presented in bold or a distinct formatting style to distinguish it from the definition.

3. **Definition:** A concise and clear definition follows each term. Definitions should be written in plain language, avoiding excessive technicality.

4. **Examples:** In some cases, including examples of how the term is used or applied in real-world scenarios can enhance understanding.

5. **Cross-References:** When a term is closely related to or dependent on another term, cross-references within the glossary can direct readers to related entries.

Significance and Benefits:

1. **Enhanced Understanding:** The glossary ensures that readers have a shared understanding of the terminology used in the document, reducing the risk of misinterpretation.

2. **Accessibility for Diverse Audiences:** Not all readers will possess the same level of expertise in AI or ethics. The glossary accommodates a diverse audience, from novices to experts.

3. **Clarity and Precision:** Clear definitions help prevent confusion or ambiguity, enabling readers to engage more confidently with the document's content.

4. **Streamlined Reading:** Readers can seamlessly integrate the glossary into their reading experience, eliminating the need for interruptions to search for external definitions.

5. **Consistency in Communication:** Authors and contributors can adhere to the glossary's definitions to maintain consistency in terminology usage, fostering a coherent narrative.

6. **Educational Value:** In educational settings, the glossary supports learning objectives by reinforcing the understanding of AI and ethics terminology.

Formatting and Presentation:

1. **Clear Labeling:** Appendix A should be prominently labeled as "Glossary of Terms in AI and Ethics" or a similar title.

2. **Alphabetical Order:** Terms within the glossary should be arranged alphabetically, making it easy for readers to locate specific terms.

3. **Formatting Consistency:** Maintain a consistent format for each entry, including the term, definition, and any additional information (e.g., examples).

4. **Hyperlinks (for Digital Documents):** In digital documents, hyperlinks can be included to allow readers to navigate directly to the glossary entry when encountering a relevant term in the main text.

In conclusion, "Appendix A: Glossary of Terms in AI and Ethics" is a valuable component of a document focused on AI ethics, contributing to clarity, accessibility, and consistency in communication. Whether used in research papers, reports, educational materials, or policy documents, this glossary enhances the reader's ability to engage with and understand the document's content effectively. It reflects a commitment to effective communication and knowledge dissemination within the field of AI ethics.

B: Notable Ethical Dilemmas in AI History

"Appendices: Notable Ethical Dilemmas in AI History" is a section within a document that serves to provide readers with a deeper understanding of the historical context and significant ethical challenges that have emerged in the field of artificial intelligence (AI). This section is a valuable resource for enhancing the document's comprehensiveness, offering insights into past AI-related ethical issues. Here, we'll explore the purpose, content, and significance of including this specific appendix in detail:

Purpose of the Appendix:

1. **Historical Context:** The primary purpose of this appendix is to provide readers with historical context. It highlights notable ethical dilemmas that have arisen throughout the history of AI, helping readers appreciate the evolution of ethical concerns in the field.

2. **Illustration of Ethical Complexity:** By presenting specific cases, the appendix illustrates the complexity of ethical challenges in AI. It demonstrates that ethical considerations in AI are not solely theoretical but have real-world implications.

3. **Learning from Past Mistakes:** Studying historical ethical dilemmas allows readers to learn from past mistakes and avoid repeating them. It emphasizes the importance of ethical awareness and responsible AI development.

Contents of the Appendix:

The content of "Notable Ethical Dilemmas in AI History" typically includes:

1. **Case Studies:** The appendix presents specific case studies or instances from the history of AI where ethical dilemmas arose. Each case study is described in detail, including the context, the ethical issue at hand, and the consequences.

2. **Relevance:** It explains why each historical case is relevant to the current discourse on AI ethics. This highlights the continuity of certain ethical concerns and their enduring impact on AI development.

3. **Resolutions (if applicable):** In cases where ethical dilemmas were addressed or resolved, this information can be included to showcase how the field responded to these challenges.

Significance and Benefits:

1. **Enhanced Understanding:** The appendix provides readers with a more profound understanding of the historical roots of AI ethics. This knowledge helps them appreciate the evolution of ethical considerations in AI.

2. **Real-World Application:** By examining real-world examples, readers can better relate to the ethical challenges faced in AI development. This makes the content more relatable and tangible.

3. **Preparation for Future Challenges:** Understanding past dilemmas equips readers to anticipate and address future ethical challenges in AI. It encourages proactive ethical thinking and decision-making.

4. **Contextualizing Current Debates:** The appendix helps readers contextualize ongoing debates and discussions in AI ethics by linking them to historical precedents. It underscores the relevance of past lessons to contemporary issues.

Formatting and Presentation:

1. **Clear Labeling:** The appendix should be prominently labeled as "Appendix B: Notable Ethical Dilemmas in AI History" or a similar title for easy identification.

2. **Structured Presentation:** Each case study should be presented in a structured format, including a brief introduction, detailed description of the ethical dilemma, and, if applicable, a section on resolution or impact.

3. **Chronological or Thematic Order:** The case studies can be organized chronologically to show the historical progression of ethical concerns or thematically to group similar dilemmas together.

4. **References:** Proper citations and references should be provided for each case study to allow readers to explore further if they wish.

In conclusion, "Appendices: Notable Ethical Dilemmas in AI History" is a valuable section within a document that enriches the reader's understanding of AI ethics by delving into historical cases. It serves as a bridge between past ethical challenges and the current AI landscape, emphasizing the importance of ethical awareness and responsible AI development based on the lessons of history.

C: Recommended Literature and Resources on AI Ethics:

"Appendices: Recommended Literature and Resources on AI Ethics" is a section within a document that provides readers with a curated list of valuable readings and resources related to the field of artificial intelligence (AI) ethics. This section serves as a reference guide, helping readers further explore the subject matter by offering a collection of authoritative materials. Here, we'll delve into the purpose, content, and significance of including this specific appendix in detail:

Purpose of the Appendix:

1. **Resource Compilation:** The primary purpose of this appendix is to compile and present a curated list of recommended literature and resources. This collection acts as a valuable reference point for readers seeking to expand their knowledge of AI ethics.

2. **In-Depth Exploration:** It encourages readers to engage in in-depth exploration of AI ethics by providing access to authoritative texts, research papers, articles, and websites.

3. **Holistic Understanding:** The resource list covers a range of topics within AI ethics, offering readers a holistic understanding of the subject matter.

Contents of the Appendix:

The content of "Recommended Literature and Resources on AI Ethics" typically includes:

1. **Categorization:** The resources are categorized based on topics or themes, making it easier for readers to find materials relevant to their specific interests or questions.

2. **Publication Details:** Each entry includes essential publication details, such as the title of the work, author(s), publication date, and the source (e.g., book, journal, website).

3. **Brief Description:** A brief description or summary of each resource is often provided. This helps readers understand the content and focus of the recommended material.

4. **Hyperlinks (for Digital Documents):** In digital documents, hyperlinks can be included to allow readers to access the recommended resources directly.

Significance and Benefits:

1. **Comprehensive Learning:** The appendix offers readers a comprehensive list of resources, enabling them to delve into AI ethics from various perspectives and depths.

2. **Efficient Research:** Researchers, students, or professionals interested in AI ethics can efficiently identify relevant materials for further study or reference.

3. **Continued Exploration:** It encourages continuous exploration and learning by directing readers to credible and authoritative sources.

4. **Diverse Perspectives:** The resource list often includes works from diverse authors and sources, allowing readers to explore different viewpoints on AI ethics.

5. **Professional Development:** Professionals working in AI-related fields can use this appendix to stay updated on the latest developments in AI ethics.

6. **Academic Support:** Students and educators can benefit from this resource list when conducting research or designing courses related to AI ethics.

Formatting and Presentation:

1. **Clear Labeling:** The appendix should be clearly labeled as "Appendix C: Recommended Literature and Resources on AI Ethics" or a similar title.

2. **Structured Presentation:** Resources are typically presented in a structured format, with entries organized logically based on categories or themes.

3. **Full Citations:** Ensure that each resource includes complete citation details, allowing readers to find the material easily.

4. **Hyperlinks (for Digital Documents):** In digital documents, hyperlinks should be active and accessible, facilitating quick access to online resources.

5. **Annotated Entries (Optional):** For added context, brief annotations or comments about each resource can be included to highlight its significance or relevance.

In conclusion, "Appendices: Recommended Literature and Resources on AI Ethics" serves as an invaluable reference tool within a document focused on AI ethics. It empowers readers with the means to further explore the subject, gain a deeper understanding, and stay informed about the latest developments in AI ethics. This curated collection of resources enhances the document's value by promoting continuous learning and engagement with the ethical dimensions of artificial intelligence.